Plant Hardiness Zone Map

THE COUNTRY GARDEN

Curved steps give gentleness and grace to this entrance
into a small country-formal garden with simple fountain.

THE
COUNTRY
GARDEN

Josephine Nuese

CHARLES SCRIBNER'S SONS

NEW YORK

To my many gardening friends who, either consciously or unconsciously, have helped me write this book.

ACKNOWLEDGMENTS

With Love and Gratitude

To Ann and Stewart Hoskins, editor and publisher of *The Lakeville Journal,* for long years of warm friendship and for releasing material from my garden column to be used in this book.

To Silvia Saunders for checking the peony article and giving it her blessing, for contributing the original sketch of how to plant a tree peony.

To my photographers, Dody Prentice and Gene Trudeau, for the countless hours they spent in pursuit of photogenic gardens.

To Timmy Foster, whose illustrations have added delight to so many garden books, for her sketch of the little tree and other drawings.

To my good friends Isabell Woodruff and Deborah Benson who helped with the final frantic typing.

FOREWORD

It has been said that the most helpful garden book for the amateur is one written by another amateur rather than by a distinguished professional who has long since forgotten his early puzzlements, his early mistakes.

If that is so then you should find this book useful, for after thirty-five years of amateur gardening I am still puzzled by various horticultural phenomena and my mistakes, both early and late, are all too apparent on our property—though I have never yet seen a garden which did not include a few mistakes, give some measure of distress to its owner. Which, in my opinion, is as it should be, for it is this distress which invites more learning, more experience. Perfection, that plastic carrot in front of the nose, can be as boring—and irritating —in gardening as in anything else. Luckily, few of us have to worry about this.

I have been asked why this book is called *The Country Garden;* aren't all gardens in the country? No, not necessarily. There are many beautiful gardens in cities, and in the suburbs of cities—the most exquisite gardens I can remember were in Georgetown, just outside of Washington, D. C.—but these are not country gardens; they are usually urban in flavor, urbane in personality. The country garden is more relaxed and informal, its character—varied, of course, by the architecture it attends—has a rural feel to it even when brushed by formality. It is this rural savor, plus greater ease of maintenance, which has endeared it to exurbanites who have escaped, they hope, into the simplicity of country living—which is not simple at all as most country dwellers can tell you.

Nor is this type of garden restricted to New England and the

East. It is just as popular, I am told, throughout the vast middle sections of the country, even in the Pacific Northwest, perhaps because it seems a throwback to the gardens our ancestors established and loved as they moved across the country.

Suggested plantings in this book are chiefly for Zone 5 which, according to the latest zone map issued by the U. S. Department of Agriculture, replaces Zone 4 as shown in various earlier maps (see endpapers). Yet no map, no official zone, can promise the hardiness of a planting in your specific area as so much depends on the placement of your property, especially in hilly sections where dryness and frost-pockets must also be considered. Everywhere, all over the country, there are "islands", microclimates, which can be either warmer or colder than the official zone. For instance, our northwestern tip of Connecticut is in Zone 5, according to this latest map, with a listed minimum temperature of 10° to 20° below zero, yet we have had drops to 30° below zero and 25° below is not unusual. And even within this tiny area there are warm pockets, near lakes or rivers, where the temperature seldom falls to even 10° below, where the climate is more like that of Zone 6, where relatively tender plants can be grown with comparative safety, plants which would surely be killed even five miles away at higher, drier and windier elevations. The presence of water is a major factor in determining the hardiness of many plants.

So you will have to work all this out for yourself according to the setting of your land, its elevation and exposure. Our property is on the northern face of one of the coldest hills, exposed to bitter northwest winds, and the plants mentioned throughout the book have usually been hardy here—or at least root-hardy—through brief dips to 30° below zero. One winter a prolonged spell of 15° below zero, with a tearing wind and almost no snow cover, killed back the top growth of English ivy in open positions and badly mauled the English boxwood (the Korean box was unharmed) but both recovered in due time. It has been my experience that many supposedly half-hardy plants can be gradually acclimated to rigorous temperatures, especially if given proper bedding and sheltered positions, so don't be afraid to experiment.

This book is concerned only with small to moderately large country properties. It does not include estates. If you have an estate you don't need this or any other book; what you need is the very best landscape architect you can find* and I can't think of a wiser use for your money.

In the beginning, about thirty-five years ago when we were mired in the confusions left by remodeling and regrading, we asked the distinguished landscape architect Helen Swift Jones to give us some idea on how to proceed. She suggested most of the basic major plantings, the bone structure, and although we have made many changes since then we are still grateful for the invaluable help she gave us. It was one of the best investments we ever made. So if you have property of any size, and don't know where to begin with what, I urge you to get professional advice. It will save you a great deal of money in the years to come.

And ours is not even an estate. I am always embarrassed when callers arrive expecting to find a magnificent country place and find instead an old remodeled farmhouse and the simple country gardens anyone can grow.

It is these gardens I write about.

* If you don't know how to find a reliable landscape architect write to the American Society of Landscape Architects, 2013 Eye Street N.W., Washington, D. C. and ask for the names of professionals in your area.

CONTENTS

ILLUSTRATIONS

DRAWINGS BY LAURA LEE FOSTER

"It has taken me half a lifetime merely to find out what is best worth doing, and a good slice out of another half to puzzle out the ways of doing it."

GERTRUDE JEKYLL in *Colour Schemes for the Flower Garden.*

THE COUNTRY GARDEN

A Time for Dreaming

Anyone who thinks that gardening begins in the spring and ends in the fall is missing the best part of the whole year. For gardening begins in January, begins with the dream.

Every garden worth the planting must begin with a dream; there is no other way of beginning a garden. Unless you are perfectly satisfied with the usual conventional plantings, the horticultural clichés, and if so there is little sense in your going on with this book.

Each January is a fresh start. You know that this year, at long last, your garden is going to be perfect: cascades of never-ending bloom, each plant superbly placed and superbly grown, no weeds, no bugs, no bare spots, no mistakes. And, of course, no maintenance. You leaf through the catalogues half drunk with anticipation. . . .

For this is the gardener's cocktail hour. And just as in the candle-lit dusk of the cocktail hour all men are brilliant and all women beautiful so, in the catalogues, all plants are enchanting, all bloom unceasingly, all are easy to grow, all suited to your area. It is one of the happiest of all delusions, putting stars into the eyes and mush into the mental processes.

It is also a time of danger to the novice in such matters and I urge you to go slowly, to order only what you can handle wisely and well. If you are an experienced gardener you already know your limitations, the limitations of your property, and you view the catalogues with a wary eye. Yet you cannot become an experienced gardener without first gaining experience, so why I go on about this is a mystery. Nobody ever pays any attention to such advice anyhow. Which, perhaps, is just as well.

Contemplating Your Property

Before you order a single plant, just because it looks so pretty in the catalogue, you should consider your property as a whole, its planning or lack of it.

If yours is an established garden of deep strength and serenity, the bone structure complete, the basic groupings of line and form, mass and texture, already in place, you can skip this part. In fact, you should probably be writing this book yourself. But few gardens are ever completely satisfying to the owners; with experience the dream enlarges and new ideas occur, with fresh knowledge comes fresh inspiration. And don't kid yourself that there is ever any end to this learning because there is not, no gardener worthy of that high calling ever stops learning. Gardening is such a limitless study, with so many areas of specialized knowledge, that it takes a lifetime to

Abiding strength and tranquility have been incorporated here through the skillful use of trees, shrubs, and stonework. Note the generous width of the stone steps, the interesting lines of the sophora trees in the foreground. This property shows the semi-formal country garden as it should be: serene, welcoming, and—above all—uncluttered.

EUGENE D. TRUDEAU

master even a small part of it. Anyone who claims to know all about gardening is either a fool or a fake and, in either case, is suffering from horticultural rigor mortis.

Any garden which is to endure and grow more beautiful over the years, give endless pleasure to the eye, the mind, and the heart, must have good bone structure. This means trees, evergreens, shrubs —and, if possible, stonework—so grouped, so placed, that there is a sense of deep and abiding delight no matter where the glance happens to fall, a quality of rightness, of belonging in that setting. This is why it is best, whenever possible, to use the planting material which is native to your section, or which has been so hallowed by traditional usage in your area that it seems native. This is also more economical in both time and money as such plants are likely to grow more happily and with less care than the exotic numbers which tempt you in the catalogues.

The simplest way to find out what kinds of plants will grow best for you is to study the terrain you are committed to. As you drive along the local roads observe, carefully, the native growths. For example, if your immediate area is open, sunny, hilly, rocky, sprinkled with native junipers (usually called red cedars) you are likely to be in a limestone section. Which is good news, for the junipers, an enormous tribe, provide some of the most beautiful planting material you could ask for and all—or almost all—are likely to thrive in the open, sunny, limey site you have to offer. And there are countless other plants, traditional in such a setting, which combine happily with junipers: apple trees and flowering crabs, lilacs, viburnums, the flowering quinces, cotoneasters, peonies—the list is almost endless.

Or perhaps you are in an acid-soil area, deeply wooded with hemlocks, spruce, pine (although most pines will grow almost anywhere), mountain laurel, native azaleas, dogwood. This opens up a different world of planting possibilities: the conifers, the hollies, all the magnificent flowering broadleafed evergreens—again the list is endless.

These, roughly, are the two basic—and extreme—types of terrain. Luckily most areas, in New England anyhow, are a mixture of both and often a blend of both so that most soils tend to be neutral in cultivated areas. Also luckily, the majority of cultivated plants are broadminded about soil, its slight acidity or alkalinity; they are usually more concerned with drainage. But most of them do have their preferences and if these are known it is a good idea to group together the plants which have similar tastes, makes for greater happiness all around.

Besides studying the native growths you should grab every chance to visit nearby gardens, see what grows well for your neighbors. Write down the names of the trees, shrubs, and evergreens which appeal to you most and, in the classic mind's eye, arrange and rearrange these on your own property using different combinations. Remember that the simplest plants can look fresh and original when thoughtfully placed.

And send for catalogues, especially nursery catalogues. There are two which I consider of special importance because they will help you glimpse the planting possibilities in your area, introduce you to new plants. One of these is the Wayside Gardens catalogue which comes twice a year, a big one in January and a smaller one in June. These are hefty, colorful jobs, well printed on good paper, full of horticultural cheesecake. But proceed cautiously, for Wayside ships to all parts of the country and not all the plants they offer are hardy in very cold areas; if you crave a certain plant best check its. hardiness and suitability with your local nurseryman before ordering. Plants which carry the recommendation "protect lightly over the winter" are definitely not hardy much below zero even with this protection. I have learned this the hard way.

The other catalogue is of a different type but just as valuable, in fact even more valuable if you are a serious gardener. This one is from White Flower Farm, Litchfield, Connecticut, and contains some of the most delightful and informative reading matter any gardener could happen upon. It is gay, knowledgeable, and witty, and assumes you are the same. No floral cheesecake, no hard sell; a limited number of charming and accurate drawings illustrate some of the plants and there are a few photographs of area plantings, plus suggested planting plans. But the plant descriptions are full and graphic, larded with fresh ideas, and the listing includes many choice and unusual varieties seldom found elsewhere. For this reason you will find the White Flower Farm catalogue mentioned frequently throughout this book, so better send for it. (A list of desirable catalogues will be found on page 243.)

This catalogue should be of special interest to gardeners in frigid sections of the country, for Litchfield is one of the coldest spots around here, and White Flower Farm is on one of the coldest hills, so anything grown by this nursery, and they grow most of their own plants, has got to be hardy to at least 20° below zero. Their plants are top quality—I know because I have many of them—and gardeners from distant regions have told me that White Flower's packing and shipping techniques are excellent.

And, of course, there are many other nursery catalogues you can send for, some valuable, some pure rubbish. So a word of warning: beware of the nurseries which flourish extravagant advertisements filled with "amazing offers", sweeping promises of "bloom all summer" (if a plant produces one tiny flower a week it can be said, quite truthfully, to "bloom all summer") and other forms of suckerbait. Many of the catalogues from such nurseries turn out to be cheaply printed, the colors misleading, the nomenclature hazy, the information inaccurate. And the plants, if you fall for the fast spiel, are usually disappointing; at least they have been in my experience. You can, of course, get your money back eventually, according to the guarantee, but this involves you in lengthy correspondence, loss of time, and mounting irritation. Such catalogues are only for the informed and experienced gardener who can thread his way around the many booby traps to find a good buy. And there are often very good buys indeed if you know how to spot them.

Then, too, there are many valuable small catalogues put out by the unsung but dedicated growers, the specialists. These are a joy and, usually, the plants are excellent. Here you are dealing not with the flashy fast-buck gentry but with genuine gardeners who devote their lives to the growing of fine plants and the pride and pleasure this gives them. The only trouble with these delightful little catalogues is that, usually, they contain few illustrations, so their educational value to the beginner is lessened. However, as you learn more about planting materials, and as your garden develops, you will find yourself dealing most frequently with these specialists.

What Is A Garden?

First of all, it might be a good idea to establish a mutual understanding of the word garden.

Many people confuse a garden with a flower bed, thinking the two are synonymous. Often they are not. A garden may include many flowers, a few, or none at all. A flower bed is a collection of blooming plants stuck in because the owner likes them—and there couldn't be a better reason!—without consideration of harmony or design; it is usually a riot of color and, as such, quickly exhausts the eye and the appreciation. If this is your idea of a garden, and it gives you pleasure, by all means go ahead and have it no matter who says what, this book included. But it is not my idea of a garden.

To me a garden is an area, or a series of related areas, wherein one finds reassurance and tranquility, surprise and delight; its beauty lies in the subtle balancing of scale and proportion, line and form, mass and texture, contrast and accord, the whole affiliated yet full of small surprises. Such a garden imparts a benediction, enlarging the mental and emotional habitation. . . .

There will now be a brief pause for the departure of those who have decided to chicken out after the above paragraph.

Or perhaps you agree with all this, vaguely, but have no idea how to go about it. Perhaps you feel that this is all very fine for the big estates but you don't have a big estate. What is more, you don't have much money. So what can you do?

Let me tell you a story:

Many years ago I knew an Italian—we can call him Tony—who found himself committed to a small, bleak back yard plot in a small manufacturing town. Like so many Italians he had been born with a mason's trowel in his mouth and a deep awareness of beauty. He was dismayed by the ugliness of his surroundings and decided to do something about this. Perhaps he could build a wall around his back yard and make a little garden . . . he discussed this with his immediate neighbors—each side and in back—and they agreed, over much spaghetti and red wine, that this would be a fine idea for all concerned. A wall with gates, so that each could enjoy Tony's garden and each use his own side of the wall for his own purposes.

So the project was started. Each neighbor, on his travels, kept a sharp eye out for rocks which could be used in Tony's wall and, one by one, the rocks accumulated. Also, Tony had a cousin who worked on the local roads and whenever a baby pine or hemlock or juniper or native azalea was due to be mowed down the cousin would snick it out and quickly wrap it in waxed paper lined with fresh grass and earth (this was before the blessing of the plastic bag) and take it to Tony for his new garden.

The vista glimpsed through the clipped yews seems endless, yet it is actually the result of skillful framing within a relatively small area.

In time the rock pile grew impressive; also the baby plants grew brisk and strong in their temporary nursery bed. So finally came the great day when it was time to dig the foundation, to buy the cement and start laying the wall, and everybody helped, either with muscle or advice or both. As the wall grew each stage of progress was celebrated with more spaghetti dinners and mutual congratulations. An old, rusted iron gate, discovered on a dump, was scraped and sanded and painted black and set in the rear wall; two wooden gates, skillfully fashioned from junk lumber by a neighboring carpenter, were contributed for the side walls; another neighbor came back from a Sunday outing with a baby dogwood tree dug from a friend's woods. Tony's garden had become a community project.

When the wall was finished it was a thing of beauty, each rock lovingly chosen, lovingly placed. A friend who worked on a big estate had begged a rooted layer of white wisteria and this was planted to—in time—curve over the black iron gate (it did, too!); for anyone else this fragment of wisteria would have died but for Tony it flourished. Then the baby evergreens were set in place; some were espaliered against the wall, some were shaped to rounded forms, a few of them Tony pegged down with his wife's hairpins to stay low and spreading. Some flat stones, left from the wall, were laid around the infant dogwood to indicate its importance, and all the neighbors came to exclaim and admire.

Then Tony's wife, who had furnished the countless spaghetti dinners, decided to get into the act and planted her favorite flowers —red and pink zinnias, orange marigolds, scarlet salvia, purple petunias, and blue bachelor's buttons—in front of Tony's evergreens and azaleas and white wisteria. So everybody was happy.

Which shows what can be done if you have the dream and the determination.

Applying the Dream to the Reality

Here are three gardens, three different ways in which you can add form and structure and interest to your property. Which one is for you will depend upon the amount of land available, your personal preferences, and the size of your purse. But all three are planned for low upkeep, now a major consideration to most gardeners. In fact, one of these gardens would take only half the upkeep demanded by the conventional bed or border; the other two would take less than half.

I. THE WALLED GARDEN

This is the most expensive, if you consider only the initial cost of a well-laid stone wall, but it is also the most enduring. Many parents plant trees as a heritage for their children and this is a fine idea, but trees are subject to storm and stress, bugs and blights, and, like all living things, need a certain amount of care, will eventually die. A beautiful stone wall, like a diamond, is forever; it will be there always for whatever the oncoming generations want to plant against it.

Furthermore, besides giving immediate form and structure to your garden, something which may take years when using plant material, an enclosing wall might enable you to grow many of the doubtfully hardy shrubs and flowers which would not survive open planting if you live in a cold section. For a walled garden becomes a sun-pocket in winter, the stones hold the sun's heat, protect the plants from bitter winds. It could be a treasury of things you have always wanted to grow. And it will need far fewer plants than a garden in the open, in fact it should have far fewer plants so that the beauty of each can be delineated against the stonework. This means that you would spend less money on planting material, less time on upkeep.

For the very small walled garden there are tiny-leafed vines with which to pattern the walls, give vertical interest: the miniature Boston ivy, *Ampelopsis lowi,* forms a tracery against stone, or cement, or any rough surface, as does the slightly coarser evergreen *Euonymus kewensis* which prefers shade. And for a spectacular mass of bloom against a sunny wall in May there is the small-flowered clematis *montana,* white or pink, which is more delicate in character than the better-known large-flowered varieties. But remember that any clematis will need a wire or lattice-type support, set out from the wall, to wrap its tendrils around. There are many such supports on the market. More about clematis later in this book.

In such a very small area all material must be kept in scale and special attention given to foliage values—color, form, and texture—as these will be viewed at close range, form an important part of the picture throughout the year. So here are some suggested planting combinations, all to take just average garden earth a little on the alkaline side, full sun to light shade. All these plants have been hardy for me here in northwestern Connecticut and blooming periods given are for this area.

Against the tracery of the *Ampelopsis lowi* (in sun) a small group of snowy Madonna lilies, for late June into July bloom, fore-planted with a semi-circle of the dwarf single peony Sunlight which stays low, under 20″, and, in May, bears cup-shaped flowers of a creamy apricot-pink . . . with and around this a massed planting of pale silver-grey *Stachys lanata* (you may know this as lamb's ears or bunny ears) spreading along to underplant the little polyantha rose The Fairy (masses of small pale pink flowers from late June to killing frost), the stachys then merging into the flat, surface-spreading juniper *Wiltoni.* . . . Set in this silvery grey-green carpet a bay of the tiny-leafed dark green evergreen candytuft *Iberis sempervirens* var. Little Gem (a sheet of dazzling white in May) neighbored by a planting of the low, ferny-leafed *Geranium dalmaticum* (masses of small, pale pink flowers amid the foliage, profuse in June and on and off all summer) . . . all this edging into a grouping of the dark, dwarf, tiny-leafed Korean box (*Buxus microphylla koreana,* Arnold Arboretum strain) . . . this, in turn, leading back into the silvery grey velvet of the stachys planting.

If you are still with me, which is doubtful, you could also

This mound of *Geranium dalmaticum* is actually only about 8″ high and 18″ across. This picture was taken after it had finished its prodigious spring bloom and settled down to its all-summer type of flowering.

EUGENE D. TRUDEAU

consider groups of low petunias, white and dark pink, to tuck in here and there where needed for July-to-frost bloom, perhaps in the candytuft bay and in front of the boxwood. The reason for restricting this color scheme to pink, white, silver-grey and dark green is that these give a sense of delicacy and space to a small area.

If your little walled garden is large enough to take a tiny tree you might think about a standard (tree form) white or pink lilac, or a white tree-form wisteria. Or, if scale will permit, a white weeping cherry; Wayside has a nice one. In any case, this little tree should go into a protected sunny corner with a wreath of pink and white petunias around its feet.

And, just for fun, you might like to experiment with an exquisite little ground cover which would be a delight if it was hardy in your area, and it might be within the protection of a walled garden; it is not hardy here. This is *Nierembergia rivularis*. It grows only about 3″ high, has dark, spoon-shaped leaves profusely studded with relatively huge, white, cup-shaped flowers which sit right on top of the leaves. There is a picture of it in the Wayside catalogue and it really does bloom, profusely, from early June to October. I carried it the first winter with layers of complicated snow-mulches, then lost it the second winter when I mulched less carefully; I doubt whether it would be hardy, without protection, north of New Jersey except along the coast, but it is well worth a trial run. It is said to like shade and moisture, a sandy loam laced with manure, but I grew it in just average soil and full sun and it flourished. If you can grow it you will have discovered an invaluable ground cover for it is a fast spreader, a constant bloomer.

Upkeep on the above plantings: except for dead-flower removal the only maintenance would be the shearing back of the candytuft after blooming (to keep it neat and shapely) and, possibly, the shearing back of the Korean box, although this, which grows only 12″ to 14″ high, is equally charming when allowed to fan out naturally. You could mulch all exposed soil areas with crushed stone to conserve moisture and keep down weeds, and the lawn center—which, of course, would need mowing—could be kept in place by that metal edging, sunk to ground level, plus a moat of sand in which are laid bricks (flat) to take the wheel of the mower. Any grasses which do creep through these barriers are easily plucked out of the sand.

In larger walled gardens, where the planting scale can be more generous, the evergreen *Euonymus radicans* will clothe your wall with patterned green in either sun or shade; this is larger-leafed than the *kewensis* but not as coarse as the better-known *vegetus* which is best used only in large-scale plantings. A sunny, protected spot against a warm wall will also give you the perfect setting for the spectacular firethorn, *Pyracantha coccinea lalandi,* with its wealth of brilliant berries in fall; this one is sometimes difficult to grow in the open. And, of course, the walled garden is the traditional setting for espaliered trees; these, when well grown, can be very effective but they are expensive to buy and need most careful pruning if they are to retain their distinctive lines. Still, to some gardeners they are worth all this and more. Most of them need sun.

In partial to complete shade English ivy makes a superb wall and ground cover—deep, dark, and glossy—and when safe from winter sun has proved surprisingly hardy, without protection, even in our dry and frigid hills. Tall white lilies (the Jan de Graaff hybrids), bedded in and backed by this ivy, would lift their ivory trumpets against this background during July and August, would enjoy the root protection afforded by the ivy and not mind the shade so long as they could get their heads into some sun, preferably morning sun. . . . In front of these lilies, to bloom in spring against the dark ivy, you could plant the white azalea *vuykiana palestrina*. All the above would enjoy deep, humusy bedding, a little on the acid side.

Nearby, but against a sunny part of the wall, a white large-flowered clematis would give a cascade of white after the azalea had finished and before the lilies started: Henryi produces single flowers of mammoth size, Duchess of Edinburgh has smaller flowers but double and more of them, *lanuginosa candida* has blossoms almost as large as Henryi and though not as profuse a bloomer in spring does keep flowering, off and on, all summer. Personally, I think that one such clematis, in such a setting, would be far more effective than several plantings but you may not agree with this. And as this clematis will want plenty of lime a good companion plant would be gypsophila, which also enjoys lime and would protect the clematis roots with its light, airy shade; you could put a massed semicircle of low pink gypsophilas Pink Fairy around the base of the clematis This gypsophila blooms heavily in late spring and, moderately, all summer. Edge this whole planting with low white petunias and flank it with the lifting, spreading grey-green of Sargent junipers nipped back to reveal the branch lines.

Within these protecting walls you should also be able to grow magnificent delphiniums, the towering English or Pacific hybrids, for here they will be shielded from their worst enemy which is wind. These delphiniums, in blending shades of blue, pink, lavender, and white, are particularly effective against stonework; they bloom first in late June or early July and then, if the flowering stalks are cut off immediately, usually bloom again in September. But be careful not to crowd them as they must have ample ventilation to stay healthy. The great spires have a dignity, almost a formality, which combines well with the dark rounded forms of English box (*Buxus suffruticosa*) and the spreading greyish-green foliage of tree peonies (*Paeonia moutan* in variety). These peonies, being among the choicest of all garden plants, have their own dignity and distinction so that this semi-formal planting in sun would balance the semi-formal ivy-lily-azalea planting in shade. More about tree peonies later.

And roses. . . . If you are a rose grower you will certainly want to have them in your walled garden, the traditional setting for roses since gardening began. I am not a rose grower (I grow only a few of the easiest ones) so if you are you probably know more about the'r culture than I do. But roses, almost any roses, would be perfect against the dark background of the euonymus, in sun.

About trees: Unless your walled garden is fairly large, and it is not likely to be, one smallish tree should be enough. But it should be a tree that carries itself with distinction, in both line and foliage, to accord with the slight hint of formality in the plantings; also, it should flower in early spring as most of the other plants, except the azalea, are late-May-through-summer bloomers.

The magnolias fill all these requirements. The ubiquitous saucer magnolia, *M. soulangeana,* is certainly one of the Fords of planting but it is also a beautiful thing with glossy leafage all summer and, usually, gracious, uplifting lines; try to get one with good lines. Besides the conventional pink it also comes in white (Alexandrina) and darkish purple (*nigra*), all to about 20′, hardy and moderately fast growing. Less well known and even more beautiful, in my opinion, is the star magnolia, *M. stellata,* which in April becomes a mass of white blossoms, before the leaves appear to clothe the interesting stem lines in dark and semi-glossy green all summer. This one, the beloved old *stellata,* is simple and slow-growing but there is a new version from the Arnold Arboretum, called Dr. Merrill, which you might prefer; it is faster and more spectacular, with more flowers, grows to about 10′ with an ultimate spread of around 8′ so should be given plenty of room. Both versions prefer sun but will take some shade and both like a deep, rich, acid bedding. Use plenty of peat moss and compost in the planting site.

Upkeep on the above plantings: with center lawn treatment same as for the smaller garden the upkeep would be, chiefly, staking the lilies and delphiniums and trimming the boxwood, lightly, each spring. Plus, of course, the inescapable dead-flower removal. The roses I leave to you; one of the reasons I don't grow them is because of the maintenance, spraying, etc., but to an avid rose-grower this is nothing, and you undoubtedly have your favorite mulch for them. The ivy ground cover will take care of that planting (use a thick mulch of pine needles while the ivy is getting established) and mulch the clematis with flat stones, under the gypsophilas, to conserve root shade. Mulch the magnolia, thickly, with pine needles— or you might try the little *Nierembergia rivularis* under it as a ground cover if you live far enough south; the white cups would be a joy, all summer long, under the dark, glossy magnolia foliage.

II. THE GREY-GREEN GARDEN

This is for the property with an already established flower bed or border which—theoretically at least—is a mass of brilliant color from the first tulip to the last chrysanthemum and has, in back of it or close by, enough space to create a small separate garden.

This area, which should be at least partially screened off from the rest of the property, can be any size or shape you choose, depending upon its surroundings and the lay of the land. But the approach to this area should be through a blaze of color and he entrance, between shrubs, flanked by beds of brilliant flowers.

The whole point of this is its shock value. You approach, the eye dazed and exhausted by all this color and, parting the shrubbery, find yourself suddenly in a hushed, half-shaded sanctuary of muted greens and greys with, here and there, splashes of white or palest pink. Against a dark shrub or evergreen there is a white bench where you can sit, for a few moments, to absorb the tranquility of this gentle spot. Then, the eye rested and the mind refreshed, you go back through the shrubbery into an open world of sun and light and color. You will be surprised to find how much more beautiful every flower seems to be when the eye is rested.

Presumably your flower bed or border will have some kind of backing—shrubbery, or the wall of a building, or an old, native stone wall—so you will have to devise some way of either using this background or working around it to reach the area selected. A short, shrub-lined path may be necessary, or there may be native plant growth you can take advantage of. If there is a tree reasonably near by take that as the major feature and build around it, using whatever shrubs or evergreens accord with its character. For example, an old apple tree would take native viburnums, honeysuckles, white lilacs, old-fashioned herbaceous peonies (white), junipers. Or a patriarchal pine, if you are lucky enough to have one, would take dark, needled evergreens, the pale pink azalea *Schlippenbachi,* andromeda, mountain laurel, low rhododendrons, perhaps a white birch. Or you might already have a woodsy patch of native growth which would need only clearing and selective planting.

If your property lies in open, sunny farm land, the rocky pastures sprinkled with slender red cedars (actually junipers, *Juniperus virginiana*) you could use these. And you could probably move them yourself if they are on your own land, or you got permission from their owners. These junipers move easily if taken when very small and with a good ball of earth, the foliage hose-sprayed daily for the first week or so after moving. I once saw them used, closely planted, as a semicircular background for a small garden and they were very good indeed. So if you must construct a background you might consider these for enclosing your grey-green garden.

White lilacs would go well with these, faced down with low, spreading grey-green junipers, either *J. Pfitzeriana compacta* or the smaller and more interesting Sargents . . . and, close by, the white flowering quince *nivalis* (sometimes listed in catalogues as *Chaenomeles* but more often, and erroneously, as *Cydonia*). This white quince with its snowy flowers and firm, shining leafage is particularly good against the soft feathered grey of the junipers.

Another plant especially effective with junipers is the glossy, shrubby *Euonymus kiautschovica* which, luckily, is better known as

E. patens. This dark and shining beauty is evergreen in gentler climates but here it drops its leaves which are quickly replaced, in spring, by new growth. It will reach 6' to 8' further south, or near water, but in our cold, dry area it stops at about 4', is happiest in deep shade and needs shelter from winter winds and sun. Mine, in a protected spot and with a heavy mulch, has been root-hardy to 25° below zero.

The perfect tree for your grey-green garden, if you need a tree, is the grey-foliaged Russian olive (*Elaeagnus angustifolia*) with its black branches and small, narrow, pale grey leaves which form a silvery cloud, give dappled shade. This is a light, airy tree to about 25', the slender twiggy branches start low but you can easily high-head it (cut away the lower branches) if you get one with a single stem; left to itself the branch lines are erratic, sometimes fascinating and sometimes not, but this can be easily controlled. It is cast-iron hardy, is used extensively in the Blizzard Belt for windbreaks, snow-breaks; prefers poor soil but good drainage, likes sun and wind, is fast growing, inexpensive to buy, and easy to plant. What more could you ask of a tree? Surprisingly, it is little known here in the East and I am constantly encountering gardeners who have never even heard of a Russian olive, who view mine with astonishment and delight.

This silvery little tree is especially effective near evergreens. If you have room for more than one so much the better. Or you could make an enclosing hedge of them, closely planted; in this case you should get small, shrubby ones and leave them unpruned close to the ground. They are sometimes difficult to find in this eastern area but the famous Rosedale Nurseries have them in specimen sizes. The hedging size is best bought, mail order, from one of the big midwestern nurseries. See catalogue list on page 243.

You will need patches of sun in which to grow the small, grey-leafed foliage plants which will be such an important part of your grey-green garden. *Stachys lanata* is one of the best—or, at least, one of the easiest—of these; the oblong leaves, varying in size, look as though they were made of pale grey-green velvet and the habit of growth is low, irregular, and fascinating. In June it sends up stalks about 12" high which bear small, pinkish flowers, but these are unimportant as the value of this plant lies in its pale, velvety leafage. It is a fast spreader and makes an excellent ground cover in poor to

Russian olives, early in May. No, they are not in bloom; that is just the silver leafage you see. These particular trees could have done with a little shaping; you can do anything with Russian olives if you have an eye for line.

average soil but must have good drainage and plenty of sun; after a few years the old woody parts should be cut out and new growth reset. Use it with junipers or with dark-leafed plants, with almost anything . . . put a sweep of it under and around the white quinces, other sweeps in whatever sunny spots you can find.

Where there is little sun the dark-leafed white-flowering myrtle makes an excellent ground cover. This, *Vinca minor alba*, is far more interesting and desirable than the common blue variety you see everywhere. It would appreciate a little humus in its bedding, and you can encourage it to spread more speedily by anchoring down the runners with hairpins. Use it in all shady areas and, where shade greets sun, its meeting with the stachys will be a pleasure to both and a delight to the viewer.

Upkeep: Almost none. Such a small and intimate garden needs no center. Let the low plantings and ground covers come right up to an informal path of flat, native stones, deeply set, which should lead from the entrance to the white bench. At first you would have to keep the weeds out of the ground covers until these become established, but after that there would be practically no maintenance.

III. THE HIDDEN GARDEN

This is the least expensive, the easiest to create, and to many gardeners may seem the most desirable. In some ways it is similar to the grey-green garden but the approach is different and the treatment is different. It can be tucked in almost anywhere, on any type of country property.

Again the idea is surprise. The late Gertrude Jekyll, who was in my opinion the most inspired garden designer of all time, constantly stresses the importance of surprise in garden planning, surprise and contrast, surprise and mystery. Miss Jekyll's own hidden garden (approached through a tunnel of yew!) was a symphony of gentle colors planned to give beauty to that secret spot for only a few weeks—but Miss Jekyll had a special garden for every blooming period throughout the entire flowering year, plus a full-time staff of gardeners to maintain all these different plantings. . . . It stuns the mind.

So here is my version of the Hidden Garden, scaled down to our smaller properties, unstaffed menages, and the necessity of making each area carry itself throughout the whole summer. It is nothing like as good as Miss Jekyll's but it will be a lot easier to create, will need almost no maintenance, and will add surprise and interest to your property.

It is a small garden. It must always be a small garden, and enclosed, so that it holds a sense of secrecy. It is a quiet, hidden place of gentle plants, and rocks, and birds that scratch around in the underbrush and make soft sounds. . . .

And it should have water somewhere. Water trickling down over a rock or dripping into a tiny shallow pool . . . the pool edged with flat stones, and ferns, and simple plants . . . nearby a low-swinging branch upon which a bird could sit to contemplate the pool, a possible bath . . . and all this come upon suddenly, surprisingly, because you followed a stepping-stone path through some bushes.

Most country properties have, somewhere, an expanse of lawn, either major or minor, with some kind of shrubbery around its edge. Often this shrubbery hides the children's play area, or the drying yard, or an incinerator, or a vegetable garden, or whatever utility makes life easier for you. Possibly such an area could, some day, be transformed into a tiny hidden garden. I know of one man who, in his later years, turned a large and labor-consuming vegetable patch—which had become shaded by surrounding tree growth—into a secret retreat of ferns and ground covers and the woodland flowers he had always loved; and a woman who made a similar sanctuary out of the play area and drying yard after her children were grown and, a little tardily, she got a dryer.

It is this lawn-edging shrubbery which is important because it can form the entrance to your hidden garden. Or, if no shrubs in the right spot, you might have to build up this entrance. A good choice for such an entrance planting would be *Cotoneaster divaricata* because it is fairly tall (to about 6') and dense, yet loose and spreading. It is also quite beautiful: a wealth of tiny pink blossoms in spring, a wealth of tiny glossy-green leaves all summer, and a wealth of scarlet berries in fall. Once established it is a fast grower, completely hardy, has no bugs or blights that I know of. It likes sun, average well-drained soil, you can get it from any good nursery, and it is not expensive. Set the plants about 6' to 8' apart (it bushes out almost that much) and, between them, sink a few flat stones to suggest a path.

Shade is going to be one of the important features of your hidden garden, so if there are no trees to provide this you will have to establish some. Usually, in a small garden, one tree will be enough, and it should be a very simple tree. Maybe a dogwood, but the common *Cornus florida,* not the Chinese or any of the "improved" versions. Or a native shadblow (tree form) which you could, perhaps, move in yourself from your own woods. Or a mulberry tree for the birds. Almost any simple tree of this size would be good if you have enough space. But there is also the matter of scale to consider; the larger the tree the larger must be the area it graces. So if your hidden garden must be tiny you had better choose one of the small, tree-like shrubs for the enclosure itself and, for the necessary shade, plant your taller tree or trees outside and to the southwest.

One of the most fascinating of these small, tree-like shrubs is the seldom seen honeysuckle *Lonicera Korolkowi* which looks like something out of an Arthur Rackham drawing. It grows to about 10′ in this area and has thin, rough, spreading, incredibly twisted branches, a strangely fey quality; it bears small, silvery-grey leaves, pinkish flowers in spring and scarlet fruits in fall. It would be the perfect small "tree" to curve over a pool in a secret garden and, like all honeysuckles, is beloved by the birds. It is hardy here, relatively fast growing, and seems content with just average soil. But, unfortunately, its life span may be only about twenty years; at least mine only lasted that long but perhaps this was because I took no care of it. Also, and still more unfortunately, it is very hard to find. I have not seen it listed, recently, in any catalogue and most nurserymen have never even heard of it. All you can do is keep asking for it.

If you can't find a *Korolkowi* there are other shrubs you could substitute until you do find one. The little *Viburnum Burkwoodi* bears the same fragrant, pale pink flower heads as the better known *V. Carlesi* but the habit of gowth is more open, airy and spreading, the leaves small, dark green, and semi-glossy; when grown on a single stem it makes a delightful small "tree" to about 8′. Another possibility might be a *Spirea Thunbergi* with its thin, lifting, arching stems (also to about 8′) which, in late April, are a foam of white blossoms, bear delicate pale green leafage the rest of the year. The only trouble with this is that, like all spireas, it will get coarse and bushy unless you keep after it, keep it thinned out; what you want for this quiet spot close to the pool is a light, open, airy affair, not a thick bush.

To enclose your hidden garden use simple, common shrubs: the large bush-honeysuckles (*L. tartarica* is a good one), the fragrant old-fashioned mock orange we used to call "syringa" (actually *Philadelphus coronarius*), the common lilacs (*Syringa vulgaris*), the simpler viburnums; perhaps a mixture of all for sequence of bloom. They are all easy, inexpensive, hardy, and will grow almost anywhere.

The interior of this hushed and secret place should be kept clear of all fussy planting if it is very small; mostly ferns and half-wild ground covers, a few bulbs. Sweet woodruff (*Asperula odorata*) is one of these half-wild ground covers, a sheet of white stars in May and a carpet of pale green whorled foliage the rest of the summer. The wild phlox, *P. divaricata*, is good next to the woodruff because its masses of pale lavender-blue flowers in May will be followed, eventually, by smooth, dark green leafage which contrasts well with the pale green of its neighbor . . . and save a spot for a drift of pale yellow primroses, the common kind, *Primula vulgaris* . . . and let spring-blooming forget-me-nots (*Myosotis alpestris*) colonize somewhere—but away from the phlox as the two blues do not get along together. The perfect blue to grow with these spring forget-me-nots is the blue of common ajuga. This is an exquisite color combination.

And let there be rocks to give strength and depth and serenity to this small area, if possible a large rock to sit on. How you are going to get the rocks there, unless they occur naturally, is your problem, but they will be well worth the necessary effort. And around the rocks use clumps of ferns grouped with the simpler daffodils; a spray of pale yellow daffodils against a great grey rock is something to delight the heart in early spring. Always combine ferns with daffodils as the bulbs will flower before the ferns wake up, then the fern fronds will arise to hide the withering bulb foliage.

Another early-spring bloomer to plant with ferns is the woodland bloodroot (*Sanguinaria canadensis*) because the snowy white flowers and heart-shaped leaves will appear while the ferns are still dormant and, again, the fern fronds will fan out to hide the bloodroot foliage which begins to look tired later in the summer. And don't forget colchicums, the autumn crocus, to supply drifts of blue, white, yellow, and lavender in late summer and early fall. All these plants will enjoy the same soil and site: soft, humusy, neutral-to-slightly-acid leaf mold bedding in filtered shade or morning sun.

If your hidden garden is large enough to take additional planting without looking junky there are several perennials and annuals which would do well in this same site and give bloom, in variety, from late spring through most of the summer: foxgloves, if they will grow for you, and mertensia, white and pink astilbes, foam flower, balsam, nicotiana, impatiens. Many of these you can raise from seed (see *February* for seed-sowing) at a fraction of the cost you would pay for plants. Also, many of these will self-sow so that each year you will have a fresh supply.

Upkeep: practically none, once the ground covers are established. With so much shade there will be few weeds.

About the pool: let us hope that your hidden garden is near enough to the house, or other water supply, to make a hose line possible; this is the easiest and least expensive way to play this. In most cases this arrangement takes only a lot of hose and a little ingenuity, and a tiny shallow pool is easily created. There are any number of plastic jobs on the market, all shapes and sizes, which you merely sink into the earth. Or you could use any shallow pan, the interior painted sand color and partially filled with sand, the edges hidden by flat rocks.

The problem is to hide the hose throughout its course, and this means snaking it through whatever planting is available between house and pool; if this hose line must cross a path be sure to sink it in a soft, sandy gully beneath the stones because otherwise it will suffer wear and tear and get tripped over. It will also have to be taken up in winter. However, I know by experience that any number of such difficulties can be overcome if you have the determination and the hose.

At the pool end: there should be a drop of from 6" to 1'—or more, if you choose, and the grade makes possible a series of rocks for the water to slide down—between the end of the hose and the pool. Rest the end of the hose (no nozzle) between two flattish stones slanted together to form a V, then put another flattish stone on top, shelving out to hide the hose end, and screen all this with ferns, or clumps of Siberian iris which are always good near a pool.

Then turn on the water, just a hair, and enjoy what happens.

If you are content with a slow, gentle drip, which is what the birds prefer, and remember to turn this off at night or whenever you are going to be away, you are not likely to need a dry well to absorb the overflow. In fact, you are better off without one because the earth around your little pool will then stay moist and this will enable you to grow, in this damp area, one of the most beautiful plantings of the whole hidden garden: the seldom-seen brook forget-me-nots (*Myosotis scorpioides* or, to most nurserymen, *M. palustris*) which so love water around their feet and will bloom, all summer long, a sheet of pale blue.

Seeds In The Guest Room

Seed starting, like child raising, is attended by innumerable theories. Each gardener has his own ideas on the subject, his own methods, and these he will describe to you at great length and tedium with or without provocation. Each system will have its own virtues and the choice is up to you. To make this decision still more difficult you will find, in almost every seed catalogue, an endless list of new "aids"—kits, mixes, containers, lamps, gadgets of all kinds— which, presumably, will help you produce fine strong seedlings with almost no work. Which to choose? Which are really helpful and which just money traps?

I can only tell you of my own experiences with some of these offerings.

For countless years I raised countless annuals in the house, each winter, without benefit of any modern luxuries and, usually, the seedlings turned into magnificent plants, far better than any I could buy. I started the seeds in pie tins (the old-fashioned kind until the foil jobs came along) and my own starting mix, sterilized the seed by shaking up a pinch of Semesan in the seed packet, kept the pans in the guest room with the heat turned low, and hustled the pans into sunlight whenever and wherever there was sunlight. When the seedlings outgrew the pie tins I shifted them into a richer mix in deeper tins (lately into the foil frozen-cake tins with always, of course, plenty of holes punched in the bottom and along the sides for drainage and ventilation) where, in the chilly 55° to 65° temperature of our winter guest room, they grew slowly and sturdily, grew fat and low and chunky with roots on them like Phyllis Diller's hair. When, eventually, I set them into the garden, nestled deep in compost, they started blooming within a week or so.

But to advocate such methods now would be like wearing skirts to mid-calf and a Coolidge button. So with some suspicion and the prune-face of the elderly I have recently been trying some of the new seed-starting aids pushed by the seed catalogues.

My first venture into modern living was to try the One-Steps offered by the Park catalogue. These One-Steps, in case you do not know them, are little patties of compressed growing medium which, when wet, expand in minutes into globes which look like individual chocolate soufflés. You sow a seed, or a few seeds, on the top, press down gently or cover lightly if seed is large, and set in a warm spot for germination. These One-Steps have their own perforated trays into which twelve of them fit neatly when wet, and these trays sit in waterproof bottom trays so that just the right amount of moisture is absorbed by the growing medium; you water the bottom tray only. This prevents over-watering.

When the little green sprouts start up you set them, trays and all, in whatever cool spot you have chosen for this project. There is enough fertilizer incorporated in the One-Steps to feed the seed-lings for about four weeks; after that you are supposed to water them with a weak solution of some soluble plant food. You are also supposed to thin out the seedlings to the strongest single sprout per One-Step so that this individual can grow to robust maturity in its own personal container. (What I do is prick off the extra sprouts and set them in some other container simply because I cannot bear to throw out a healthy plant no matter how small. But let us hope that you are more callous and intelligent about this than I am.) When planting-out time comes you just set the whole One-Step into the garden where it takes hold immediately. This avoids transplanting shock to the seedling.

I had a lot of fun playing around with these One-Steps last summer. They grew the best delphinium seedlings I have ever raised, and I have raised many. They also worked magic on cuttings in the fall. The growing medium is held together by a plastic net so the little chocolate puffs are easy to handle individually and you are overjoyed to see roots bristling through this net. The delphiniums I set out in September in a protected growing-bed where, covered with vermiculite, they came through the winter in fine condition. The cuttings (Boston daisies and impatiens) I potted up and they soon started blooming in the house. Incidentally, the trays mentioned above are a lasting investment, can be re-used endlessly with fresh One-Steps which may be ordered separately. All highly recommended.

Next I tried Park's Seed Starting Mix and this also I recommend. It is sterilized, so you don't have to bother with Semesan in the seed packet, and is a joy to use; you just pour it into the seed pan, set this pan in water to soak up moisture, sow the seed, and you are all done. Although the One-Steps may be easier if you are a beginner, or attempting difficult seed, I personally prefer the seed-pan method as I enjoy pricking off the tiny seedlings and setting them in my own home-made growing mix. (Park also offers a Growing Mix which I have not tried but which might be easier if you don't have your own ingredients handy; I squirrel mine away in the fall, keep them in the cellar.) To me, handling plants is a deep pleasure, the feel of the earth, the soft yet gritty feel of a good soil mix. Also, manual dexterity with plants is something you are going to need all your life if you intend to become a serious gardener, and one of the best ways to develop this dexterity is to transplant tiny seedlings. At first you feel as though you were operating with mittens on, but you soon outgrow this stage and the sight of a pan filled with brisk, bright seedlings is cause for pride. I transplant mine when very small, find they come along better than when allowed to crowd each other in the seed pan.

I have proved time and again, at least to my own satisfaction, that seeds germinate faster and more completely in a shallow container, such as a pie tin, than in a deeper one. I well know that all garden books, all seed-sowing directions, recommend seed pans two or three or more inches deep, but I have made tests on this, have sown half a packet in my shallow (1″ deep) pie tins and the other half in deeper containers, then subjected both to the same germinating conditions to see what happened. Invariably the seed in the shallow container has produced more sprouts faster. Possibly this is because of more air, better soil ventilation, for I punch holes not only in the bottom for drainage but also along the sides for air vents. Throughout this whole book you will find constant harping on ventilation for it has been my experience that this is essential to the well-being of almost all plants in all stages of growth. I have found, also, that cuttings will strike faster if the container holding the growing medium is well ventilated along the sides. I use foil containers for certain cuttings too.

So, as far as containers are concerned, I suggest that you save money here and use these foil ones which come free, in all sizes, depths, and shapes, under any number of frozen foods; they are feather-light yet strong, easy to poke holes in, and most are just about the right size to take six to ten seedlings, thus providing you with extra pans to give away to friends—and no worry about getting

Planting Suggestion to Consider: This shows what wisteria can do for a simple garage-and-toolshed combination. Or it could be used on a garage alone, any bare wooden wall in sun, and is particularly effective in winter. The wisteria branches, trained when young into pleasing lines, are held in place by telephone wire fastened, loosely, to large, strong staples driven securely into the wood. This allows the necessary air space between vine and wood, also allows for growth of branches. Wisteria is easy to train when young and pliant. Use purple wisteria on a white building, white wisteria on anything else.

THEODORA M. PRENTICE

your containers back. Also, the rectangular ones fit nicely on a cookie sheet with raised edges, which makes a fine light tray both for bottom watering and for moving your seedlings outdoors when hardening-off time comes. These cookie-sheet trays will also hold, and neatly, a large number of those square peat pots in case you prefer to transplant your seedlings into these; you fill them with a growing mix, insert the seedlings and, later, plant pot and all as the roots grow right through the peat. These, like the One-Steps, save transplanting shock. Very inexpensive.

It has been my experience that the most important factor in the successful raising of seedlings, indoors in winter, is room temperature; that seedlings subjected to the customary comfort of the American home—70° or over if the inmates are elderly—grow tall and weak and spindly with almost no roots, whereas seedlings grown under chilly conditions—a daytime high of 65° and a nighttime low of 55° or lower—grow far more slowly but with strong roots and a squat, vigorous top growth.

Yet, mysteriously, this important matter of temperature is seldom stressed, or even mentioned, in most gardening books or seed catalogues. You are told to start slow seeds "under glass", which is fine if you have a greenhouse, or even a cold frame (which you can get to through the snow!) but few gardeners do. The next recommendation is the "sunny windowsill" which, at a temperature of 70° or over, merely intensifies the heat. And in case you are wondering how your grandmother could raise such strong, healthy seedlings on her kitchen windowsill just remember that your grandmother did not have an oil furnace which kept going all night. That kitchen was mighty cold when she came down in the morning to stoke the range and get things warmed up, and those cold nights were the secret of her fine plants.

So your first concern should be to find some place in your house where these low temperatures can be maintained. Under such cool conditions the strength inherent in the seed will go first into root development, which is what you want, for the future health and flowering of the plant depends upon its root strength, its feeding apparatus which enables it to utilize the nourishment in the soil; without this ability to feed itself it can do nothing. This is why so many windowsill seedlings amount to so little when set outdoors.

Light, preferably sunlight, is just as important as cool temperatures but a lot harder to find in winter, so my next sampling of
la dolce vita was to try one of those plant lamps. As these represent
a considerable investment to most gardeners I pondered long and
thoughtfully, decided to try a small experiment: grow one pan of
annuals under the lamp and another pan—same seed, same growing
medium, same everything—without benefit of lamp, see which produced the best plants.

For this experiment I chose one of Park's Gro-Lamps, table
model, a double tube Bloom Lamp, having been told that this was
more effective than the single tube one. Beguiled by the photograph
in the catalogue which shows a family in summery attire admiring
the fine plants under their lamp, I set up this enterprise in a room
kept at normal temperature (65° to 75°) as seemed indicated by the
picture, and for this mistake I should have had my head examined.
I don't know what kind of plants they are growing in that picture at,
presumably, comfortable room temperatures, maybe house plants or
tropicals, but I soon found it impossible to grow good annuals in
such warmth. Or what I consider good annuals. My pans of ageratum and salvia *farinacea*, both normally very slow growers, shot up
far too fast, grew tall and skinny with almost no roots. Meanwhile
the control pans in the cold room were showing almost nothing
above ground, the tiny seedlings very busy making roots.

So I moved my lamp into the cold room, started fresh pans of
the same seeds, and this time got excellent results. The new seedlings came along far more slowly, but strongly, obviously making
good root growth. And the tops, encouraged by the lamp and
strengthened by the cold, grew brisk and firm. In about six weeks
they had caught up with and passed the seedlings sown earlier
but grown without benefit of lamp. When set into open ground
later in the spring these lamp-grown seedlings were much larger and
stronger than the others, some were even budded.

All of which has convinced me that a Bloom Lamp is a very
good investment indeed, and that the old-fashioned ways are not
necessarily the best no matter how swathed in nostalgia.

Here are some miscellaneous tips on seed sowing in general,
fruit of my own experience. You will find that some of this advice
differs from that found in other garden books so take your choice.
I do not claim that my system is The Way—other gardeners raise

excellent plants through quite different systems—but it is the way which has proved best and easiest for me.

1. Keep all seed packets in the ice box until moment of sowing.

2. Be sure to mark each seed pan as soon as sown. My method, using foil pans, is to punch a hole in the rim of each pan and, using a wire twister, fasten the seed envelope to the pan, adding date of sowing; this will give you a check on how soon to expect germination. When seedlings are moved into a deeper pan, with suitable growing mix, transfer this envelope to the new pan, again using the wire twister. This is a far more secure way of marking your seedlings than the stuck-in plant label method.

3. Always fill seed pans all the way to the top, preferably mounded up a little. This insures better aeration around the seedlings; seed pans filled only partially are more apt to invite the dreaded damping-off. This damping-off (seedlings wilting at soil line and toppling over) is not likely if you use a sterilized soil mix, or shake up a pinch of Semesan or Rootone in the seed packet, but even with these precautions you can sometimes get damping-off from over-watering, inadequate drainage, insufficient air around the seedlings, or too rich a soil mix. If you see seedlings toppling over, looking pinched at the soil line, take these out immediately and destroy. Then water the soil surface with a Semesan or Rootone drench (directions on package). Or if you don't have either of these dust surface with sulphur. Or if no sulphur mix two tablespoons of vinegar in a cup of water and drench surface with this. Sometimes these remedies will save the remaining seedlings and sometimes not.

4. I use a thin layer of vermiculite on top of all seed pans after the seed has been sown. This provides a sterile, ventilated covering which allows air yet conserves moisture, prevents the surface from drying out. And I use a slightly thicker covering of vermiculite around all seedlings when they have been pricked off into the deeper pans, the growing mix. This seems to give them comfort.

5. Most seeds of annuals need a bottom heat of about 70° to germinate. Easiest way to provide this is to use a folded bath towel on top of a radiator which has been turned low. The seed pan should be covered with newspaper or a paper towel during this germination period and kept out of sun or strong light. If the germination period is lengthy (ten days or more) check moisture

content of pan every few days. To do this remove paper covering, then cover pan tightly with a piece of plastic wrap, wait a few hours and see what happens; if plastic shows a mist of moisture underneath then no further watering is needed at the moment; if plastic remains dry set pan in shallow water for a few minutes, then lift out, remove plastic, restore paper covering, and return pan to radiator.

6. If you use a very shallow pan, such as a pie tin, germination is likely to occur far sooner than you expect so, after a couple of days, check this daily. I have had seeds of fast characters, such as marigolds, germinate in three days when sown in pie tins, take the usual five days in deeper containers with less ventilation. As soon as the little green sprouts start popping take the pan off the radiator, remove covering, and keep at normal room temperature (around 70°) for a few days more until germination is complete. Then put in the cool room and expose, gradually, to light, finally to direct sunlight. Or put under your plant lamp. (Note: you will find, to your further confusion, that all this differs from the advice given by the manufacturers of these lamps. I suggest that you try both methods and see which works best for you.)

7. Hardening-off: seedlings which have been grown slowly in cool to cold temperatures need comparatively little hardening-off as they are already tough and sturdy with good roots, accustomed to chill. However, they have not yet met up with wind and rain so should be exposed to these gradually, to gentle spring breezes and light spring rains, to night temperatures down to 40° and, later, to almost freezing. So for a few weeks you will be busy taking the pans out and bringing them in. This is where the cookie-sheet trays, mentioned earlier, will be invaluable as you can get so many pans on each tray.

I have found that the best hardening-off set-up is saw horses, with boards laid across them, on the sunny, protected side of a building or wall; shade-loving annuals can be hardened off on a porch. But when leaving pan out all night be sure they are high off the ground to protect them from night prowlers. Skunks and rabbits may investigate them otherwise, and raccoons will sometimes dump a pan of seedlings apparently just for kicks.

Well, I warned you at the beginning of this chapter: get any gardener started on his own system of seed-sowing and he will continue indefinitely. I am no exception.

Some Annuals and Fast-from-seed Perennials
You May Not Have Met

Every gardener has his favorite annuals, and this is as it should be, for if everyone grew the same flowers gardens would be tiresome indeed. Also, every gardener has his favorite seed catalogue and this, also, is as it should be. All the same, it is often profitable to check other catalogues as prices can vary enormously even for the same seed, and higher prices do not necessarily mean better seeds. Also, each grower has his own specialties, his own originations which are usually not listed in other catalogues. Often these are interesting, worth a try anyhow. I urge you to make the acquaintance of at least one new annual and perennial each year.

As you may have gathered by this time, the Park catalogue is my own favorite, though I often try specialties from other growers. The list of annuals and fast perennials which follows will refer to Park seed, unless otherwise specified, and will include only those which I return to year after year having found them endlessly useful. It is not intended to be a comprehensive listing.

AGERATUM (half-hardy annuals). These are easy but very slow. Best started in February, or March if you use a Bloom Lamp. The low blue varieties, your choice, are all valuable for edging, or for massing as a summer ground cover in sun; nice with dwarf white petunias. But my favorite ageratum, and one I call to your attention, is the tall variety *Mexicanum* which is listed as growing to 2′ but, for me, grows to almost 3′, spreading and bushy, with fluffy flower heads of an exquisite blue. This is a wonderful blender in the perennial bed. I believe it acts like a perennial in the South.

ALYSSUM (hardy annual). This is the popular sweet alyssum (Violet Queen, Carpet of Snow, et al.) which is so useful as edging. You are told to sow it, outdoors, right where it is to bloom, then thin out the seedlings. But I find you get earlier bloom if you start it in shallow foil pans, kept in the cool room, or on a sunny porch except in bitter weather; then, when the spring earth is ready to work, cut out small chunks about the size of a dime and set these where you want them to bloom. All alyssums bitterly resent any root disturbance but don't seem to mind this chunk system, a few of the tiny sprouts will die but enough will survive to give a good display, both fuller and faster than from individual seedlings sown outdoors. Also, these clumps will usually self-seed generously, and these self-sown babies are so much stronger that, the following year, they can be moved individually without trouble if you take up enough earth with their roots. All alyssums do best in full sun, average well-drained soil.

ARCTOTIS (half-hardy annual).   *A. grandis,* the blue-eyed African daisy, is a delight, and easy. It has pearly white petals around a blue center, has uprising, silvery-grey leaves, beautiful in themselves. I have found it fairly fast when started in the house in early April, set out after all danger from frost. It likes a hot, dry, sunny spot and is most effective when grouped in clumps between other plants as the stems are apt to be a little weak. It is excellent for cutting.

BALSAM (hardy annual).   These are among the most useful of all annuals as they bloom well even in considerable shade, the small, waxy, camellia-like blossoms nestling amid glossy dark green leaves. They come in a variety of colors and heights, from 2' down to the 6" Tom Thumbs, the little plants bushy and vigorous. Park has them in the separate colors which are usually so hard to find. You could use the very dwarf 6" ones as a ground cover in partial shade. I have found all these balsams easy, fast, and simple to transplant. When set out they prefer a moist, rich soil and protection from hot sun.

CHRYSANTHEMUM, Korean Daisies (hardy perennial).   These early-September-to-frost bloomers are easy from seed, quick enough to start flowering the first year, and the color range is a luscious blend of muted autumn shades—cream, buff, bronze, pale to deep yellows, soft pinks and wine reds—which are dandy for cutting and combining with the soft blues of autumn asters. They are best grown in the cutting garden as they are vigorous spreaders, like most chrysanthemums, though they need less attention; you can let them go several years without division if you have the room. Thoroughly hardy here and the flowers survive several frosts. Park's

Korean Sunset, mostly singles with some semi-doubles, is the best blend I have found so far. They like sun and good drainage, almost any soil.

CLEOME (hardy annual). This feathery charmer, suffering from the unfortunate name of spider flower, is an airy, bushy affair often growing 4′ high and 3′ across. Once established it will, if happy, self-sow year after year so that you have a continuous supply in that area. It is a little weedy for the small perennial bed or border, for any small garden viewed from close by, but makes a soft and delicate background for a more spacious planting. Easy from seed, reasonably fast, and does not mind moving when small; likes plenty of sun, average soil. Pink Queen is the best in my opinion.

COSMOS (half-hardy annual). The only cosmos I grow is the white (Purity, to 4′) because it is so useful for tall background masses, also for cutting. It is easy but a little slow and, when frost danger is over, should be set out, singly, in an open growing bed in full sun until the little plants strengthen and grow tall enough to survive in back of other plants in the border. They then show up best when closely massed as, individually, they are thin and spindly. Give them plenty of sun, average soil, and work in a little potash to strengthen the stems.

CYNOGLOSSUM or Chinese forget-me-nots (half-hardy annual). For this one I switch to the Burpee catalogue for their Blanche Burpee mixture which is seldom listed elsewhere. I usually dislike and distrust mixtures but this one is a really beautiful blend of different blues, from the palest to the deepest. But it should be used in masses, partly because the colors are so lovely together and partly because, individually, the plants don't amount to much. Try a deep swirl of these blending blues in front of a feathery crescent of pink cleome and white cosmos in a relatively distant planting. It is easy from seed, fairly fast, does not resent moving, prefers sun but will tolerate some shade.

DELPHINIUM, Connecticut Yankees (hardy perennial). This new and smaller version of the older delphiniums is a blessing to the gardener with limited space for the plants grow only about 2½′ high. The flowers are single, quite open, and well spaced on the blooming stalks, come in heavenly shades of blue, the little plants bushy. It couldn't be easier from seed and is so fast—for a perennial —that if you sow it in February or March it will likely bloom in September. At least it has for me. After that you are all set for several years if you protect it a little over the first winter (see article on delphiniums in *July*). Almost all seed catalogues now list it.

HESPERIS *matronalis* or sweet rocket (hardy perennial).   If you don't have this somewhere on your property you should start it, and after that you can forget about it for it will take over and bring late-spring beauty to all those odd areas you never knew what to do with. It blooms from late May well into June, grows about 3′ tall, and looks like a poor relation of phlox, but when it naturalizes in great sweeps it is a lovely thing to gaze upon. It is easy from seed, but order only the white because the self-sown seedlings will often be pale pink, or pale lavender, or darker lavender, and it is this blend of related colors which make it so effective when massed. It is, usually, too weedy for most perennial beds—though I use it, grouped, at the half-wild end of a very casual one—but when used in cultivated plantings it can be cut down after flowering to form a coarse but pleasant clump of dark green leafage against which to grow low annuals, and sometimes it will bloom again in late summer. However, I should warn you that it is scorned by many gardeners. Be that as it may, I get great pleasure from the fragrant flowering of this simple country plant.

HOLLYHOCK, *Althea rosea* (hardy annual or perennial).   This should, properly, have been listed under its botanical name, but as most gardeners know altheas only as shrubs (Rose of Sharon) it seemed less confusing to use the common name. Everyone knows hollyhocks.

But did you know that there is a dwarf form, an annual, relatively quick from seed which grows only 4′ tall? This one is bushy and compact, has semi-double flowers. Park has this in separate colors. Burpee also has an annual hollyhock but in the tall form, to 6′, mixed colors only. And, of course, there is the traditional perennial type; these come in singles, doubles, carnation and powderpuff forms, all to around 6′. All hollyhocks are easy from seed (I suggest you use the One-Steps mentioned earlier) and will self-seed lavishly if happy. There are few other plants better suited to the country garden.

IMPATIENS (half-hardy perennials). If you have shade problems you should try these as they are fairly fast and very easy, but they are certainly not hardy here. They come in various heights, from 2' down to 6", and in a wide range of colors. Park has an extensive listing, in separate colors, and you can start them at almost any time of year as they also make fine house plants. I set them out in spring for all-summer bloom and then, when heavy frost is expected, pot them up and bring them in the house where they will continue blooming on a windowsill. Cuttings can be taken at any time and will even root in water.

Sweet rocket gone wild near an old barn with weathered siding. Once you get sweet rocket started you just let it go; positively no upkeep. And it is very fragrant, fine for cutting if you have a simple house.

EUGENE D. TRUDEAU

MARIGOLD (half-hardy annual). Nobody needs to be told how fast and easy these are; nothing seems to bother them except rabbits. The tall (to 30″) pale yellows are nice with the soft mixed-blues of *Salvia farinacea,* with all white flowers, and are good for cutting; the low ones are useful for edging where you want a line of bright colors. The most flowerful of these edging marigolds I have yet discovered are Burpee's Nuggets which give an incredible amount of bloom, unceasingly, from early June until killing frost. These Nuggets are mules so do not pause to set seed, which accounts for their uninterrupted bloom. They grow about 10″ tall, bear relatively huge flowers, and come in bright yellow, gold yellow, and orange. You can take them up in the fall, pot them, and they will continue blooming for several weeks more in a sunny window. Burpee catalogue for this one.

MATRICARIA or Feverfew or Camomile or *Chrysanthemum Parthinium* (hardy annual or perennial). This is usually listed in most catalogues as an annual, perhaps because it blooms the first season from early-sown seed, but for me it acts like a short-lived perennial lasting two, sometimes three years; then the old growth should be discarded and the new, outside growth planted afresh. It seems quite hardy here and is certainly one of the country-garden classics, beloved by our ancestors to whom it was a cherished plant both for its medicinal uses and its simple flowering charm. But the newer forms, and it now has many new forms, are far more flowerful while still retaining their gentle country character. The standard 2′ form now comes in both double and ultra-double versions which bear incredible masses of small white flowers all summer long. And there are dwarf forms (to about 8″) in pale yellow (Lemon Ball), bright yellow (Golden Ball) and white (Snowball) which are also masses of bloom all summer. And there is a little 6″ number called White Stars which is literally a mound of same. All of these are invaluable to the country gardener for they can be used in so many different places in different ways and are so easy to grow in just average soil and sun.

NICOTIANA (half-hardy annual). This is another valuable bedder for light to partial shade, easy from seed and moderately fast. The old-fashioned white *affinis* (to 2′) is still the most fragrant, and

Nicotiana Limelight used as summer filling for a partly shaded corner in front of a Japanese tree peony, the shrub-althea William R. Smith in the background. Earlier, white Madonna lilies rose up behind the peony, gave flowering interest before the nicotiana and Mr. Smith got going. This is the young peony which produced the blossoms pictured on page 118.

the most desirable for areas which are used in the dusk of evening when it opens up and perfumes the air, but it does little in sun. There are now varieties which stay open in sun, a tall white called Daylight and a greeny-yellow called Lime Sherbet, also a dwarf White Bedder, but none of these are as fragrant. The only trouble with most nicotianas is that they are inclined to flop and so look best when supported by other plants. The trick here is to get them to self-seed for self-sown seedlings are far stronger and more flow-erful, so watch the area carefully the following spring to see if there are any babies. If so you are lucky, and best leave them alone as they resent human interference.

PETUNIAS (half-hardy annual). I used to raise all my own petunias, but they are so slow and fussy that I now buy them ready-made. However, if you want to experiment there is one petunia which I found relatively easy. This is Blue Lace, which I believe was a Park introduction but is now listed by other catalogues as well. This is a good violet-blue with darker veinings, grows about 18″ tall, the plants stronger and with more substance to them than most petunias. It is a heavy bloomer with considerable spread and the foliage is excellent.

PHLOX *divaricata* (hardy perennial). You might be interested to know that this invaluable plant, which is mentioned so constantly throughout this book and can be used in so many ways, can be raised from seed. Park lists it, and this is the only listing of this seed I have ever seen in an American catalogue. As I have never tried it from seed I do not know whether it is easy or difficult, and I imagine it is very slow, but it might be fun to try if you are going to need a lot of it.

SALVIA *farinacea* Blue Bedder (half-hardy annual or peren-nial). Another plant I consider invaluable. For some reason this is usually listed as Wedgwood blue, but the ones I have raised turned out to be a heavenly blend of blues, from Wedgwood to pale blue, mostly pale blue. It is easy from seed but slow, very slow, and should be started in February, even with a lamp. But it is a delight in the perennial bed, makes everything around it seem more beautiful, and does not take up much room as the plants should be closely massed. Try it with phlox—any color—or almost anything else which blooms in late summer. I believe that in warmer climates it can be grown as a perennial but it is not hardy here and so should not be set out until after hard frosts.

ZINNIA (half-hardy annual). The fastest and easiest of all an-nuals except, perhaps, marigolds. As you well know, zinnias come

in all sizes, shapes, models, and colors, but here is a word of warning which may or may not interest you: the tall, bushy zinnias can
harbor horrendous spiders, so if you feel as I do about spiders be
very, very careful. Once, dumping an armful of tall zinnias into the
pantry sink for floral arrangements, I saw a moving object emerge
which at first I thought was a dark, hairy crab. . . . This was five
years ago and the memory still sends me into shock. I have not
grown these zinnias since, especially as I have heard similar horror
stories from other gardeners. There seems to be something about
zinnias which attracts spiders.

Imitation Shrubbery—Fast—From Seed

This is such a switch from the conventional characters listed
above that to append it here is like putting an anteater's tail on the
family beagle, but it is quite possible that you do not have the conventional garden, or any garden at all, in which case this information might interest you. It is for the home owner who is faced with
bare, new property and a bare, new house and no money.

CASTOR BEANS, *Ricinus* in variety (tender annuals). Did you
know that seeds of castor bean plants, poked into the ground after
frost danger has passed, will give you almost instant shrubbery?
That these plants will grow from 3′ to 8′ tall, bushy and quite
handsome? Like junk jewelry, which they resemble, they are not
going to fool anyone, but they will decorate your property in an incredibly short time and at a cost of less than one dollar for the
works. Recommended for temporary use only, just until you can
save up enough money to buy those shrubs and evergreens you
dream of.

Though I have a friend who grows these astonishing plants
regularly to keep out moles (see *April* for mole control) and they
are certainly striking. The speed at which they grow is unbelievable,
by midsummer you can have your own jungle. Or, of more importance, you can have screening, or backgrounds for other annuals,
or what might be referred to, merrily, as "foundation planting". If
you think I am making this up take a look at the picture in the Park
catalogue (1969 edition anyhow) above the castor bean listing. Park

offers a variety of sizes, shapes, and foliage colors; in fact, the only reason you grow these plants is for their foliage, the huge, tropical leaves ranging from dark red to dark green.

My friend gets her seed from Harris, their *Zanzibarensis* mixture because this includes the smaller 3' forms as well as the 8' ones. She says it is easy to tell which is which because the smaller plants come from the smaller seeds so you know which to put where; if you want a tall screen you put the big seeds 4' or 5' apart, or if you want a low—well, comparatively low—edging you put the little seeds about 3' apart, or spot them wherever you want them to grow. Or it might be possible to start these seeds a few weeks earlier, in the house. I would suggest One-Steps for this adventure, also advise you to be ready to run for it when the plants start chasing you, but this would give you well-started plants to set out without root disturbance when warm weather arrives. They like heat, and sun, and well-drained soil.

However, there is one danger which you should be aware of: the poisonous character of these plants which eliminates moles will also eliminate anyone who eats the berries, so if you have toddlers who like to sample such things better think twice. Older children could be warned, and if they have had any experience with castor oil they would have no desire to sample the plants.

Actually, although these tropical giants would look ridiculous near a country farmhouse or any traditional form of fine architecture —unless your sense of humor is even more distorted than mine— they look startlingly right near the stern, strong lines of many new houses, especially the contemporary types which flaunt tradition so courageously. So if you are young and gay and adventurous, with a brave new house to plant, by all means try these far-out characters. You might want to grow them every summer just as conversation pieces.

MARCH

Delusions of Spring

In our cold, mountainous part of northwestern Connecticut March is a month you treat with greatest caution. There are warm, almost hot days when you sit out on the steps lifting a pallid face to the spring sun and wondering whether your legs are still good enough to wear shorts again this summer (when you start questioning this the answer is probably No) and then, that night, the temperature drops to almost zero and you wake up to a blizzard. On our hill we don't take snow tires off until May.

The very real danger which lurks in these false spring days is the urge to get started on the garden, to rake and dig, remove the trappings of winter. After months of mostly sitting, punctuated only by purposeless walks, you have the figure of a woodchuck and the mentality of a stuffed owl; you can't wait to get out into the spring and employ your mind and your muscles in some meaningful work.

But—at least in northern sections—it is far too early for many of these activities. Innumerable plants are killed each year by eager gardeners who try to beat the spring and end up doing more harm than good. So the next few paragraphs will be a series of Don'ts, to be applied at your discretion to your own climate.

DON'T whip off winter protections—baskets, screens, mulches, etc.—until the soil beneath the plant has thawed out. This applies especially to young evergreens and all fall-planted material. The reason is because strong March winds and warm March sun, both dehydrating, can drain from such plants the essential moisture which the still-frozen roots cannot replace. Long established and hardy trees, shrubs, evergreens, etc. have, presumably, gotten their roots down below frost level and so can tap the waters under the earth, but such characters would not have needed winter protection in the first place. And don't be misled by the shallow surface thawing which, in sunny spots, often follows a few warm days; take a stick and gently poke around the roots and if you hit ice a few inches down leave all coverings in place for another week or so and then test again.

And, above all, don't remove ground mulches this early in the naïve belief that you are helping the soil warm up; you may help it warm up so fast that after the next hard freeze and subsequent thaw your plants will be frost-heaved clean out of the ground to die of root exposure. Even if they are not tossed out the roots can be fatally torn by this upheaval, or the resultant earth-cracks may admit air which can be equally disastrous. This applies especially to semi-hardy plants, shallow-rooted ones, or anything set out late last fall. Many plants need a long period of growing weather to get their roots firmly anchored.

Even when the hard freezes are over you should remove mulches very slowly, a layer at a time, waiting several days between each operation. Do not remove the final layer until the earth beneath has thawed out entirely. This, which will vary according to exposure and soil texture, can be determined by more pokings with the stick.

DON'T attempt to work wet earth, wait until all the frost has gone out of it. This will seem like a maddening and senseless delay, with the sun so warm on your head and your hands itching for spade or trowel, but if you touch that frost-wet earth you will destroy its tilth, cause it to become hard and compacted. Good growing earth in good tilth is an active, breathing thing made up of innumerable tiny air passages which allow circulation of oxygen and soil nutrients, assist drainage. When you work wet earth you close up those air passages and the result, when dry, is a heavy, lifeless, cement-like material which feels dead when you handle it. This is loss of tilth, and once tilth has been destroyed it is a long time rebuilding. This applies especially to the average garden soil which is usually deficient in humus.

So no matter how great the temptation keep away from those wet flower beds. Don't even step on them; wait until the soil has dried out naturally. The way to find out when this drying has occurred is to take a small handful and compress it gently in your fist; if, when you open your hand, the earth is soft and crumbly it is ready to work; if it remains in a lump it is still too wet.

DON'T rake out all winter leafage from under shrubs and hedges in the spring urge to clean up—that is, unless you plan to re-cover these areas with a good feeding mulch. The fall of leaves is designed by nature to nourish and protect plant roots, to provide food and conserve moisture. If you remove this natural mulch without replacing it with a reasonable facsimile you are depriving the plants of the materials they need to maintain health.

Many tidy gardeners feel that leaving winter leafage under a shrub is akin to leaving dust-mice under a bed; the difference is that you are growing live roots under the shrub and you are not, presumably, growing anything under the bed. If you must tidy up your shrubbery you can rake out the winter debris, putting it on the compost pile, and replace it with real compost or with store-bought humus laced with dried cow manure. This will not only benefit your shrubbery but will give you the feeling that you have done something important, which you have. Most shrubs and hedges are starved for such attentions and that they continue in even reasonable health is a miracle.

And now for some of the early-spring activities which will benefit both you and your property.

LAWN RAKING. This simple chore, which would bore you witless at any other time of year, seems interesting and invigorating after a winter indoors. At least you can make it interesting if you look for twigs and branches which you can use later on in the garden. Such material, usually strewn over lawns by winter winds, has a variety of uses.

I have found twiggy branches invaluable for guiding young clematis shoots upon their way towards the more major supports they will enjoy later on. These branches can be stuck in the ground, lightly, close to the clematis roots and the delicate tendrils introduced into the twiggy growth which they will accept with pleasure. Later, as the shoots grow taller and reach the lattice or trellis or chicken wire or whatever you use for clematis, the twiggy material, having served its purpose, can be clipped away.

Or you may find tall, outspreading branches which can themselves be used as permanent supports for clematis. One benefit of

using such branches instead of structured supports is that they are
less obvious, give a more natural appearance as the unused parts can
be clipped away. Also they cost you nothing, which is still another
thought.

Smaller twigs can be used to support the many perennials and
annuals which need support. Such twigs, stuck in the ground, are
soon completely hidden by leafage and give a far more natural and
graceful mien to the plant than the stiff and obvious stakes so commonly used and misused; often the foliage can be distributed over
the branching twigs to give form and structure to a weak-stemmed
plant which has neither. Though if you find too many weak-
stemmed plants it may be that your soil is lacking in potassium, or
potash if you prefer. An easy and inexpensive way to introduce
potash is to use wood ashes from your fireplace or scratch in a good
sprinkling of sulphate of potash. More about wood ashes later in this
chapter.

Still another use for this twiggy material is on seed beds or on
just-set-out seedlings: a light covering of small, much-spiked twigs
will support yet hold down a length of cheesecloth (or an old thin
organdy or nylon curtain) which, unsnagged, would soon blow
away. This is the easiest way to screen seed beds and infant plants
from sun and wind as the cheesecloth admits beneficial amounts of
light and moisture while keeping out injurious excesses of both. On
very windy days it is wise to anchor the edges of the cheesecloth (or
curtain) with stones.

PRUNING.   This is a good time to go over shrubs and small
trees with sharp clippers, lopping shears, pruning saw, and an
equally sharp eye for better lines and more graceful growth. Grape
vines, I believe, should be pruned even earlier, and fruit trees soon
thereafter to produce maximum harvest, but as both need special
treatment they are out of my bailiwick. Look them up in your garden books.

Small flowering trees (don't attempt a major tree yourself; get
a good tree man) should be looked at with an eye for branch lines.
Often such a tree will get cluttered up with incidental shoots which
are best removed as they not only interfere with the symmetry of
the tree but also sap its strength. And it is wise to start this elimi-
nation while the tree is still young, for not only will the job be

easier but you will get a more graceful and flowerful tree. Early spring, before the leaves appear, is the best time for such pruning as you can see more clearly what needs doing.

Flowering shrubs usually need thinning rather than pruning. Most shrubs tend to thicken up over the years with interior growth and the selective cutting out of this clutter improves both looks and ventilation. Usually it is the older and woodier stalks which should be cut away, close to the roots, but sometimes the new growth is so thick that some of this should be cut out too; often a shrub which is allowed to produce a forest of stalks will furnish more leaves than flowers. And, again, it is wise to start this cutting-out early in the plant's youth for an old shrub which has become a thicket is almost impossible to redeem, and no one knows this more bitterly than I do.

The cutting back of flowering branches which have gotten too long is usually postponed until blooming time so that these blossomy sprays can be used for the house, and often this takes care of the shaping. However, any major topping job, such as is often necessary on old lilacs, should be done far earlier, before the plant starts into growth. Occasionally these very old lilacs, especially some of the French varieties, have stern and beautiful lines which are treasured by the owners, but all too often they are merely skinny stems with a few tufts of growth on top. Such lilacs should be cut back approximately one third each year or so, allowing at least one growing season between each operation so that the plant has time to recover.

In any major pruning enterprise never cut back, or out, more than one third of the entire plant or it is likely to suffer shock. Of course, there are many woody plants which will survive far more drastic cutting than this but until you learn which is which you had better play it safe and stick to the one-third rule. Also, after any pruning operation always feed the plant liberally to help it regain health. A thick mulch of good compost, or compost mixed with dried manure, should be applied to the entire root area which usually extends out to the tips of the branches; many gardeners believe they are feeding a tree or shrub if they put a little circle of nourishment around the base of the trunk, but this does almost no good as the trunk itself has no way of absorbing the food and the feeding roots are further out, usually under the branches. So if you are going to feed a shrub or tree best put the food where it will do the most good.

THEODORA M. PRENTICE

Flowering crab, in blossom, shaped to give background outline to the mass of cotoneaster *divaricata* which, in turn, will give background to groups of tall white trumpet lilies in July. More white lily tulips were planted against the dark background but the puppy ate them.

Do you know the proper way to prune a woody plant? If not, better look this up in your garden books before you cause more harm than good. But, generally speaking, the procedure is simple: you cut, closely, just *above* a node or bud or incipient shoot which is heading in the direction you want the plant to take. Never cut carelessly between those nodes or buds as this will leave an ugly stub. Also, when cutting away any branch or shoot from a major part of the tree always cut flush with the main stem, or as flush as possible, so that no stump remains.

When cutting any branch large enough to necessitate a pruning saw always cut *upward*, from underneath, first of all; then start sawing downward, hoping that the two cuts will meet. The reason for this is to separate, cleanly, the under part of the branch from the main stem so that when the almost-severed limb falls from its own weight it will not tear down the bark of its former host.

In any major pruning operation it is wise to apply tree paint to the wound as soon as possible. As a general rule, any cut large enough to need a saw also needs tree paint. The purpose of the tree paint is to sterilize the wound until the tree has had time to take care of its own healing. This tree paint, which can be bought at any nursery or garden supply store, is thick, black and gooey; it comes in a can and the easiest way to apply it is with a small, stiffish pastry brush, preferably one with a rounded end. But better wear your rattiest apparel when handling this paint because it has an uncanny ability to get where you don't want it; cleaning fluid will remove it from your person but only a pair of scissors will remove it from your clothing.

When applying tree paint to a wound be careful to keep it away from the outer rim of the cut. This rim is called the cambium, it is the active, sensitive growing tissue between the bark and the wood and is important to the healing process; its mission is to grow out over the wound to seal it, and this it cannot do if sterilized by the paint, for a tree is a living, growing thing. So paint the central portion of the cut but NOT the outer rim, which you can easily recognize.

About suckers: many shrubs, and some trees, develop these and they should be removed, not only for looks but because they sap the strength of the host. Most authorities tell you to pull them out but this, I have found, is easier to write than to do. I usually end up by cutting them, as close to the roots as possible, which is not supposed to be good gardening but by the time I reach that stage of exasperation I don't care. There is also the theory that if you keep stripping off all leafage, year after year, the suckers will eventually give up and die. I have not tried this because I cannot decide which is the lesser of the two evils, the suckers clothed or the suckers unclothed. This is something you will have to decide for yourself.

About hedges: March is a good time to remodel your hedge if it needs remodeling. All hedges, whether evergreen or deciduous, should always be shaped on a slight slant so that the top is narrower than the bottom. There is a reason for this, as for most rules in gardening, and if you know the reason it is always easier to remember the rule: the slanted sides enable the foliage to catch rainfall and channel it down into the interior where it will do the roots the most good. A hedge cut straight down, perpendicularly, cannot do this; the only rainfall such a hedge can acquire must come through the top, and often this top becomes so matted with age that it acts almost like an umbrella, allowing little moisture to reach the roots. Consequently, such hedges suffer from dryness—especially as they are so seldom given a comforting mulch—and the interior becomes thin and meager. This is particularly true of deciduous hedges; the needles of evergreen hedges admit more rainfall through the countless interstices and present more open tops to the sky but even such hedges do better if cut on a slant.

SPRAY FOR SCALE.   March is—or used to be—the time when one sprayed for scale on euonymus, lilacs, quinces, and various other plants. Whether this picture has been—or will be—changed by the introduction of systemic pest controls is still uncertain. However, as the ground must be open, unfrozen, when such controls are applied it may also be a matter of geography.

The systemic pest controls (more about these later) are a new and important break-through in garden hygiene. The material is introduced into the soil around the roots and is absorbed by the plant throughout its entire system, rendering it immune to many chewing and sucking insects for periods ranging from six weeks to two months. Thus no need to spray. At the time of writing this the systemic controls now on the market affect only insect life—and not all of that—but I understand that scientists are not only enlarging the scope of present insect controls but are also working on a systemic which will control fungus and bacterial infections as well. By the time this book reaches you such controls may be available.

However, at the moment, scale, although a sucking type of insect in its earliest stages, is not listed among the pests controlled by the systemics now on the market. So perhaps you had better play it safe and use the old-fashioned spray method. There are several scale sprays to choose from, most of them poisonous, but the good old miscible oil is still one of the most effective, and certainly the safest to all concerned except the scale. Personally, I never use poison sprays; I disapprove of them on principle and have had some frightening experiences with them. But miscible oil contains no poison, it kills the scale insects by merely suffocating them in oil.

THEODORA M. PRENTICE

Planting Suggestion to Consider: You may not have a stone toolshed with slate roof but you could build a small arbor over the door of whatever you do have and train a flowering vine to grow over it, thus adding beauty to an otherwise dismal building. Wisteria is shown in this picture but a clematis *montana,* a climbing rose, a silver lace vine, or even an old-fashioned honeysuckle would be faster, lighter, and easier to control.

There are several different kinds of scale but don't stop reading because I am not going to describe them; if you want to know more about scale, which is doubtful, look it up in your garden encyclopedia. All you need to know right now is that scale, roughly speaking, is a collection of swarming bodies somewhat like the Grand Central Station at rush hour and that it attacks various ornamental plants. Sometimes the injury is unimportant, sometimes it is serious. With euonymus it may be fatal unless controlled in time.

During the first warm days of spring, which usually occur in

March in our climate, the soft scale bodies emerge from whatever they emerge from and can then be killed by the gentle miscible oil spray. Soon after this the hard shells develop and, in this stage, they cannot be killed except by violent poisons, and sometimes not even by these. So, to my mind, it is questionable whether systemic controls will ever be effective against scale in northern regions where the ground is still frozen when the scale insects are, briefly, vulnerable. However, I could be wrong. Perhaps when this book comes out I will sound like those sages who said that the Wright boys were just a couple of kids with a crazy dream.

Miscible oil is sold under various trade names and at various prices, but you can get it most cheaply at your nearest Farmer's Exchange or whatever agricultural co-op functions in your area. And you need only a small amount as the March (or dormant) dosage is one part oil to thirty parts water. Or forget this and follow the manufacturer's directions. You will also need a sprayer with a nozzle which adjusts to fog spray (try the 5 & 10, or the emporia which used to be called the 5 & 10s) and a gallon jug to mix the stuff in. Some moral fibre may also be necessary to get you started on this job but, once organized, it can be fun just getting out in the warm spring sunshine and doing something useful. And pick a warm spell as this spray should be applied only when the temperature is above 40° and likely to stay above freezing for about twenty-four hours.

The evergreen varieties of euonymus should be your first concern, and why some plantings are attacked by scale while others fairly close by are not is one of the sweet mysteries of gardening. I know of an extensive planting of *E. vegetus* which has never been sprayed and never known scale, while another planting a short distance away must be sprayed every year.

My own euonymus plantings—*vegetus, repens, acuta, minimus,* et al—receive varied treatments. Those in outlying areas are pruned back each winter by rabbits who eat every single leaf. At first I was distressed by this until I found that, each spring, these plantings burst into fresh, young, scale-free growth of unusual beauty and vigor. So now I am grateful to the little bunnies for maintaining the best euonymus plantings on the place. But the euonymus close to the house is not attended by rabbits and this used to show scale, needed spraying, until I started mulching it each fall with dried manure. Since then (two years) it has shown no scale. You figure this one out for yourself.

Speaking of rabbits—and they will be spoken of frequently as they are part of the country way of life—I have heard that if you supply these small creatures with plenty of this euonymus forage (*E. vegetus* is their favorite) they will not chew the stems of young trees and shrubs which, presumably, they eat only in final desperation. I do not know how true this is but I do know that in our own areas generously planted with euonymus the trees and shrubs are never touched.

But back to the actual spraying: you will probably need a helper. Most varieties of evergreen euonymus, except those plastered flat against a wall, send out long sprays of growth each year and these are the ones most apt to show scale, most in need of thorough spraying. The function of the helper is to hold out these shoots so that you can maneuver around in back to get at the undersides of the leaves where scale is most likely to settle. You will probably spray the helper as well as the shoots but as the spray-mist is harmless to humans this will be of no concern. Except perhaps to the helper, for miscible oil has a peculiar smell which is not noticeable at first but which later on, like the dead mouse in the piano, creates a haunting fragrance. So best not ask your teen-age daughter to help you if she has a date that night.

WOOD ASHES. Do you save the ashes from your fireplace? You should, for they are of great value to the earth, especially in the spring. Not only do they supply a certain amount of lime in a quickly available form but they are also an excellent source of potash (potassium), that essential mineral which strengthens stems, helps protect the plant from fungus troubles and bacterial diseases, and regulates the balance of other minerals. Most garden soils have a potash deficiency.

To be effective wood ashes should be applied dry, as they come from the fireplace. Ashes from an outdoor fire which has been rained upon are almost worthless as so much of their mineral content has been leached out. Hardwood ashes are best, but even softwood ashes are better than no ashes at all.

I have found that the easiest way to save these wood ashes, over the winter, is to put them into those large plastic bags which are sold as garbage pail liners. This is far more convenient than storing them in the usual cardboard cartons for, when you clean out your fireplace, you can put the wide-open mouth of the bag right into the ashes and push them in gently so that there is comparatively little dust; you then close the top of the bag with a wire twist. Also, these bags are lighter to move and easier to store than the boxes. More convenient to handle later on, too, when you distribute the ashes upon the earth; you simply allow a small opening in the mouth of the bag and waft.

Almost all forms of plant life—trees, shrubs, lawns, vines, bulbs, and most perennials—enjoy wood ash, in varying degrees, each spring. The only plants which do not like its alkaline properties are the acid-loving characters, notably the broadleafed flowering evergreens to whom lime in any form is often the kiss of death, and many of the woodland-type needled evergreens. There are also many small evergreen-type treasures, not commonly grown, which can be killed by lime: the heaths and heathers, andromedas, bearberry, shortia, and a lot more I can't think of at the moment; but if you grow any of those plants you are probably familiar with their culture. Yet some evergreens do like lime; the junipers relish it, and boxwood likes it in moderation; the yews and the whole euonymus tribe couldn't care less so don't waste any wood ashes on them.

Lilacs are greatly benefited by wood ashes in early spring, preferably on top of the snow; spread a thin layer over the entire root area, which is often extensive. Later, when the snow has gone, give a feeding mulch of compost laced with dried manure. Flowering quinces and cotoneasters will also appreciate this attention.

Most mixed-planting flower beds need the potassium content of wood ashes, and as the majority of popular bulbs and perennials either like lime or are indifferent to it this would be a good place to distribute some ashes. Be especially generous around clematis and gypsophila as these are lime addicts. Other plants to include in this largesse would be peonies, delphiniums, campanulas, pinks (*Dianthus*), candytuft, and whatever grey-leafed numbers might occur in such a bed; stachys is very fond of lime and so are the artemisias, *A.* Silver King especially needs the stem-strengthening properties in wood ash. The German or bearded iris would like a sprinkling but NOT—repeat NOT—the Japanese iris, *I. Kaempferi,* to whom lime in any form can be fatal; if you have any of these tall, stately beauties they should be grouped by themselves, not only to show to best advantage but because their soil preferences—moisture and acidity —differ from those of most mixed-bed perennials.

A great many perennial beds include spring-flowering bulbs and the majority of these would be helped by wood ashes. Especially tulips, as the potash will strengthen stems, improve color, and help protect the bulb from disease. But you can skip lily bulbs as most of the tall garden lilies, such as the Jan de Graaff beauties, care little about lime; one of the few exceptions is the lovely Madonna lily, *L. candidum,* which likes lime very much indeed and if you are not completely confused by this time it is no fault of mine. Every plant family has its odd-balls but you soon get to know them, and with no effort at all, as any experienced gardener can tell you.

If you believe that lawns should be limed every spring (some should and some shouldn't, depending upon how limey your soil is naturally) you can use wood ashes before the grass starts into growth; but not afterwards as this ash can burn tender new leafage, which is something to keep in mind throughout all these operations. Best wait until the snow has gone and then, allowing a small opening in the mouth of your wood-ash bag, walk slowly back and forth, wafting as you go.

However, this involves personal problems. Wood-ashes are feather-light, can be distributed upon your person by the slightest current of air, so it is well to wear some kind of enveloping garment, such as an old raincoat. Protection for the hair is also advisable—a large shower cap is fine—and as this ash can irritate the nasal passages if too much is breathed in you might want to add a towel draped yashmak-fashion over the nose and mouth and fastened atop the head with a safety pin. This ensemble is particularly bewitching if you happen to wear glasses.

Incidentally, getting yourself rigged out in such a costume is one sure way to invite unexpected callers. The only surer way is to have a dusty house full of dead flowers and unemptied ashtrays.

Compost, Anyone?

> The King asked
> The Queen and
> The Queen asked
> The Gardener:
> "Could we have some compost for
> The Royal flower bed?"
> The Queen asked
> The Gardener,
> The Gardener
> Said, "Certainly,
> I'll go and tell
> The Cow
> Now
> Before she leaves the shed."
>
> With profound apologies to
A. A. Milne. . . .

Well, if there are any readers left after the above I can tell them that cow manure, either fresh or stored under cover, makes the best, fastest, and cheapest compost. Even a relatively small amount added to your compost heap will work wonders. Assuming, of course, that you have a compost heap, and if you haven't you should. Such compost, used regularly in all planting and mulching operations, will not only give you healthier plants, more flowers, and tastier vegetables but will also save you a lot of money.

The reason cow manure used for compost-making should be either fresh or kept covered is because, when left outdoors for any length of time, the vitally important nitrogen leaches out of it and it is this nitrogen which heats up the pile, starts decomposition of the materials. So you want this nitrogen to leach out into your compost, not elsewhere.

Most country dwellers can usually wheedle a few pailfuls of fresh cow manure from a local farmer who, though well aware of its value—never underestimate the intelligence of a farmer—is apt to regard such a small amount with some amusement. On most well-run dairy farms the manure is taken out and spread on the fields every day, so you would have to arrange with the farmer when to call for your treasure. Occasionally there is a trifling charge for this bounty but usually you are welcome to help yourself for free. Depends on the farmer. But most farmers are nice people.

Or, if you don't fancy this fresh manure bit you can use dried cow manure, the packaged kind now available everywhere; this is pleasanter to handle but will cost you more money. Or you could use any of the many packaged products which "make" compost; some of these are organic in character and some are not, and all are relatively expensive. I have seen what looks like excellent compost made with these but many organic gardeners scorn them.

Some valuable information you should have on hand is contained in the little booklet "How To Make Compost in 14 Days" issued by Organic Gardening and Farming, Emmaus, Pa., 18049. This booklet is available only as a bonus with a subscription to *Organic Gardening,* a magazine devoted to this method, and could be particularly important to you in early spring when you need compost fast. Briefly, the secret of this speed method is shredding the materials first, which you can do with your power mower. But better get the booklet and read about this for yourself. Full directions are given for every step of the process together with many other tips on composting.

There has been an enormous amount of trash—or what I consider trash—written in the name of organic gardening. At one time a good deal of the literature extolling this system was filled with references to Healing The Earth's Wounds, to Rebirth, to The Wheel of Life, The Bosom of Mother Earth, and such nauseous verbiage (always with caps) which gave the whole idea the unpleasant aroma of a mystic cult. Also, some of the activities recommended were not only misty-eyed but misty-minded, such as mulching your garden with "kitchen wastes" (i.e. garbage) which is certainly an open invitation to rats and skunks. All this antagonized a lot of gardeners who might otherwise have maintained an open mind on the subject.

But this pseudo-spiritual approach has been largely overlooked recently as more and more gardeners are finding out for themselves the practical and economical benefits of using natural organic materials to replenish the earth, have found that this thrifty, old-fashioned method does actually produce healthier and more disease-resistant plants, better flowers, and more flavorful vegetables. Also, the study of organic gardening has moved out of the hallelujah-tent into the laboratory where the relationship of soils to human and animal health is being investigated scientifically.

One of the scientific groups studying this subject is The Pfeiffer Foundation, Inc. which conducts a research laboratory in Spring Valley, N.Y., another in Stroudsburg, Pa. This study, started by the late Dr. E. E. Pfeiffer, has produced a method which is called Bio-Dynamic Farming and Gardening. One product of this study is a light, granular, all-vegetable material called B. D. Compost Starter; about one tablespoon, dissolved in water and diluted, will compost one ton (1½ cubic yards) of rough material such as garden refuse, weeds, leaves, etc. It is available only by mail from The Pfeiffer Foundation, Inc., Threefold Farm, Spring Valley, N.Y., 10977, is sold in "units" (a unit is about one tablespoon) and is very inexpensive. I have not tried this myself but have heard enthusiastic reports from those who have. If you write to The Pfeiffer Foundation at the above address you will receive an envelope filled with information about this study, price lists, and complete directions for using the B. D. Compost Starter so you can see whether this method appeals to you before ordering.

PLANNING YOUR COMPOST OPERATIONS

Many gardeners, starry-eyed in the spring of the year over the dream of home-made compost, soon get discouraged because, gradually, the heap becomes so large that it gets out of hand, spreads and spills and doesn't "cook". It becomes a sprawling eyesore which merely sits, and the turning of this mess is a herculean job, exhausting for a man and impossible for a woman.

This problem can be avoided if instead of one huge heap you plan several small piles, or bins, to be used in rotation as each

matures. This is a far more practical method especially if you are
a woman alone, dependent upon male brawn for the heavy work;
there will always be plenty of other jobs for the handyman to do,
and what further masculine companionship you can get you would
probably rather employ in more interesting activities than the turning of compost.

Personally, I favor the bin method as neater and more easily
controlled. These bins can be constructed, either singly or in a
row, with metal fence posts and hardware cloth; this hardware cloth,
in case you haven't met it, is a strong metal-mesh job which comes
in different widths and is sold by the linear foot. You can get both
posts and cloth at any hardware store. Or, if you prefer, you can
use cement blocks to build your bins (open ends laid horizontally
to guide in ventilation) but these are clumsier and take up more
room, sometimes shift.

If you decide on the permanent, no-upkeep metal construction
get the 5′ posts, which cost around a dollar apiece in this area, and
drive them in deeply enough to have a little over 3′ above-ground
height. This will take, neatly, the 3′ width of hardware cloth (the
¼″ mesh is best) which costs about 50¢ per running foot around
here. In measuring the amount of hardware cloth you will need to
allow an extra 3″ for each corner as this metal mesh is too stiff
to bend sharply.

You then fasten this mesh to the outside of the posts (which
have holes in them) with the thin, pliable wire you buy for this
purpose. But I advise you to handle this wire with caution, to wind
it on a stick before you attempt to use it, for it comes in a coil and
once this coil is opened up you will find yourself entangled in endless convolutions of wire with no visible ends. You can waste half
an hour just trying to unsnarl this mess.

The front opening of your bin, which will swing outward like
a door for easy loading and working, can be finished with a vertical

LAURA LEE FOSTER

board to give strength and stability; have this board extend a few inches above the metal mesh so that it can be loop-fastened to the corner post. If the front opening is more than 4′ wide two or more such vertical boards may be necessary.

SIZES

Most compost-making directions recommend a medium-sized heap or bin: a height of from 3′ to 5′, a minimum width of from 4′ to 6′, and whatever length seems desirable. Smaller heaps or bins dry out faster and do not heat up as well. However, a bin 3′ to 4′ wide (front to back) and about 4′ to 6′ long is the maximum size a frail woman can handle with ease. If you consider yourself more stalwart, or have a lot of material to compost, regulate the measurements accordingly. But it is better to underestimate your abilities than overestimate them, better to plan a bin which will be easy to work than one which will soon become a dreaded chore. Two bins of moderate size should supply enough finished compost for the average small property.

LOCATION

Shade is recommended as it helps conserve moisture. If you must use a sunny area you can shade the materials with pine branches, or coarse-weave burlap, or an old window screen, for compost should never be allowed to dry out completely. What is just as important to you as to the compost is that a dry heap or bin gives birth to a particularly vicious species of tiny ants which will swarm up your legs when you approach. So best keep your compost moist—not soggy wet, just moist—then no ants.

Actually, a compost heap or bin will bless any spot it occupies as the gradual seepage, working down into the ground, will be eagerly enjoyed by whatever plant roots are nearby. Thus you could put your bin on the shady side of a shrub border, or under a tree. I once put a compost heap under an old and exhausted pear tree, simply because it happened to be the handiest spot, and was astonished by what happened to the tree. It took on new life and the pears, instead of being small, gnarled, inedible rocks became big, juicy, and luscious.

Or you could make your compost bin a lovesome thing God wot by setting up a tall trellis on the sunny side and planting this trellis with flowering vines—roses, clematis, morning glories, or whatever—to partially shade the bin and screen off anything you wanted to screen off. Or you could plant tall shrub roses around your bin. It seems a pity that most compost is made in a hidden and dreary area where the surplus nutritive values are wasted.

ABOUT MANURES

If you use animal manures there are certain facts you should know. Most compost-making directions do not distinguish between the various kinds of manure but there are important differences and you can get into a lot of trouble if you are not aware of them.

Cow manure is known as "cool" whereas horse, sheep, and poultry manures are "hot". These hot manures should not be used, when fresh, on compost—or anywhere else—as the heat can become so intense that it kills the beneficial bacteria. Also, such an over-heated compost pile will take a long time to cool down and can be dangerous to use until this cooling is complete. I learned this the hard way. And I know one gardener who ruined his beautiful compost heap by adding a couple of bushels of turkey manure, fresh from the turkeys, which not only cooked all the earthworms but turned the entire thing into a grey, lifeless mass.

Nor should these hot manures be used, when fresh, even as garden dressing. This, also, I learned through bitter experience having once killed off a whole planting of English delphinium seedlings by mulching them with too-fresh horse manure. The only place these manures might be used, when fresh, is possibly around deep-rooted and long-established trees and major shrubs. Or maybe I am being unnecessarily timid about all this—many gardeners will think so—but, to me, it seems wiser to be over-cautious than to risk disaster.

However, I do remember, out of my childhood, an old-fashioned chicken yard wherein grew the most magnificent peach tree I have ever known, its roots constantly fertilized by the chickens, its peaches the size of grapefruit and so juicy they exploded when bitten into. I have never forgotten those peaches nor seen the like of them since, so maybe fruit trees should be treated this way.

If you are given any of these hot manures while still hot the safest procedure is to store them in some unimportant spot until the heat has gone out of them, a process which may take from six months to two years depending upon the type of manure and how fresh it was to start with. A good deal of their mineral value will, of course, leach out but, when mellowed, they will still be beneficial as garden dressing. Horse manure is supposed to be the best, or horse-and-cow mixed. This is the "well-rotted manure" of legend, the handmaiden of beautiful gardens throughout gardening history. You can do anything with it: use it as a mulch, a dressing, incorporate it in plantings, or simply stack it up as a status symbol.

Cow manure, however, although too strong to be applied to plant roots when factory-fresh, cools very quickly, is gentle in action. Its chief value is on the compost pile but it can also be used as a winter dressing for the garden (its fragrance is a little too potent for summer use) where, come spring, its mellowed goodness will seep down into the earth.

Dried cow manure, the packaged kind, can be used the same way but the most effective and economical way to use this is as manure tea: make a cheesecloth bag (or cut up an old, thin curtain) big enough to hold about a cupful of dried manure, tie the mouth tightly with a piece of string with a long end to it, and let this bag soak for several days in a pail of water, the end of the string hanging over the edge. Then take it out and peer at the resultant brew. It will probably be too dark, in which case you dilute it with water until you have a pale amber liquid. This you apply with a watering can and it will be relished by almost everything in your garden. Particularly good to encourage second bloom on roses, delphiniums, Miss Lingard phlox, campanulas, etc. In fact, any number of early blooming perennials can be induced to bloom again if cut back after first flowering and given an invigorating snack of manure tea. This disappears into the ground without odor.

METHODS OF MAKING COMPOST

Detailed directions for the making of compost are found in almost every "complete" garden book or encyclopedia. Usually you are told to arrange specific materials in layers, so many inches of this and of that, to turn it thus and so and when. Undoubtedly this method produces excellent compost. But I, and countless other experienced gardeners, have made very good compost indeed without observing any of these formalities. We—many of us, anyhow—simply dump in the garden trash as it occurs, the used-up earth from seedling flats and pots, whatever manure is handy (usually dried), plus a little seasoning of lime or bone meal or wood ashes as the spirit moves; occasionally, when in the vicinity, we give the whole mess a stir, turn under what needs turning under, add a little water if indicated, and then go away and forget about it. In due time we get compost, and very good compost too.

So here is one garden book which tells you to make your compost by whatever method appeals to you most. Some people like to follow a ritual, some don't. But it is my contention that compost which is easy and pleasurable to make, to complete, will do your garden a lot more good than compost which becomes so complicated, such a dreaded chore, that it never gets finished.

From all the above you may have gathered the impression that, as an apostle of organic gardening, I disapprove of all chemical fertilizers, disdain the quick-and-easy "miracle" products. I do not. I use them myself whenever the need arises. But most of these are merely stimulants, the quick pick-up, the double Scotch after a long, hard day. They do indeed, just as the ads say, inject new vigor— or the appearance of new vigor—into an ailing plant and for this purpose they are admirable. But if a plant is ailing it shows that there is something basically wrong with either its bedding or its nutrition, that it needs the root-freedom supplied by humus, or the balanced meat-potato-and-vegetable nourishment which only the regular use of compost, rotted manure, or other organic material can provide over a long period.

So don't be afraid to use the chemical fertilizers now and then, especially on annuals. But don't depend upon such products as a way of gardening life any more than you would depend upon alcohol as a way of personal life. Both can be invaluable upon occasion but dependence upon either, unless balanced by proper nutrition, can lead to big trouble.

If you don't want to bother with composting your own plant foods look around your area for a feeding humus which can be used in place of compost. Such a humus differs from peat moss in that it is rich in active bacteria, trace minerals, and plant nutrients whereas peat moss has very little food value and takes a long time to break down, is useful chiefly for its spongy, soil-softening and water-retaining qualities. We have such a feeding humus in our northwestern part of Connecticut, it comes from a local bog and we consider it unique, but I have been told that such mineral-rich bogs occur in many other parts of the country where similar rich, black, compost-like humus is sold under various names.

Our local product, called LaFontan Humus, comes from South Kent, Connecticut, is a clean, odorless, completely organic material which looks like minced black velvet, has a wonderfully springy, alive feel to it. It is entirely vegetable in character, contains no animal products, yet is so rich in natural minerals and plant nutrients that even a small amount of it added to the poorest soil will produce spectacular results. It can be used like compost to feed, soften, aerate, and enrich the earth, the only difference being that its continued use should include, annually, the application of a small amount of organic phosphates and potassium. Ground rock phosphate (or bone meal) and green sand (or sulphate of potash), mixed together and dug in lightly over the earth, would be the least expensive for large areas, or you could use Fertrell for small properties. No other fertilizer of any kind is needed and, furthermore, plants grown in this humus are remarkably resistant to bugs and diseases.

This LaFontan Humus is the decomposed remains of a forest millenniums old. The power shovel will bring up great sections of huge tree trunks, the rings of their ancient growth still distinct, which will crumble at a touch. Just a little of this humus will turn hard clay soils into soft garden loam, yet its action is so gentle that it cannot burn plant roots: seeds can be sown in it, tender seedlings bedded in it, cuttings rooted in it, in each case with remarkable results. Even the seepage from this humus can cause startling growth; one spring Mrs. LaFontan left a bushel basket of it on a patch of sandy clay soil where the so-called "lawn" had died out for lack of nourishment, and when she remembered it several weeks later the basket was ringed with lush green grass, a small oasis of fertility in a barren area.

The LaFontans, discovering this humus on their property, at first dug it out by hand, used it only on their own gardens (it grows vegetables of extraordinary size and flavor, so rich in vitamins and minerals that the LaFontans maintain a remarkable health record) and as gifts to friends and neighbors. But news of this humus soon spread and gardeners in surrounding areas begged to buy it. Now it is taken out by power shovel, put through a shredder, and either packed in strong plastic bags to be sold at the shed or piled up to be called for by truck. Yet, surprisingly, it is not expensive. This is still a small family enterprise and the LaFontans are not greedy. Like so many gardeners they are glad to share their bounty with other gardeners—a characteristic of gardeners everywhere—and the generously filled 50 lb. bags are, at this writing, only $1.20 each (no shipments), the bulk humus $7.00 per yard when called for. The LaFontans will deliver, when possible, within a fifty-mile radius on truckloads of 15 yards or more but in this case the trucking charges—which are considerable—have to be added to the price. It is far cheaper to do your own trucking.

So if you are ever in the neighborhood you might like to stop in and sample this unusual humus for yourself. South Kent is part of Kent, Connecticut, to the east of Route #7 which runs north and south through the state. If approaching from the north on Route #7 you would turn left at the Kent stop light, then immediately right, following the signs to South Kent for about three miles. If approaching from the south you would leave Route #7 just after crossing the Gaylordsville bridge, turn right, then left, following South Kent signs for a little over two miles.

South Kent itself is a tiny hamlet you could whip through without even realizing it; there is a post office housed in a frame building but the sign over the door is so small you can't read it from the road. However, there is a big "LaFontan Humus" sign at the driveway which leads up to a small stone house. You drive up and around to the back door—for this is an informal family affair— and Mrs. LaFontan herself will probably step out to greet you if she knows you are coming; better telephone first, the number is (Area Code) 203–927–3446. She is a woman of great warmth and great enthusiasms, has been studying organic and biodynamic gardening for fifteen years and is always eager to talk to another gardener. You will enjoy meeting her.

Dept. of Wildlife

In the spring of the year the little animals emerge from their various winter retreats and make a lot of trouble for the country gardener; they tear up or tunnel through lawns and gardens, chomp on buds and tender new shoots, frolic through plantings breaking down stems. How to deal with them, mercifully, is a problem.

Here are a few suggestions which might help you.

MOLES. Contrary to popular belief, moles do not eat bulbs (tulips, lilies, etc.). It is mice which eat bulbs, often using the mole runs as a handy turnpike. Mice will also establish their own runs, lured by the scent of a delectable bulb—the more expensive the bulb the headier the scent and the more luscious the taste, apparently— but this damage should not be blamed on the mole who is going about his own business, which is searching for grubs. and earth- worms, and couldn't care less about your bulbs. What to do about mice will be taken up at bulb planting time, in *October,* as these voracious wee timorous beasties do most of their damage during the winter.

When moles burrow through your lawn they are searching for grubs, usually Japanese beetle grubs (their favorites) which are obviously nestled under the sod. In this activity they are doing you a big favor for without their help these grubs would turn into still more Japanese beetles to propagate their kind ad infinitum. Skunks are also looking for grubs when they dig those holes in your lawn so both of these animals are, actually, beneficial to the gardener. It is certainly annoying to have your nice smooth spring lawn heaved up, dug up, but this is a comparatively minor problem, you can always tramp down the ridges and fill in the holes with no permanent harm to the lawn.

However, when moles start tunneling through the garden in search of earthworms, opening up possibly fatal air spaces around plant roots, the problem can become a major one and something has got to be done about it. Well, here is a way to get rid of moles in the garden without resorting to those dreadful traps which skewer the little things and hold them there to die in pain. To be at once a gardener and a lover of small animals is a most unhappy combina- tion.

I have a friend, a superb gardener, who for years has been building up her soil with all the goodies known to organic garden- ing. Consequently her plants are magnificent, her flowers incredi- ble, the soil deep and dark and soft and teeming with earthworms. Also teeming with moles.

At least it was until she read somewhere about the castor oil caper. It sounded absurd but she decided to try it—and it worked.

This is what you do: take equal parts of castor oil and a liquid detergent, add a little warm water and with a beater (egg or whatever) whip up this repulsive mess until it is afoam. Then put two or three tablespoons of this into a watering can of warm—repeat, warm—water, mix well and, using the sprinkler cap, douse the soil wherein are the moles. Best time to do this is when the soil is wet, after a rain or hosing, so that the oil can penetrate more deeply. And saturate the area, really soak it, not only the mole runs but the adjacent soil as well. Apparently moles dislike castor oil as much as you do and take their activities elsewhere. Two or three dousings may be necessary where mole infestation is heavy but all this does no harm to the plants involved. This treatment will keep the area mole-free for from three to six months depending upon how serious the mole problem and how heavy the earthworm population.

Which makes one wonder whether building up your soil to such a high pitch of fertility is a good idea after all, considering the earthworms which are part of this package deal. These humble tillers of the soil are supposed to be of great value in a garden as they aerate the earth, keep it soft, and constantly enrich it with their minute droppings, but when they get so numerous that the moles flock in after them their mass value becomes questionable. My friend gets great pleasure from the extraordinary beauty of her flowers, the health of her plants, yet her life is plagued by this mole-earthworm problem. Well, my own plantings are nothing like as spectacular as hers but I have far fewer moles and far more peace of mind. Or maybe this is just sour grapes. . . .

But there is one gimmick in this castor-oil program you should be braced to meet: you go into a drug store and ask for a gallon of castor oil and not only will the druggist do a double take but everyone within earshot will turn to look at you with awe and sympathy.

My friend has also discovered another way to use this castor oil idea. She grows castor bean plants, wherever space permits, and this takes care of all the moles in that area for the entire summer. Castor beans (see *February*) are tender annuals, easy from seed which is listed in almost every seed catalogue, grow to astonishing heights (3′ to 8′) and have enormous tropical-type leaves which can be startling and quite decorative when well placed. These plants, which are very fast growers, make a quick and interesting temporary screen in case you are in need of same. However, they are poisonous, not only to the moles which shun their vicinity but also to humans. Not recommended for properties where there are children who like to sample plants.

GRUBS.   While on the subject of moles and their prey I can tell you how to rid your lawn of the grubs which the moles burrow after and the skunks dig up. This is a product called DOOM which spreads the milky spore disease through the soil killing every grub it encounters. It is also self-perpetuating as each diseased grub disintegrates to spread a fresh supply of milky spores throughout the area to infect still more grubs which in turn disintegrate, etc., etc. Yet this disease is harmless to other forms of life, both animal and human, and does not kill the earthworms and beneficial insects as do the violent poisons usually recommended for grub control. Also, and again unlike the poisons, DOOM is completely safe to use.

Late summer or early fall is the best time to use DOOM as that is when the grub infestation begins. This product is a powder and you apply it to your lawn, every yard or so, by inserting about a spoonful under the grass roots (it should be used only on lawns, not on flower beds). This is a tedious job but, once done, the results are long lasting. I used it first about ten years ago and had no further beetle trouble (or mole runs) until last summer when a few beetles appeared. Apparently when the milky spores run out of grubs to perpetuate them the disease dies out, then when a new crop of grubs arrive you apply fresh DOOM and the cycle starts all over again. I expect to use it again next fall as it worked so well before.

If you cannot find DOOM at your nursery or garden center you can order it direct from the Fairfax Biological Laboratory, Clinton Corners, N.Y., 12514. As I remember, it was moderately expensive but certainly worth it.

BUGS AND SLUGS.   Here are two little nuggets of information which might interest you. (1) A strong tea made of geranium leaves, sprayed on your plants, will keep bugs away. I have not tried this but am told by those who have that it works surprisingly well. And it figures, for geraniums are never bothered by bugs. (2) To keep slugs away from delphiniums and other soft-crowned plants circle them, generously, with rough coal ashes; these should be applied either in the fall or in earliest spring. Reason this works—and it really does—is because slugs, being tender-bodied, will not crawl over scratchy material which injures them. Where you are going to get coal ashes is your problem, but I suggest calling your local fuel supplier to find out who still burns coal in your area; most coal users would be charmed to have you cart away their ashes. When you get these ashes put them through a fairly coarse screen and use only the sharpest and scratchiest.

And now for the larger forms of wild life:

YOUR FRIENDLY NEIGHBORHOOD WOODCHUCK; THE LITTLE BUN-NIES. The problem of how to keep woodchucks and/or rabbits from chomping on your spring garden has given birth to any number of kooky ideas, from raising a soy bean patch to distract their attention to decorating your plantings with dried blood, gallon jugs, and old sneakers.

And, recently, I heard of two more:

1. You crumple up that crackly plastic wrap and tuck it under the plants you want to protect. The theory here is that when the little stranger in paradise investigates this phenomenon it emits a frightening crackling sound. Frightening, that is, until the investigator realizes he is being had. What do you mean, dumb animals?

2. The other is to get someone to shoot a woodchuck (or rabbit, depending on your problem) and arrange the corpse tastefully amid the plants. This, of course, is simply another version of hanging a dead crow in a corn field, which I believe really does work. But, unfortunately, your garden is apt to be a lot closer to your living areas than your corn field, a dead woodchuck or rabbit a lot juicier and more pungent than a crow, and a few days of good hot sun will heat up those once-cold remains to such a peak of fragrance that you and your guests will be kept away if not the little animals. What you do then, I gather, is get a fresh corpse and start this one in a new spot. Your garden, thus treated, will gradually acquire an over-all and haunting effluvium.

Very funny. But what is so mysterious is that each gardener

has complete faith in his own star-bright remedy, swears that it really works. Well, to each his own. It is a little like vitamins, you get buttonholed by a health nut and you feel the mind and eye gradually glazing over—as many of my friends know all too well— because what works for another may not necessarily work for you.

Take dried blood, for instance. This is the ancient and honorable animal repellent, yet my rabbits thought it was delicious, especially on petunias. So then, harkening to a friend, I tried the gallon jugs half filled with water (the theory here is obscure) which had worked so well for her; my little bunnies were fascinated, played hide-and-seek around them. Next I tried the old-sneaker gambit; in this one you place old and very ripe sneakers amid your plants so that the human smell (understatement) permeates the area. My woodchucks nosed them away to get at the plants. That year, with a house full of small children, I had plenty of sneakers and my garden was certainly unique.

As far as I know the only thing which will keep woodchucks and rabbits out of your spring garden is chicken wire, coiled, twisted, or spread out. Apparently the animals think this is a trap—and with good reason for they can get caught in it—and will usually give it a wide berth. Until they get used to it. For this reason it is wise to rearrange the wire every few days so that it presents a different shape, different threat. Though whether the dubious decorative value of this wire is worth the unnibbled plants is for you to decide. However, you will need it for only a few weeks.

But there is one very real trap in this chicken wire bit—for you, not the animals—which you should be aware of: you take out the coil of chicken wire, plus wire clippers, and cut off the lengths which seem suitable, lay them on the grass while you select and arrange the various pieces in various contours. But chicken wire, laid flat on the grass, becomes almost invisible and you may leave a piece, forgotten, where it will remain dormant until the approach of the power mower when it will rise up to do battle with the blades. And what your husband says to you for lousing up the power mower is unprintable even in this era of relaxed censorship. After a few such experiences you learn to pick up your chicken wire. Easiest way is to take out a lot of newspaper, spread it out, and put your wire pieces only on this paper. You can then be sure no wire has been left on the grass.

SKUNKS. Know what I recommend doing about skunks? Nothing. They are, unless frightened, the most courteous of all animals, operate on a live-and-let-live basis, do no harm to your plantings—except digging up your lawn for the grubs you now know how to cope with—and are valuable residents of your property. Rats will seldom venture into an area patrolled by skunks because they know the penalty involved in any dispute over domain. Skunks come out, usually, only at night and if you have reason to go out into the dark, presumably with a flashlight, you merely bid them a pleasant Good Evening and pass by on the other side. They will do the same, unless you give them reason for alarm. If, through a misunderstanding, the worst happens to either you or your dogs, make a sloppy paste of LaFontan Humus (or its equivalent in your area) and apply thickly to the affected parts. This humus contains so much chlorophyll that it is even more effective than the classic tomato juice.

SNAKES. Never kill these unless you are very sure they are poisonous. Harmless snakes, and most snakes are harmless to humans, are your best protection against rats and mice. Like skunks, they are naturally courteous and will leave you alone if you leave them alone. A bulb planting near a snake den is seldom troubled by mice. Snakes are said to go after birds, but we have lots of snakes and lots of birds and I have never seen an encounter between the two.

FOR THE BIRDS. One April, while still high on the seed catalogues, I wrote a column piece on sowing seeds of hardy annuals outdoors, right in the open ground. This was something I used to do years ago before I discovered the greater pleasure, speed, and convenience of sowing seeds indoors. Also before I put up the battery of bird feeders.

Anyhow, it was a very helpful article, according to readers, and I was so enchanted by my own advice that I decided to follow it.

The annuals I chose for openers were Iceland poppies and sweet peas, and the site a warm, sunny spot just outside the kitchen windows so I could observe the progress of the little sprouts. The fact that the bird feeders were also just outside the kitchen windows did not register at the time.

The birds watched this seed-sowing operation with great interest, and as soon as I went into the house a flock of chickadees, juncos, sparrows, cardinals, and various unidentified characters settled on the poppy-seed bed, scratching and picking. They couldn't have cared less about the expensive sunflower seed and other goodies which burdened the feeders.

And the jays took care of the sweet peas. Watching from distant trees their telescopic sights had recorded in the memory banks the exact location of each seed, and within minutes their computers started to roll.

So this was my latest—and last—experience with outdoor seed sowing, and when visitors exclaim over our wealth of feathered friends my smile grows a trifle frosty.

Clematis Pruning—Dept. of Utter Confusion

It is early April and you put on your old galoshes and go out to prowl around, see what has happened since yesterday. Happiness is the sun on your head, another tulip not eaten by mice, a budding clematis you thought was dead. Should clematis be cut back? You can't remember. And nobody seems to know for sure anyhow.

You are quite right, nobody does seem to know for sure. It is one of the many garden problems authorities disagree on. Depends on which book you read. The following will explain why, when I am asked about this, I look around for the nearest exit.

According to most authorities the small-flowered types of clematis (*montana, paniculata,* etc.) should not be cut back as they bloom on old wood—though a great many gardeners have learned through experience that a good sharp pruning will often do wonders for an elderly clematis of this type. The large-flowered varieties, however, are definitely a bunch of individualists and which to cut back and which not to cut back is one of the sweet mysteries of life to many gardeners, this one included.

Theoretically, it is simple: you cut back those varieties which bloom on new wood (the *Jackmani* type) to stimulate new growth, and leave alone those which bloom on old wood (the *patens* type). So, apparently, all you have to do is look up the variety you are dealing with—assuming you know what it is—to find out which type it belongs to. Then on further reading you discover that there is still another type, the *lanuginosa,* which blooms on new shoots from old wood and should be "pruned lightly".

With all this information swirling around in your head you pursue the matter further, which is a mistake, to find that the authorities disagree on which varieties belong to which type. For instance, one authority will tell you that Gypsy Queen, Countess de Bouchaud, Madame Edouard André, Star of India, Crimson Queen, Duchess of Albany, Elsa Spath, Henryi, Lady Caroline Neville, Lord Neville, Mrs. Cholmondeley, Nellie Moser, Prins Hendrik, Ramona, Sir Garnet Wolesey, Ville de Lyon, William Kennett, Jackmani *superba,* and Snow White all belong in the Jackmani group which should be cut back sharply.

So you think you know which is which? Then consult another authority, open another garden book—or, for peace of mind, don't—and you will find that the above is incorrect, that Nellie Moser and Sir Garnet Wolesey belong to the *patens* type (no cut back) along with Fair Rosamond, Lady Loudesborough, and Miss Lateman; that Crimson King, Henryi, and Lady Caroline Neville belong to the *lanuginosa* type (cut back lightly) along with Beauty of Worcester, Blue Gem, Fairy Queen, Lady Northcliffe, Marie Boisselot, Mrs. Hope, and William Kennett. Best thing to do now is to take a couple of aspirins and decide to grow morning glories instead.

After chasing this subject through five or six garden books I have emerged with only one morsel of definite information: the only variety all authorities seem to agree on is good old Belle of Woking. Apparently she is a steady, dependable girl blooming on old wood and I only hope the same can be said about me.

From the above snarl anyone would think that the lovely large-flowered clematis was a complicated plant to grow well. Which it is not, if given the soil and site it prefers: a deep, rich, well-drained loam well laced with ground limestone, and a spot where its roots can enjoy a cool root-run and its top parts enjoy the sun. The north or east side of a fence or low wall is recommended by most authorities, but I have grown it successfully in full sun and happy ignorance, shading the roots and lower parts with small, light-feeding and shallow-rooted plants—such as stachys, gypsophila, or the low artemisias, which also enjoy lime—plus flat stones laid over the root bed itself; if, after a cool rain or hosing, you cover these stones with a mulch of compost or lime-flavored humus they will stay cooler as the mulch absorbs much of the sun's heat.

Thus treated, and pruned mostly by ear, the majority of my clematis plants have given me a wealth of flowers each year, and if yours have done the same for you I advise you to forget you ever read all this and keep right on doing whatever you have been doing.

How To Visit A Nursery

From late April on through May you will probably be visiting all the nurseries in your area, searching for trees, shrubs, and perennials. (More about buying plants in *May*). This will be a happy time for you, and I beg of you to make it a happy time for the nurserymen also. An incredible number of normally courteous and considerate people display shocking carelessness and discourtesy—if not worse—when visiting a nursery. It must be that they simply do not realize the consequences of their thoughtless acts.

First of all, try to remember that spring is the Time of the Ulcer for all those who make a living—if you will forgive the euphemism—from the sale of plants. It is the time when, within a few short weeks, hundreds of trees, shrubs, and evergreens must be carefully dug, carefully balled and burlaped, and moved into their display area . . . . when thousands of baby perennials must be fed, cultivated, and/or shifted into containers and moved into their own display area. It is the time when the weather can spring fatal surprises . . . . the time when machinery breaks down . . . . when the hired help either gets sick or decides to take an easier job. It is the time when nurserymen's wives have babies and don't ask me why. Maybe you think you yourself are busy in the spring of the year but, my friend, you are lying on a park bench with a newspaper over your face compared to a nurseryman.

So here, for the sake of all concerned, are a few DON'TS to keep in mind when visiting a nursery.

1. DON'T take dogs into a nursery; leave them in the car. A male dog will, with unerring taste, select the most valuable evergreens upon which to bestow his compliments; a female dog will choose a bed of choicest seedlings for similar attentions. Both, if intrigued by the scent of bone meal, are likely to start excavating and the resultant root damage can be fatal to the plants involved.

I have seen all these things happen and have had great trouble keeping my mouth shut. Of course, some nurseries have resident dogs but you can be very sure that these animals have been well schooled in nursery behavior—which your dogs have not.

2. DON'T let small children run wild in a nursery. Long, planted rows fascinate most children and in their happy romping countless plants are likely to be stepped on or broken. If the nurseryman seems a little grim while listening to sounds of childish glee from a distant area it is because he has learned through bitter experience what he is likely to find there later. But he must operate on the popular fallacy that the customer is always right, so please, out of simple consideration for him, try to keep track of your lusty young.

3. DON'T pick the pretty flowers. It seems incredible that any thoughtful, well-mannered adult would do this but I have seen otherwise charming people tear sizable branches from flowering trees and shrubs because they were "so pretty". If you ripped off part of a dress in a dress shop the manager would certainly make you pay for the damage and some nurseries have, in self defense, adopted the policy. So don't get light-fingered about the plants.

4. DON'T insist upon seeing the owner or manager, who may be desperately busy far afield, unless your problem is obviously beyond the abilities of the helper who is attending you. If a plant which looks like a Pfitzer juniper is clearly labeled "Pfitzer Juniper, $7.50" you don't have to call a Board Meeting, just pay the lad and have him put the plant in your car. However, if you have real landscaping or horticultural troubles don't hesitate to ask for expert advice; most nurseries are very glad to supply this. You may have to wait a little while for this expert to arrive from the far field, and you should be prepared to buy from him at least some of the materials he recommends, but the help and information you receive should make this well worth your while.

Above all, do remember that a nurseryman's time is his most precious commodity in the spring of the year so don't waste it on chit-chat. He couldn't care less what your Aunt Edith grew in Greenwich fifty years ago, or how gooseberries used to give you the hives, so just transact your business and get out of there as speedily as possible. Okay?

On behalf of the National Association of Nurserymen I thank you.

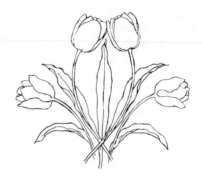

Garden Tour

Ideas are always disturbing, especially new ideas. Most normal, charming, intelligent adults have learned to leave their minds alone and so are immune to new ideas. But not gardeners. These unfortunates are susceptible to every new idea carried by the winds of chance. Let even a sober and settled gardener glimpse a new way of handling an old garden problem and unrest is upon him and within him until he has tried this out for himself. I feel sorry for anyone who has to live with a gardener.

One of the most unsettling experiences is to go on a garden tour, so don't miss any of these junkets for you will come home so filled with new ideas that you will be utterly miserable. Your own plantings will, by comparison, seem so dull, so lacking in imagination. Why didn't you think of making a little rock garden out of that stony slope? Or carpeting that woody spot with primroses? Or using tulips in drifts and swirls instead of tight little bunches? Or underplanting shrubs, maybe trees? You prowl your property so feverish with all these new ideas that you forget home, family and meals. You can be very difficult to live with.

This divine discontent is one of the healthiest things which can happen to a gardener and I recommend at least one garden tour a year to increase your knowledge of plants and how they can be grown, to sharpen the vision and stir up the horticultural circulation. I also recommend that you take along a notebook in which to write down the names—if possible the full botanical names—of plants which especially delight you so that you can look for them in catalogues or local nurseries. And don't be fooled by the ignorant notion that botanical names are unimportant, merely affectations tossed off by certain gardeners to impress other gardeners, for nothing could be further from the truth; they can be vitally important if you are trying to track down a plant which may be known by three or four different common names in various parts of the country. Also, many fine nurseries, many specialists, list plants only under botanical names so you must have those names if you expect to find the plants.

This is particularly true of the dedicated brethren who specialize in choice rock plants, and in May you will probably be driven out of your mind by rock gardens. Although it may be too late now to catalogue-order major plants such as trees and shrubs for spring planting—in this area the planting season ends June 1st for most such items shipped bare root—the majority of rock-plant specialists send their small treasures carefully potted so they can be safely planted at almost any time of year as there is little root disturbance. Or, if the plants you want are not too unusual, you could try the local nurseries which may carry such items in containers. More about this later.

Rock Garden Fever

This is a virus which attacks almost all gardeners in the spring of the year. Sometimes the victim recovers with the onset of summer and sometimes he does not. If the infection is serious he is likely to become a rock-plant addict, spending more and more time and money on rock plants no matter what happens to the leaking roof, the car insurance, or the children's teeth. This type of gardener is a breed apart with permanent stars in the eyes, a permanent dream in the heart. No rock gardener ever grows old no matter what happens to the flesh.

Luckily—or unluckily—I recovered. Once upon a time I had a tiny and exquisite rock garden, part of my own hidden garden, but that was when I had a full-time staff in the house and a part-time staff outdoors. Now that I have neither I have had to give up many of the plantings I so loved: the rock garden, the hidden garden, the primrose garden, the trial gardens, the propagating beds, et al. It is a sadness.

I learned a small something about rock plants during that

period. Finding a natural rocky outcrop in the area I had chosen for my hidden garden I immediately, and in joyful ignorance, ordered a lot of rock plants, not knowing which was which and caring less. Among these were some *Androsaces* which I picked out of a catalogue because they looked so pretty; I stuck them into a rock crack and, in due time, was rewarded by masses of little gray-green rosettes with white flowers sitting right on top. This was viewed with awe by informed rock gardeners for, apparently, I had in all innocence picked a variety which was supposed to be difficult to grow. Such beginner's luck happens frequently in gardening, especially rock gardening. If it happens to you be humbly grateful for the experience but don't let it give you delusions of knowledge.

I enjoyed these delusions for several years, during my rock gardening period, and even wrote articles about rock plants, designed rock gardens for friends. Through sheer luck, probably, the rock gardens turned out pretty well and the articles apparently did no harm, but when I realize how little I knew about the subject, which is a lifetime study, I get goose pimples. This is why, knowing so much more now, I refuse to write about any but the easiest rock plants, the kind anyone can grow, given a few rocks. These will be mentioned often throughout this book in association with rock settings, for there are many commonly grown garden plants which are far happier with a few rocks around their roots. But if you want real rock garden information I advise you get the books which give this in detail and with authority.

There are many such books, excellent ones, some old and some new, but here are two which I consider particularly valuable.

One is H. Lincoln Foster's *Rock Gardening, A Guide To Growing Alpines And Other Wildflowers In The American Garden*. Mr. Foster's clear and gentle prose is a delight to read and Mrs. Foster's delicate, accurate drawings a delight to study. Besides giving detailed instructions on just how to build a rock garden, or a planted rock wall, or cope with a rocky bank—each step illustrated with easy-to-follow diagrams plus full cultural directions—Mr. Foster also lists over 1900 rock plants, describes each one and tells you how it should be grown, tells you which are easy, which difficult. It is a hefty volume and one which could save you any number of costly and heartbreaking mistakes if you are contemplating a rock garden of any type.

Two of the areas which form part of the famous H. Lincoln Foster rock garden which is at its most beautiful in May.

The other book is Gertrude Jekyll's *Wall and Water Gardens*. This one, alas, is out of print and a collector's item; if you ever see it in a second-hand book store snap it up because it is a treasure. It is not as practical for the American gardener as Mr. Foster's book but it will launch you into far, high dreams which, if you live in a section which resembles England in climate, could very well come true. In fact, many of the plants she describes are hardy even in this chilly area, so get this book if you possibly can. It will give you pure delight if nothing else.

A Garden of Primroses

When I am an old, old woman with long grey moustaches, a baggy tweed suit, stout boots and a cane, (what do you mean, when?) I shall have a whole garden of primroses. All kinds. Each growing in its preferred spot. For some primroses like wet feet and some do not, some like to grow in a gravelly bank, some like to nestle between rocks in a shadowy woodland, some like a touch of sun. Most of them want a deep, rich, humusy bedding a little on the acid side but some, like the *auriculas,* are happy only in lime-flavored gravel.

My primrose garden will be a swale of fairly open woodland with rocks, flickering sunlight, ferns, a spray of primrose-footed white birches at the far end against a great grey boulder . . . there will be a little stream where, along the damp sides, will be white, lavender, rosy-pink drifts of the very early primrose P. *denticulata* neighbored by small ferns whose fronds will unfurl later . . . further down the stream, edging out into the morning sun, will be groups of the taller and later P. *japonica* in white and deep pink . . . and all along these moist edges, spilling into the water, will be masses of the pale blue brook forget-me-nots (*Myosotis palustris*) to bloom from late spring all through the summer.

And there will be a little path, not even a path, just a way of going, meandering towards the stream and the half-glimpsed birches beyond. Here and there along this path, among rocks, will be occasional groups of simple native azaleas footed by clumps of the great-leafed Bergenia (*Saxifraga cordifolia*) which shelter carpets of the tiny *juliana* primroses—white, purple, apricot—and a good-blue strain of *P. acaulis* merging, further back, into drifts of the white, cream, and pale yellow garden primrose *Polyanthus* set among ferns . . . this, in turn, lifting to a low bank of rocky, humusy, limey gravel studded with the evergreen tufts of *auriculas*—yellow, buff, pink, purple . . .

If you can take the above and still keep on reading, look up primroses (*Primulas*) in H. Lincoln Foster's *Rock Gardening* and glimpse the further and almost infinite variety of primroses which you can dream about as you become more experienced with these gentlest of all plants. The kinds listed above are among the easiest.

For, contrary to popular belief, most primroses are very easy to grow if you give them even a reasonable facsimile of the soil and site they want. There are, of course, difficult ones which will be a little querulous at times but most of them are remarkably sweet tempered. All of them are best bought from primrose specialists who offer not only the best plants but also the best colors, widest assort-

Primroses (*Primula polyantha*) in a half-shady spot.

THEODORA M. PRENTICE

ment of kinds to choose from. A list of such specialists will be found on page 243.

They are also easy from seed. Some authorities recommend that you freeze the seed (just stick the seed pan in the freezing compartment of your ice box) and this is advisable if you are dealing with seed of uncertain age, but fresh seed, I am told by primrose growers, does not need this treatment.

But I know from my own experience how easy they are from seed, how loving and forgiving, for once I grew a panful which survived a traumatic experience. I had frozen them as above, they had sprouted generously and, believing they liked cool temperatures, I had stuck them in the cold pantry for further growing. Shortly thereafter, through some accident, the cat got shut up in the cold pantry overnight and decided that the earth-filled pan was a new kind of sandbox. When I released him the next morning the tiny primroses had been scattered far and wide, most of them with their roots up. I fixed a new pan, stuck them into fresh soil, and they picked up right where they had left off. They are that easy.

Another delight in growing primroses from seed is that they often produce sports (i.e., mutations, variations in form, habit or color) which may turn out to be a primrose the likes of which no one has ever seen before. This is one of the most exciting experiences which can happen to a gardener and sets you up among the experts—in your own estimation anyhow—from which elevation you can afford to be gracious and a little condescending to other primrose growers. This does a lot for your morale if not for your popularity.

A garden of primroses is especially recommended for the elderly because it needs little care. The small plants are so light and so easy to handle, so easy to divide every few years, need so little attention, that most primrose-gardening can be done sitting down; all you need is a trowel and a low stool. There is none of the deep digging, hefting of large plants, which accompanies most other forms of gardening and, in the shaded area where most primroses like to grow, there are few weeds. Primroses are for those who, for one reason or another, have had to give up heavy gardening.

If you are in this category, consider primroses. Buy just a few to start with, then begin raising your own from seed, and before you know it you will be launched upon the primrose path which, as everyone will tell you, leads to the skids.

Contemplation of Tulips

Tulips are to the May scene what sweaters are to *la belle poitrine;* they accent and enhance the beauty of whatever setting they grace. Even a very few, well placed, can bring drama to the dullest garden.

Personally, I consider most tulips so beautiful in themselves that I dislike them packed into those tight mixed plantings which seem so popular; such plantings are apparently based on the theory that if one drop of perfume is good, a whole bottle is better. I prefer tulips in gentle, swinging, blended drifts—where space will permit—or in small loose groups, one color to a group, and underplanted so that the eye is progressively refreshed and delighted by the subtle color combinations.

Here are some of the ways you can play this:

Suppose you have a long and deep perennial border which, right now in May, looks as though it was just climbing out of its winter underwear. Stand back and try to visualize a long drift of tulips, variations on a single color scheme, underplanted with blending—or contrasting—material which can either be removed later on or left to be interplanted with annuals.

For instance, if you love the pink-purple tones you could start at one end of your bed with palest pink tulips blending into pink-lavender, then into darker lavender, into deep purple, then back into lavender but with the blue tones predominating, ending the drift in pale lavender-blue. Then underplant this drift with blue, lavender, and pink carpeting; ajuga, forget-me-nots, pink arabis . . . where peonies are lifting their spring leafage, use white violas which can stay on all summer to enjoy the partial shade caused by the peony foliage. This color scheme is good with white and purple lilacs nearby.

Or perhaps you prefer the yellow coloring. Then start at one end with creamy white tulips, gradually deepening the yellow tones into orange, then back through the yellows to cream white. This color blend could be underplanted with bright yellow alyssum Basket of Gold at the cream-white ends merging into the pale yellow alyssum *citrinum* and double-white arabis (*A. flore-pleno*) around the orange center. Low evergreens, such as the bronzy junipers, and the white flowering quince *nivalis* with its bronze-tinted foliage, would go well with this color scheme as would tall white lilacs back of the orange tulips.

Or you could play around with another version of the drift idea; this one is for the smaller perennial bed, needs less length. Use small loose groups of tulips, one color to a group, in differing but congenial shades—pale pink, wine red, deep purple, pale yellow, white, lots of white—which move in and out among the awakening perennials, and underplant all this with only one carpeting material to tie it all together, soften the spottiness. Forget-me-nots are very good with mixed tulips, or you could use the pale blue phlox *stolonifera* Blue Ridge which leaves a close, dark, glossy-green carpeting all summer. This type of tulip planting is usually better where there is a solid one-tone background such as a wall of woven fencing to give it serenity.

Remember, too, in planning any planting which is usually viewed from a distance that the white and pale yellows will show up better, tend to bring everything closer, contribute drama. In plantings which are customarily viewed from close by you need fewer of these whites and yellows, can use more of the subtle tulip colorings, the bronzy-purples, the smoky blends. These amount to a whole lot of nothing when viewed from a distance.

Another way to use the tulip-drift idea is in front of a shrub border; just remember to leave ample space—at least 2'—between the shrub roots and the tulips; as a planting of this type is usually seen across an expanse of lawn this gap is not noticeable. One such planting I remember high-lighted a long swinging shrub border which curved around a great lawn. Tall shrubs and small flowering trees, laced with evergreens, formed the background against which rose an almost continuous drift of tulips; the pinks and wine-reds, lavenders and purples lifted against the delicate pastels of the May-flowering shrubs to blend into the white, scarlet, and pale yellow tulips which foreplanted the evergreens and summer-flowering shrubs. Yet all this was so skillfully merged into a whole that there was no discord, no spottiness. Later, the dying tulip foliage would obviously be screened out by the masses of low evergreens and midsummer-flowering shrubs which edged this whole border.

Still another tulip planting I will long remember was a small, sunken, hollow square (with lawn center) done entirely in scarlet and white tulips underplanted with pale blue pansies and edged with white candytuft (*Iberis sempervirens* var. Snowflake). The background was old, weathered stone—the walls had been the foundation of an ancient barn—against which, here and there, fanned out the delicate dark tracery of *Euonymus kewensis* with groups of bush form euonymus (*E. patens* and *E. radicans Sarcoxie*) in the corners. I was told that this scarlet, white and pale blue color scheme was continued throughout the summer by using white iris, single white peonies (late), white phlox (both early and late), shasta daisies, scarlet gladioli, scarlet and white petunias, with masses of pale blue *Salvia farinacea.*

If you don't have the space for a long tulip drift, or an old barn foundation for a setting, it is wise to use tulips carefully and sparingly so that you won't be left, in June, with masses of dying tulip foliage which, on a small place, can be difficult to hide. For, as every garden book will tell you, this foliage must be left as is to ripen and feed the bulbs for next year's bloom; it should never be cut down, or shaded too heavily by other plants as it needs at least some sun to complete its feeding cycle.

Many gardeners, blest with a philosophical outlook, are not at all disturbed by this morning-after scene. They accept it as one of the inevitables of life along with TV commercials and rebellion in the young; just close your eyes and it will go away in time. If you belong to this happy brotherhood you can skip the next few paragraphs. If not, here are a few suggestions for dealing with the chilly remains.

Gypsophila (or baby's breath if you have a strong stomach) makes one of the best tulip screens as it is feathery enough to hide what it is meant to hide yet allows considerable sun and air to come through. This gypsophila rises up in June, which is just when you need it, and comes in white or pale pink, very pleasing when mixed. All gypsophilas love lime. A good companion planting, towards the back of the bed, would be the lower delphiniums, the beloved old *Belladonna* (light blue) and the *Bellamosum* (dark blue), and, towards the front, the still lower—and newer—Connecticut Yankees which come in mixed blues, all lovely. (See seed sowing in *February*). In this area delphiniums start blooming in early July.

Or, if you are given to forethought, you can sow seeds of hardy annuals—such as larkspur or annual poppies—in late fall right over your tulip bulbs; then, when these annuals appear along with the tulips, thin out the former. This is highly recommended by many garden books, many gardeners, but Old Sourpuss here, who takes a dim view of most open-ground seed sowing, has found that the little seeds are apt to wash away over the winter and come up everywhere except where you want them. But best pay no attention to me in the matter of outdoor seed sowing as countless gardeners sow seeds this way and, for them, it works out very well indeed.

I have found that the surest system, if you are going to use annuals as tulip screens, is to set in well-started plants in May. One friend of mine, each spring, simply buys dozens of heliotrope plants, greenhouse-grown to blooming size, and inserts them among the tulips. The result is instant enchantment which continues all summer as the delicate heliotrope shades seem to make all neighboring colors more beautiful.

Or perhaps you prefer to avoid this whole tulip aftermath by digging up the bulbs as soon as they have finished blooming, replanting the area with something else. This seems to me a costly and time-consuming way to operate for not only are tulips difficult to dig out of a mixed planting but, if you do not let them mature, you have to buy fresh bulbs next fall. I have heard gardeners claim that tulips are no good after the first year, and indeed they will deteriorate fast if left unfed, but it has been my experience that most tulips will last for years, and bloom more beautifully each year, if given generous amounts of bone meal washed down with manure tea either before or after they have completed their flowering. I once had a tulip planting, starting with six single bulbs, which in ten years increased the output to four or five major blossoms per bulb.

I am not recommending by name any special tulips for the plantings suggested above because I think you will have more fun going through the catalogues and selecting the ones which appeal to you most in each color range. But there is one group of tulips, relatively new, which I do call to your attention: these are the bouquet-tulips which, remarkably, produce four or five blossoms per bulb, even the first year. The flowers are slightly smaller than the classic Darwins, more graceful, the form and colors, delightful. Especially good for small gardens, small properties, as they seem simpler, less formal, and produce many more flowers in less space. So far I have seen these listed only in the Park catalogue (fall edition) but by the time you read this other growers may be offering them.

Here are some suggestions for using tulips—different kinds—on small country properties where there is little room for extensive plantings: (1) If you happen to have a great rock, or an old grey barn, use a small clump of bright scarlet Red Emperor tulips (species) against this background. But don't use too many; three Red Emperors against a rock, maybe five near a corner of the barn with masses of white arabis in front (both are early bloomers). This vivid scarlet is so powerful that you need only a spot of it, too much is merely stupefying. (2) Try a planting of tall white lily tulips, maybe five, against dark evergreens or dark-leafed shrubs; or palest pink tulips against the grey-green of junipers. Foreplant either or both with *Abelia grandiflora* if this is hardy in your area. (3) If you have an old tumbled-down stone wall you don't know what to do with, clear out the junk and plant groups of tall, pale yellow tulips in a sea of pale blue phlox *divaricata;* later set in masses of marigold, both tall and dwarf, in all shades of yellow and orange. (4) Or if you have a woody edging to your property, foreplant this with massed groups of the small, wild species tulips (your choice) with phlox *divaricata* as a blender.

Incidentally, this might be a good place to explain why phlox *stolonifera* is recommended for some plantings, phlox *divaricata* for others. *P. stolonifera* Blue Ridge is lower, tidier, a less rampant spreader, has closer, glossier summer leafage and so is a better choice for cultivated areas; *P. divaricata* is the wild phlox, taller and looser, less tidy in habit, a better choice for wild or semi-wild settings. Both bear, in great profusion, masses of pale blue flowers in May.

All the above suggestions—the swirls, the drifts, the color harmonies, the special plantings—sound dreamy on paper, but how to achieve this dream can take years of trial and error. I have seen it done, really well, in only a very few gardens and am still working on it myself without, so far, much success. The chief block seems to be the time span between the vision of what needs doing, in May, and the actual ordering and doing, in the fall. By the time the bulb catalogues arrive in late summer you have not only forgotten what tulips you meant to order, you have forgotten what tulips you already have and where they are.

This is where the Notebook comes in. All garden authorities stress the importance of the garden notebook and I agree with them heartily. It is the only way to keep track of your plants, especially tulips which, unlike other characters, disappear from the scene leaving no reminder of their existence. So, in May, with the whole picture before you, jot down in your notebook what new tulips you will need for where, what colors, and how many.

It is also most helpful to mark, in the earth itself, the exact spots where these new tulips should go. I have found that evergreen clippings—yew, box, juniper, whatever is handy—stuck into the ground in May will pinpoint these spots for fall planting. The little green sprigs are inconspicuous and when you find them, in October, you will know where to dig. Also, these small clippings will often root themselves over the summer so you get an unexpected bonus: rooted cuttings to move into a nursery bed for further growing. I have several fine evergreens which started life in this way.

So do I keep a garden notebook? I certainly do. I buy one each year, write in it profusely for several weeks and then, caught in the whirlpool of spring work and summer entanglements, forget about it for the rest of the season. Consequently, when fall-ordering time comes I am just as confused as anyone else and only hope you are a better gardener than I am in this respect.

Have You Tried Underplanting?

This will give you double beauty, double interest in a small space. You can have two levels of bloom, or two separate periods of bloom, or a dark, serene carpet of shining leafage. It is easy, inexpensive, and can add the invaluable quality of surprise to your property. Also, it can be adapted to any planting scale, any type of landscape design.

For openers let's start with the smallest scale: the very small property, the small house, the simplest type of landscaping. Such a layout would take the tiny paving-stone garden. Don't attempt this one on larger properties with sweeps of lawn, masses of shrubbery, for it would only look picky and precious, a little silly. Though it can sometimes be used in the small, intimate hidden spots which are often such a delight on large properties which have been lovingly landscaped.

THE PAVING-STONE GARDEN. This simply means that you wreathe a shrub or small flowering tree with little plants tucked in between a footing of flat stones, preferably native stones. Actually, many garden authorities recommend such stone mulching of trees and shrubs to keep the roots cool, conserve moisture, discourage weeds, so besides benefiting your major plant you are getting a tiny extra garden which is practically self-supporting. Also, the soft grey of the stone provides a show-case type setting for the small plants, causing each one to seem more beautiful and important.

The actual construction of the paving-stone garden is relatively easy. You simply dump a load of good garden earth—well mixed with coarse sand, compost, bone meal, perhaps ground limestone or peat moss—over the entire root area of your chosen tree or shrub and rake it smooth, being careful to keep any build-up away from the trunk or stem where ground level must be maintained. It is impossible to say, exactly, how much of any of these materials should be added as this depends on the type of garden earth you are dealing with; heavy soils would need more sand than light soils, sandy soils might need more compost or humus; also you should consider the type of small plants you intend to grow. Experienced gardeners seldom measure anything accurately, they go chiefly by feel: bedding for the sun-loving, drainage-loving rock-type plants should feel soft, gritty, and crumbly; bedding for the shade-tolerant humus lovers should feel soft, gritty and spongy. But don't worry too much about this as you will soon learn to play it by ear.

I have often heard gardeners claim that most plants will "grow anywhere" and indeed most of the popular ones will, though not always to perfection. But as almost all plants have their individual likes and dislikes it seems to me only reasonable to give them the soil and setting they like best if you expect them to do their best. Thus if you were underplanting a tree or shrub which prefers a rich, humusy, slightly acid soil—dogwood, mountain ash, the conifers, the magnolias, roses, etc.—you would add extra compost and a little peat moss (for acidity) to your soil-mix and choose small plants with similar taste such as the heaths and heathers, common primroses, violas, pansies, and most of the shade-tolerant annuals. Or if underplanting the trees and shrubs associated with open, sunny, dry areas—and this includes most of the popular cultivated items such as flowering crabs and quinces, lilacs, cotoneasters, the viburnums (in variety), mock orange, the smaller fruit trees—you would add extra bone meal, maybe a touch of ground limestone if your soil is on the acid side, and choose guest plants such as arabis, the aubrietias, iberis, the alyssums, low gypsophila, most of the common, sun-loving dwarf annuals.

When placing the flat stones it is best to begin at the outside, under the perimeter of the branches, and work towards the center, using the best and largest stones first as these will be the most conspicuous and it is easier to fit in the smaller ones as you near the trunk or stem. Where you will get these stones is, of course, your problem, though this is certainly no problem in New England where stones are mammals and breed like rabbits. Arrange the stones so that, where they meet, there are planting pockets and these pockets should be, roughly, 4″ or 5″ each way to accommodate the plant roots; the foliage will soon spill out over the stones, hiding the edges.

When you have achieved a design which pleases you, lift each stone and, underneath, stir in a couple of inches of gravel such as is used for driveways. This is for drainage, to prevent frost-heave over the winter. Then wiggle the stones down into this gravel to settle them; don't worry if some of the gravel works out between the stones or into the planting pockets for in a bed of this kind the more drainage the better. Then set in your little plants, firming the roots down well. When these are bedded, fill all unoccupied cracks with sand (to discourage weeds) and give the whole thing a long, gentle, thorough watering. If it is a sunny or windy day cover the small plants with flower pots or strawberry baskets. Repeat this watering every few days for about a week, adding more sand to the cracks if necessary.

How you finish off your paving-stone garden is up to you. You can leave it as is, and if the setting is deep-country casual this looks simpler and more appropriate. Or you can rim it with a tiny low hedge. Evergreen candytuft, *Iberis sempervirens* var. Little Gem, is one of the most useful and delightful of such hedging materials as it not only gives a wealth of white bloom in May but also provides neat and permanent evergreen edging; the variety Autumn Snow blooms twice a year, in May and again in October, but it is taller and more sprawly, more difficult to keep tight and neat. In a half-shady spot with a woodsy background where such a trim little

LAURA LEE FOSTER

hedge would look out of place you can blend your garden into the surrounding area with casual groups of tiny ferns, hepaticas, violets, etc.

If your paving-stone garden occurs in a lawn area it is a good idea to install a moat of sand around the outer rim. Into this you can sink that metal edging (comes about 4″ wide) which, theoretically at least, will prevent grass from creeping into your planting and your plants from creeping out into the grass. And/or you can set narrow flat stones, or bricks (flat) in this sand to take the wheel of the mower. Such a sand moat is a great labor saver as it discourages cultural exchange between the two areas and makes for easier maintenance.

All this sounds far more complicated on paper than it actually is when you get going on it. Several years ago I did a paving-stone garden around an old apple tree, and, once the materials were assembled, the whole job took only about an hour. This ancient, twisted tree was the one interesting feature of a small area the owners wanted to turn into a terrace, so we decided to play it up. White, pale blue, and deep purple pansies (compost bedded) were used between the stones to coincide with the apple blossoms; then the pansies were replaced by low petunias, white and strawberry-pink, the whole thing circled by Little Gem plus the sand moat with flat stones for the mower wheel. The old tree was sufficiently high branched to allow considerable sun to reach most of the petunias which bloomed profusely all summer, aided by snacks of manure tea, and the little evergreen hedge was pleasing when viewed from winter windows. Apple trees are easy to underplant.

So are their smaller cousins, the flowering crabs. But often these start branching so close to the ground that there is not enough light or ventilation for the plants beneath. If underplanting is contemplated, the lower branches should be cut away to give a headroom of at least 3', more if this can be done without spoiling the shape of the tree. Also, as the foliage is often so dense that little sun gets through it is a good idea to prune out some of this interior growth. This will also benefit the tree itself by providing better ventilation. Many shrubs are improved by the same treatment.

Few small plants will flower all summer in complete shade, though many will keep going in light, partial, or filtered shade. The violas are invaluable for such half-shady spots, will often bloom continuously if given the rich compost bedding they love and a shot of manure tea when they start to drag their feet in midsummer; they come in a wide range of colors and many can be raised from seed. Another dependable bloomer in part-shade is the impatiens clan; these can now be obtained in many forms and colors, doubles and semi-doubles as well as the old-fashioned singles. They are easy and sweet-tempered from seed, though this should be started early in the house if you want bloom the first year. I lift these in the fall, carry them over the winter indoors, and set them out again after frost-danger is over. They are also idiot's delight from cuttings taken in the fall. Balsams (dwarf varieties) enjoy some sun but will accept partial shade; these are best used where they can be seen from close by as the exquisite little camellia-like flowers are often somewhat hidden by the glossy foliage. These, too, are easy from seed, and quite fast; they like a rich, humusy soil.

Here, to start you off, are a few suggested combinations for paving-stone gardens: pale yellow primroses under a white dogwood,

or white and wine-red primroses under a pink dogwood; the primroses can be replaced, after blooming, with dwarf white and pink impatiens . . . pale blue and dark blue pansies under a pale yellow
Father Hugo Rose (*Rosa Hugonis*) later replaced by white lobelias
. . . white and pale blue pansies under the shrub rose Betty Prior
(a rose-pink single floribunda which blooms all summer) followed
by low white petunias . . . white and pale yellow violas for all-
summer flowering under a star magnolia (*Magnolia stellata*) . . .
white violas under pink or red weigelas . . . white pansies under a
pink or red flowering crab followed by dwarf pink and white impatiens.

Or try white arabis, the double variety *flore-pleno,* under an
old-fashioned scarlet flowering quince; the silvery mounds of arabis
foliage will be lovely all summer under the bronzy-green quince
leafage . . . use dwarf pink gypsophila under a grey-leafed viburnum
Carlesi, candytuft edging . . . use almost anything pale yellow under
a Russian olive tree (*Elaeagnus angustifolia*) with its black bark,
silvery foliage, and tiny yellow flowers in June . . . underplant
lilacs, almost any color, with aubrietias in shades of lavender from
dark to light, replace with low white petunias.

About lilacs and underplanting: the tall, uplifting French hybrids are the most suitable for the paving-stone garden as they
usually admit ample sun to the root area, enabling you to grow
sun-loving annuals throughout the summer; the common lilacs,
Syringa vulgaris, sucker too persistently to be worth bothering with,
and most of the bush lilacs (species) are too large and heavy.

But there is one species lilac which seems especially designed
for underplanting, either the paving-stone garden or carpeting, because of its open, airy grace and simplicity. This is the Daphne
lilac, *Syringa microphylla superba,* which blooms twice a year. In
May and again in August its slender, willowy branches are laden
down with soft-pink trusses, very fragrant, and better for cutting
than most lilacs. White arabis is enchanting under this, either as
paving-stone planting or as carpeting, for the arabis flowers have the
same quality of gentleness and the silver foliage is beautiful throughout the summer, especially with the August bloom of the lilacs.

The Wayside catalogue currently carries a picture of this
Daphne lilac which is completely misleading. The photograph shows
a short, chunky bush of no distinction whatever bearing stiff,

Daphne lilacs *(Syringa microphylla superba)* in May. The August bloom will be only a little less profuse. In the background is a tall white French lilac.

washed-out lavender flowers, and why Wayside persists in using this libelous picture is beyond my understanding. Especially as the text describes this lovely lilac as graceful and slender with mahogany-red buds which soften to pink. So pay no attention to this photograph. Another inaccuracy is Wayside's statement that this lilac seldom grows over 5′ tall. Well, mine—I have had three of them for several years—are all over 8′ tall. But they are a joy to own, easy and completely hardy. Most of the better nurseries now carry them.

While speaking of lilacs let me call your attention to one of the most rewarding: this is the old-fashioned Persian *(Syringa persica)* which many modern gardeners seem unaware of, at least around here. It is massive and magnificent, one of the most prolific bloomers of the entire tribe, yet not coarse like so many large bush-lilacs as the leaves are smallish and faintly glossy, the rounded bush-form quite graceful. The books say it grows to around 8′ but mine are well over 12′ and almost as wide. Each May they are covered with fragrant flowers of a good clear lavender which last almost two weeks. This is quite a display and visitors, agape, ask me what I do to make them bloom so profusely. The answer, I am ashamed to say, is "Nothing." But Persians are like that, they forgive more neglect .than any other plant I know of. At least mine do. They like a heavier soil than most lilacs.

These are, of course, far too big and heavy for individual underplanting but I once saw them well used as a background for a large, circular, paving-stone garden set with small, creeping plants and entirely rimmed with a low, clipped, silvery-grey hedge of Arctic willow (*Salix purpurea nana*); this circular form was pleasing

Persian lilacs (*S. persica*). These are now over 12′ high and almost as broad, have been blooming like this for twenty years without the slightest care.

EUGENE D. TRUDEAU

with the rounded forms of the lilacs. In the center of this paved
area was a simple marble bird bath, and this seemed particularly
appropriate as birds love these Persian lilacs for nesting, each spring
mine are bird hotels. This design was startling in its simplicity and
took almost no upkeep. It would be far too large in scale for the
small property but something to keep in mind if you have ample
space.

THE FLORAL CARPET.   This is for larger properties which take
a larger planting scale, from the average country layout (remodeled
farmhouse type) with its old apple trees, beat-up stone walls, and
reasonable facsimile of greensward to the·distinguished architecture
of a really fine house with its sweeping lawns, shrub borders, and,
perhaps, a single magnificent maple rising from a huge circle of
pachysandra which stretches to the tips of the branches. This verges
on the estate type of property and is where my bailiwick ends. At
this point you should consult a professional.

But probably your property lies somewhere between the small
plot which takes the paving-stone garden and the spacious estate
which takes the landscape architect. If so, consider the floral carpet,
which is a very simple way of adding personality to the average
country property which couldn't be less interested in grandeur.
It differs from the paving-stone job in that it is more generous and
relaxed in feeling, more country-casual, is usually viewed from a
comparative distance, is not precious with show-case type planting.
For example, an old gnarled apple tree could rise from a great circular bed of country myrtle (*Vinca minor* Bowles var. if in a lawn
area, *V. minor,* the common periwinkle if further afield). Or, if
your property has a woodland background, a spray of white birches
could be footed with clumps of daffodils set in a sweep of phlox
divaricata.

All such carpet plantings should be left as is throughout the
summer with no attempt to fuss them up with dinky annuals; presumably if you have this much property you have other spots in
which to grow the summer bloomers. Also, one such carpet planting
is enough in any one area, let it present a single serene statement.
If you must have summer color somewhere in this scene, use another type of planting and keep it as far as possible from your
carpeted tree.

This leafy carpet is far easier to install than the paving-stone garden. You simply spread a thick blanket of appropriate bedding over the entire root area of the tree—again being sure to keep any build-up away from the trunk where ground level must be maintained—and set in your carpet plants. This bedding soil should be the type preferred by the host tree, and the carpet plants should share the same tastes, but the bedding should be richer in compost or rotted manure than for the paving-stone garden as most major trees are heartier eaters than shrubs and there will be more guests to feed.

Maples and beeches are notoriously difficult to underplant but I know this can be done as I have seen such trees beautifully carpeted and a state of well-being enjoyed by all concerned. The secret seems to be plenty of humus (compost or whatever) and ample nourishment; one tree owner told me that each spring the entire area was thickly sprinkled with dried manure, hosed in.

Pachysandra is the customary, almost inevitable, underplanting for such trees but, personally, I consider this one of the horticultural clichés and suitable for only public buildings. Myrtle is a little less trite, has a longer flowering period (especially the Bowles variety), grows just as well in shade and is more country in feeling. The white form, notably Miss Jekyll's White, is especially effective under copper beeches; this one is a less rampant spreader and a little more difficult to get started but well worth the effort. Another charmer under major shade trees of this type is sweet woodruff (*Asperula odorata*) which is a foam of white in spring and a sea of whorled, light green leafage thereafter. This is a good choice if your property is near woodlands.

The needled evergreens—hemlock, spruce, pine, et al—are usually easy to underplant. These are fond of acidity so peat moss should be added to the blanket bedding. For deep shade under a spruce or hemlock the most beautiful underplanting you can choose is European ginger (*Asarum europaeum*) with its low glossy leafage which spreads a shining carpet; don't confuse this with the common wild ginger which is taller, duller and less tidy.

Another shiny carpeter, this one better for old, high-headed pines, as it needs sun, is bearberry (*Arctostaphylos uva-ursi*). This bearberry, which you may not recognize by name, is that low, glossy, small-leafed creeper which forms mats along the sand dunes of the

eastern seaboard, especially Fire Island and Cape Cod. But this one
does best in poor, sandy soil, so if you have an old pine growing in
such a setting, all you need to add is more sand, well mixed with
pine needles. Bearberry must have perfect drainage, likes acidity.

A very special beauty which loves to grow under pine trees,
likes some sun though it will take partial shade, is the tiny, creeping
species iris *I. cristata.* This little gem is best used in intimate areas
where its delicate, exquisite beauty can be appreciated; it has iris-
type leaves, only 3″ high, upon which sit relatively enormous iris-
type blossoms, mid-blue, pale blue, or white; the white form is
particularly choice. It creeps by runners and will, in time, form
solid carpets which are an unbelievable delight in spring. Unlike
most rhizomed iris it prefers a slightly acid soil and is particularly
fond of pine needles in a soft, gritty, well-drained bedding. This
tiny iris should be planted almost on the surface, the minute
rhizomes barely covered with a dusting of earth and pine needles;

European ginger *(Asarum europaeum).* Flat, low, and shining, this is
the most beautiful of all ground covers for shade, though sometimes difficult to establish. Shown here, in a close-up, beside a rugged stone step.

THEODORA M. PRENTICE

it will die if set too deeply. If you have an old pine tree, close by, this is for you.

So now go out and contemplate your trees, decide what carpeting to put where. By this time you will probably be sorry you ever started this book. Your family may be even sorrier.

ON BUYING PLANTS

This is for when you start off in the car on a bright May morning, your eyes full of stars and your head full of popcorn, to buy a lot more plants. As inexpensively as possible.

If you are an experienced gardener you can skip this section because you already know what I am going to say. But if you are a beginner, with only vague ideas as to what a well-grown plant should look like, how it should be offered, you had best read this very carefully. In my many years of nursery-hopping I have witnessed countless heartbreaks in the making because of the innocence of the purchaser, the ignorance—or cupidity—of the seller.

Probably your best insurance against being taken for a horticultural ride is to go to a large, well-established nursery of excellent repute. Yet even these will, occasionally and unintentionally, offer you poor plants. Often such a nursery will become so over-extended that it is impossible for the owner to check on the care given each plant, so that many fine offerings may have deteriorated by the time you arrive. I have greatest respect—and sympathy!—for nursery owners and am very sure that the majority of them would never, knowingly, sell you a poor plant, but often the temporary hired help couldn't care less. So it is up to you to know which plants are worth buying and which are not.

There are also, and everywhere, small nurseries which offer superb plants. Most of these nurseries are still so small that the owner, who is usually a dedicated and experienced gardener, can supervise the handling of each item offered. Some of the best plants I have ever bought have come from such nurseries. Also, in a small nursery you are usually allowed to wander through the growing fields and select the individual plants you want, have them freshly dug for you. In most large nurseries this is impossible, you must take what has been stacked in the display area, and if you cannot distinguish a good plant from a poor one that is just too bad.

So here are some check points to keep in mind.

At this time of year, from late April on, all pre-dug trees, shrubs, and evergreens should be either balled-and-burlaped, or canned, the treatment usually given the smaller shrubs. Earlier in the season, while they are still dormant, many shrubs and some trees can be moved bare root but once these have started into active growth the roots must be protected. Yet, incredibly, I have seen well-started shrubs and trees—even evergreens!—offered bare root by roadside stands, lashed to car bumpers or fenders to be transported hundreds of miles, judging by the license plates, with wind whipping through the exposed roots. By the time these poor things got planted, most of them would be deader than canned mackerel and the buyer would have no come-back as the seller could always claim, quite truthfully, that the plants were alive when sold.

When considering a pre-dug balled-and-burlaped plant of any type observe the size and condition of the root-ball. It should be of generous size in proportion to the top growth, tightly packed, firm and slightly damp to the touch. Never buy a plant, especially an evergreen, with big top growth and a tiny root-ball, or one with a loose, shifting, dry root-ball. The first indicate that the grower is ignorant of good digging practices—or thinks you are—and the second means that the plant has suffered neglect, been allowed to dry out. For some plants, notably evergreens, this could be the kiss of death. If most of the plants offered by this nursery or roadside stand show either of the above conditions, best get right back in your car and go elsewhere.

Perennials and roses, unless freshly dug for you, should be either canned or potted in containers of adequate size. Like certain shrubs, many of these can be safely sold bare root early in the spring before they start into growth, but it is too late for that now as growth has already started. Roses should show signs of leafage; perennials should have good top growth, thick and chunky. Also observe the type of soil which—presumably—the plant was grown in; it should be reasonably dark and friable. But if you are dealing with an unknown seller watch out for a booby trap here, and scrape away the top layer of earth to see what lies beneath. I once was suckered into buying some "bargain" plants, potted, and found when I got them home that the top layer of good soil was a fake, that underneath was the miserable sandy clay the plants had been grown in through forcing. The roots were so weak and meager that it took weeks of intensive care in a humus bed before the plants amounted to anything. Of course, no reputable grower would resort to such trickery but apparently there are fast-buck artists who do.

When buying annuals look for short, brisk, chunky, bud-filled top growth. Avoid tall spindly offerings, especially if these bear tiny, misshapen flowers, are presented in shallow containers of obviously poor soil. I have seen innocent gardeners offered such worthless plants and listened to the sales spiel—"Lookit, it's bloomin' already!"—with a sick heart. They were indeed blooming, in a pitiful fashion, for when a plant is about to die it will make one last effort to fulfill a basic law of nature, propagate its kind by setting seed. But this is usually its swan song. Such a badly grown plant will take weeks of intensive care before it regains its health, if it ever does. If you are offered annuals of this type, distrust the seller. He is either a fool or he thinks you are.

But do not confuse this type of "flowering" with the robust, full-sized blooms often produced by annuals such as petunias, marigolds, etc. when grown in good soil, in containers of adequate size and depth. Most reputable nurseries display racks of these, and if you peer into the thick, vigorous top growth you will find innumerable buds ready to pop when set into your garden. These are good buys, even if they do seem more expensive than the "bargains" you have seen at roadside stands.

About prices: never begrudge an established and reputable nurseryman the prices he asks for well-grown plants of any type. It takes knowledge, skill, and endless care to produce such plants and they are usually well worth the price asked. A nurseryman is going to keep this price as low as he possibly can—for, obviously, the lower the price the more plants he is going to sell—but his expenses keep going up all the time and he is certainly entitled to make a small profit, though sometimes this is a very small one indeed. I have often heard inexperienced gardeners complain about the prices of plants, especially evergreens, but let such critics try raising such plants themselves and they will soon glimpse the problems involved.

When buying pot-grown plants always up-end the pot to see what is happening at the root end. Many nurseries buy in such material from growers who may or may not have had time to shift the little plants into pots of adequate size. Consequently, such plants may have outgrown their containers, become pot-bound. This is bad, because pot-bound plants often become stunted, may never recover from this injury. If, when you up-end the pot, you find a hard, woody root protruding from the hole, the plant has probably been pot-bound for some time, is a poor risk. If you find only a network of fine roots there is still time to reclaim the plant; set it— unpotted, of course—in a bed of sandy humus to encourage root relaxation and, in a week or so, give it a shot of fast-acting "miracle" fertilizer. Such fertilizers are often very effective when setting out annuals or perennials which have been poorly grown. Devout organic gardeners will have to forgive me this one.

Late Spring Homework

Now begins—or, rather, continues—the gardener's most frantic period. In late May or early June, depending on where you live and whether spring was early or late, there are several chores which must be done promptly to ready the garden for the summer. Many of these cannot wait upon your social life, which is probably even more hectic than your horticultural life, so this confusion you will have to work out for yourself.

One of the first chores is the trimming back of arabis, an early spring bloomer. In this area arabis starts blooming in latish April and usually continues well into May. But as soon as it stops flowering, and before it sets seed, it should be sheared back so that it can expend its last spring strength in growing that tight frosted-silver foliage which makes it so valuable in the summer garden as a foil for the dark leafage of most perennials and annuals. If neglected at this time it will soon become leggy and it is then too late for cutting back; or rather, the stems will take far longer to fill out as the plant's strength has been used up in seed setting. After shearing, scratch in a little bone meal around the roots.

The same applies to any number of low spring bloomers, notably candytuft, which flowers throughout most of May. This, unless trimmed back right after blooming, will develop long spidery legs which are still slower to fill out. It seems a pity to let these plants, capable of such compact and decorative summer foliage, get sprawly and untidy for want of a little attention at the right time.

Another May chore, possibly an April one in your area, is lifting and dividing fall-blooming asters, both cushion and Michaelmas-daisy types. This should be done while the plants are comparatively dormant so that they have time to reestablish themselves. These perennial asters are hearty eaters, can exhaust in one summer most of the nourishment around them, so lift, pull apart, and replant the divisions in fresh soil rich in compost or you-know-what plus a handful of bone meal and a little sand; asters like plenty of moisture but they also like drainage. Use only the young, outside roots and discard the center. You will probably have more divisions than you can find room for so these you offer to friends or to your garden club. This will give the impression that you are most generous, a lovely person. It does no harm to let people think this.

Primroses, also, should be divided at this time, or as soon as they have finished blooming. This is not necessary every year, of course, but if the clumps are allowed to get too big they will not bloom as well. Lift, pull apart gently, and reset the divisions in appropriate bedding (see primrose article) saving out those you cannot use to give away. As primroses are considered quite special by most gardeners this will make you appear even more gracious.

And have you fed your tulips yet? This can be done at almost any time during the spring—if you can find that time!—but the last call is after the faded flowers have been cut off (always cut them off, never let them go to seed). Follow the bone-meal-manure tea procedure mentioned earlier, or if you don't have time to brew the manure tea, combine the bone meal with dried manure and water in thoroughly. Other spring bulbs such as daffodils, jonquils, hyacinths, and even the tiny ones like snowdrops and crocuses, would be most grateful for—and enormously surprised by—such attention as, being socially unimportant, they are usually forgotten.

Back in *March* I alerted you to the systemic pest controls which now are relatively new on the gardening scene, though by the time you read this they may be well known to every gardener. I have sampled one of these products and it worked very well indeed. To save you hunting through *March* for this information, here it is again, for now is the time to get started on this program if you haven't started already.

Basically, it is very simple: the material, usually granular, is introduced into the soil around the plant roots and watered in well, is then absorbed by the roots and circulated throughout the entire plant system, rendering all parts immune to most of the chewing and sucking insects for a period of six weeks to two months. The first application is supposed to be made when the plant has an inch or so of new growth, so when you start this program depends on where you live; in southern states early April might be the time, in northern states, May or even early June if spring has been late, for the earth should have had time to warm up a little. But—and this is so important I put it in caps—DO NOT USE ANY OF THESE SYSTEMIC MATERIALS AROUND VEGETABLES, FRUITS, OR ANYTHING YOU PLAN TO EAT. This also includes herbs, but as most herbs have their own built-in insect repellents they would not need such systemics.

For, unlike sprays, this systemic material cannot be washed off; it is inside every leaf, flower or fruit, and remains there until gradually diluted by other soil properties absorbed by the roots. This is why the application should be repeated once or twice during the summer for plants, such as roses, which are particularly subject to insect damage. And there is a systemic made especially for roses which also contains a balanced fertilizer so you don't have to give separate feedings. It is made by Ortho and called Rose And Flower Care.

This is the one I tried last summer, and with fairly spectacular success as I didn't get around to it until late July when my roses had already been chewed up by a lot of free-loaders. Yet within a few days after application, all visible insect life had disappeared and the new growth, which appeared shortly, was completely clean and remained that way throughout the rest of the summer. I have never had such fine September bloom as those roses produced, so I am sold on this product anyhow. Ortho also makes a systemic which does not contain a fertilizer in case you want to pursue your own feeding program. This one I have not tried but I intend to.

To me the greatest blessing of these systemic controls is that they do away with spraying, a chore I detest above all others and consequently seldom get around to. However, if you are a determined sprayer Ortho also makes a spray which introduces the systemic material directly into the top growth to be absorbed by same. This I have not tried nor do I intend to.

Now for some garden trickery which might amuse you. The

first concerns phlox, the tall, summer-blooming garden phlox, *P. decussata*. If you are facing a wedding, big party, or similar wing-ding in early September and want your phlox to be at its superb best, this is what you do now, in late May or early June: lift each plant, leave it out of the ground for about half an hour, and then reset it in enriched soil. This will delay its bloom for from ten days to two weeks. Choose a cloudy or rainy day for this operation. Or, if you have an extensive phlox planting which always blooms at the same time, lift every other plant and reset; this will stagger the flowering period, give a gentler but more prolonged display.

Still another trick with phlox—certainly one of the most loving, forgiving and long-suffering of all perennials—is to nip off, in June, every other uprising stem, slanting this nipping so that the stems are lower in front than in back. The nipped stems will be slower to bloom, the entire flowering period will last longer, and the effect will be a soft vertical display instead of a horizontal one. But re-member that phlox is a hearty eater, also a thirsty one, and needs plenty of compost or manure in its bedding, plenty of water (around the roots, not on the leaves) during a dry spell. This garden phlox will take more abuse and neglect than any perennial I know of, but it will also repay your loving care most generously.

Here is a trick with zinnias, the tall giant types. Whether you do this now or later in June depends on how far along your zinnias are. While the young shoots are still soft and pliant, bend them down, towards the front, and fasten to the earth with wire hairpins (remember hairpins?), the ends bent back for anchorage. You will thus achieve a low foreplanting of these huge zinnia flowers which will mystify other gardeners. Can be quite effective, these huge blossoms, poking out unexpectedly among low plants along the front of the border, for these zinnias will often stem-root themselves and bloom more profusely than at their normal altitude. Try deep rose-pink zinnias with a white lobelia edging, or pale yellow zinnias with a foreplanting of artemisia Silver Mound. I haven't tried this trick except with zinnias but have been told that many other tall annuals will respond to the same treatment—or maltreatment—if it is done early while the stems are still soft.

MULCHING.   Have you decided whether you are going to sum-mer-mulch your plantings this year? If you are this is the last call, for such mulching should be done while the earth still retains a good portion of spring moisture. Actually, this mulching is best attended to earlier, where possible, but in many cold sections with late frosts it is risky to set out tender annuals until early June, and these should be in place so that they, too, can be protected. Around here we often get a hard freeze over Memorial Day. I remember going to one Memorial Day picnic in a ski suit. I was the only comfortable person there.

A summer mulch on perennial beds, special plantings, and around shrubs will keep roots cool and conserve moisture. This could be particularly important in case of a long, hot, dry summer; if there is a prolonged drought such a mulch could even save the lives of your plants. Also, a summer mulch will cut down on maintenance, almost eliminate weeding, for what scattered weeds do appear are easily plucked out of the soft blanket. But, of course, many gardeners do not like the appearance of a mulch. They prefer the traditional look of bare, immaculate, cultivated earth. This is fine if you have the time or labor to maintain such elegance but most of us do not. Nowadays it's like having a butler with white gloves.

There are many different kinds of mulches to consider. Also, different types of plants take different types of mulches. Most grey-leafed plants, which usually want a dry, lean bedding and super-drainage, like a mulch of pebbles or crushed stone. This is a very practical mulch to use under any number of small, low plants as it prevents mud-splashing after a hard rain. Most rock-type plants also prefer this kind of mulch.

For perennial beds and special plantings which like a well-fertilized soil, a feeding mulch takes care of several chores at once; it contributes humus, supplies nourishment, conserves moisture and, to a certain extent, cuts down on weeding, though its very character will encourage whatever weed seeds alight on it or may have been contained therein. But if you are watchful these strays are easily removed and there will be fewer and fewer of them as the summer goes on.

The best feeding mulch you could use would be compost or well-rotted manure, so well-rotted that it is almost odorless. Unfortunately, these mulches are not always pleasing to the eye for to be effective they should be applied thickly and this gives a somewhat coarse appearance which some gardeners consider unsightly. Such mulches are best used around shrubs in outlying areas. For plantings which specialize in gracious living a bacteria-rich humus, such as the LaFontan Humus mentioned earlier, makes a nutritive but genteel mulch, your plantings look as though they were swathed in black velvet. This one is especially recommended for roses and lilies which relish its faintly acid contribution to their welfare.

Peat moss, that most popular of all mulches, I consider one of the poorest except in deep shade around evergreens; in fact, when innocently used around the wrong plants it can actually be dangerous. It has almost no feeding value, is slow to break down, and in bright sun is apt to cake, forming a crust which sheds water like an umbrella, thereby preventing moisture from reaching the roots. You can forestall this caking by covering the peat moss with a thin layer of earth, but this entails the extra work of providing the earth. Also, peat moss has a very acid seepage and can, in time, injure lime-loving plants. I was once called in to adivse on a peony planting which had stopped flowering and found that it had been lovingly mulched each summer with peat moss. Removal of the peat moss, plus doses of wood ashes, lime, bone meal and manure tea (the idea that you should not use lime and manure together is disputed by many experienced gardeners) finally restored this planting to blooming health but a hard time was had by all. And I know of one gardener who almost killed her clematis by continuous use of peat moss mulches. Her piteous cry "Why didn't somebody tell me?" is the reason I have gone into this at such length.

Lest peat moss devotees be aghast at this criticism of the woman they love, let me assure them that I love her too—in her place. Peat moss is invaluable in all deep-planting operations because of its ability to hold and disperse quantities of water, to soften and condition and aerate the earth, encourage root growth. It also makes an excellent and economical mulch in shade around acid-loving plants, and as most plants which enjoy shade are either acid-loving or acid-tolerant you don't have to worry too much about which is which. But, so far as I am concerned, these are the only valuable services rendered by peat moss. I am always shocked to find the wholesale and indiscriminate use of peat moss mulches recommended so often by garden writers.

For use in sunny social areas where appearance is important, vermiculite (get the horticultural grade) makes a fine mulch. It presents a soft, grey-beige blanket which is pleasant to look upon and it is a terrific insulator; could be especially valuable in those hot, dry spots which bake in summer. Being sterile it has no feeding value so best feed the plantings first with a sprinkling of dried cow manure mixed with bone meal, water this in thoroughly and then cover thickly with the vermiculite; the manure will soon become odorless after the mulch is applied. Being neutral in character it causes no soil reaction and so is safe to use anywhere around anything. Buckwheat hulls can be applied the same way, are not quite as effective for insulation but present a brownish appearance which you may prefer. These dry out more quickly than vermiculite and sometimes blow away in strong winds.

These are the only mulches of this type I have had experience with but there are probably others, native to your area, which would do the same kind of job and perhaps be less expensive; just check on their soil reaction before using too generally. Chopped pine bark makes a fine mulch around evergreens, especially flowering evergreens, in either sun or shade; I know of one superb gardener who prefers this because it mellows down to a good earth-color and looks so well near lawns. Or if you live near piney woods you might use pine needles which you could probably collect for free, a happy thought. These seem particularly right near wooded areas and give a lovely smell. However, both of these pine products cause a slightly acid soil reaction in time, so be a little careful where you use them.

Now for the homemade mulches: both coffee grounds and spent tea leaves can be used for mulching; but don't just dump them wet; spread them out so they can dry before they turn mouldy. Both produce a faintly acid reaction but not enough to bother most normal plants, and, in time, can be built up into a respectable mulch which you will enjoy, thinking of the money you have saved. This enterprise is best conducted close to the kitchen door as you will soon learn for yourself.

And here is an economy mulch if there ever was one. Grass clippings. They work wonders when poked down, thickly, among perennials and annuals; the results are almost as miraculous as those produced by the famous hay mulches used in vegetable gardens. I discovered this last summer by accident. Being faced with a morbid expanse of dried grass clippings, too heavy to leave on the so-called lawn, I bundled them up and stuffed them down around a planting of nicotiana and petunias in the nearby border; this was at the far end of the border where, I figured, the dead clippings wouldn't show too much. I then forgot about the whole thing and was mystified, a few weeks later, to see that end of the border blossoming more profusely than any other part, even though it got less sun. Investigation showed that the mountains of grass clippings had settled down into a thick, light, fluffy blanket, now almost hidden by foliage, and that the soil beneath was soft and moist, the plants stronger and more flower-filled than similar but unmulched plant groupings further along the bed. And this mulched section needed no watering or other attention throughout the rest of the summer.

So I give you this information for whatever it may be worth to you. Such a mulch is certainly not beautiful but it does produce better plants and more flowers. You may want to use it in the back of perennial borders or in the cutting garden. But be sure to let these clippings dry completely before you gather them up, and then apply thickly, don't just sprinkle. And do this only in spring when heavy cuttings should be removed from the lawn anyhow. Later on, in the heat of summer, it is best to leave the clippings to protect the grass roots from hot sun.

There are also the living mulches to be considered, the flat, shallow-rooted, ever-spreading ground covers which, in time, will provide a wall-to-wall carpeting for plantings, keeping soil cool and practically eliminating weeds. These ground covers take a while to get established but can save an enormous amount of maintenance. Sweet woodruff, the myrtles, ajuga, several others suitable for informal country settings have already been mentioned, but for formal or semi-formal areas in deep to partial shade ivy is one of the best. European ginger is even more desirable but is also more difficult to establish.

English ivy (*Hedera helix*) makes a glossy and beautiful living mulch, is particularly good around lilies and evergreens, or shrubs which have a shady footing. It is easy to establish in shade if you give it a deep, rich, humusy bedding (compost, peat moss—lots of peat moss—and sand, well mixed) and keep it cut back at first until it thickens up. It is said to be doubtfully hardy in very cold, dry sections such as this but most of mine, in shade, has been root-hardy for over thirty years and to 30° below zero; a few times it has killed back to the roots during especially hard winters with little snow, but has gradually resumed growth in spring. The Baltic variety, *H. baltica,* is supposed to be hardier but, personally, I consider it less desirable.

If ordering this English ivy, it is wise to get it from a northern grower where it has already been exposed to cold winters. The individual clones seem to vary a good deal in hardiness and, I have been told by ivy-growers, can be conditioned to withstand progressively colder temperatures. This seems to have been the case with mine, propagated from the original plants which succumbed during one early and bitter winter, perhaps because they were badly placed in sun. Their progeny, however, now accustomed to our below zero temperatures, seem far tougher.

Once you get this ivy established it will go to town, swarm over everything, until you have such billows of the shining stuff that you can start complaining. These complaints will get you little sympathy from other gardeners who may have tried, unsuccessfully, to establish this ivy in hard, dry soil, sunny spots. But a word of warning: keep ivy away from all wooden structures as it will sneak under clapboards to loosen them. When this happens you have to cut out armfuls of it every fall and, as you can't bear to throw it away, you go around offering it to anyone who will take it. This is a good way to lose friends. Every November people run when they see me approaching.

More about this ivy in *November,* how you can root it in the house over the winter, how beautiful the sprays will look on your mantelpiece.

To Peonies—With Love

I think these are my favorite plants. One of them, anyhow. I know of few others which flower so generously, offer such strong, serene foliage over so long a period, ask so little of the gardener. In our area peonies bloom, in one form or another, from the middle of May into July, so perhaps June should be the month in which to lay my heart at their feet.

The first to flower are the herbaceous species *P. tenuifolia, P. Mlokosewitschi, P. macrophylla* and their hybrids. Some of these are: Daystar (single goblets of clear pale yellow), Playmate (bright rose flowers, ferny foliage), Nova (pale yellow, dwarf plants), Seraphim (a shining white, profuse bloomer), Gwenda (tea-rose goblets, rosy edged) . . . . followed by their close relatives, Nosegay (salmon-rose, tall plants), Diantha (light pink, dwarf), Roselette (deep pink, unusually tall), Chalice (immense pure white flowers, dark glossy leaves), Serenade (pale pink flush with spray of golden stamens), Halcyon (white with crimson flares), Picotee (rounded white petals edged deep pink), Rushlight (warm ivory with golden heart) and Rose Crystal (ivory petals, twisted and pointed like cut glass, rose edged). All of these are very early (VE) to early (E).

Then, from late May on into June and overlapping some of the VEs and many of the Es, come the tree peonies, first the Japanese and, later in June, the *lutea* hybrids. Also from early June on into July come more of the herbaceous hybrids in endless colors, shadings, forms: Edward Steichen (dark red, semi-double), Campagna (pure white goblets, greenish shadows, golden center), Frances (a pale peach-pink single), Legion of Honor (flaming cherry-scarlet, tall plants), Madrigal (palest pink, semi-double), Postillion (scarlet crimson), Gillian (a silvery salmon-pink single) and Laura Magnuson (a coral-pink single).

And these are only a few picked at random out of the Saunders catalogue, not even touching the tree peonies! The late Dr. A. P. Saunders of Hamilton College was one of the first hybridizers, and certainly the most famous, to create through his skill and knowledge and unfailing taste the exquisite forms and colorings which still distinguish the Saunders hybrids from all others. Now there are many more peony breeders—Gratwick-Daphnis, Auten, Glasscock, Mrs. Freeborn, Nicholls, Brand, to name a few—all with their own originations, their own catalogues for you to delight in.

Did you have any idea there were so many new and unusual peonies to choose from? And you are still growing the same old faithfuls everyone else grows? How about finding new homes for a few—anyone with new property to plant would probably welcome such a gift—and replacing them with some of the choice beauties listed above? But if you do this be sure to give the newcomers entirely fresh soil in their bedding.

In my opinion the Saunders hybrids are the most beautiful, the most unusual in forms and colorings, but perhaps this is only because I know them better than the others, and also have the good fortune to know Dr. Saunders' daughter, Miss Silvia Saunders of Clinton, N.Y., who for many years has been continuing her father's work. Miss Saunders is, herself, a unique person—warm and gay and generous, and a very great lady. She is a delight to know and to deal with. Unfortunately she is now in the process of retiring from the nursery business, will probably be fully retired by the time this book reaches you, and this is a sadness to everyone who has ever come in contact with her.

However, the Saunders stock and the Saunders tradition is being taken over by a young man Miss Saunders herself hand-picked for this job. He is Dr. David Reath (a veterinarian) of Vulcan, Michigan, a trained geneticist who has been working with peonies for several years. I suggest that you write for his catalogue (see page 246).

All the peonies mentioned so far in this chapter are herbaceous, which means that the tops die down in winter and come up from the roots in spring, and their forms range from the ethereal singles to the semi-doubles and full doubles. Personally, I consider the singles and semi-doubles far more interesting and desirable than the ordinary doubles and bomb-types; not only are they less work to grow as they seldom get bogged down by rain, need no staking, but they are also far better for cutting. Even I, whose idea of a flower arrangement is some nice daisies in a milk bottle, can work wonders with single peonies. Some are so huge—to 8″ when fully opened!—that just one, floated in a shallow bowl with a few leaves, is all you need.

Herbaceous peonies are invaluable in the country garden, they are part of its summer structure with their great blossoms in late spring and their dark, semi-glossy leafage the rest of the season. This leafage itself can be important, giving strength to a perennial planting which might otherwise be weak, giving emphasis or punctuation, providing a frame for some special plant grouping; try such a frame for a planting of *Platycodon* (balloon flower or bell flower), double form, in white, shell pink, and deep pink . . . or for *Matricaria* (feverfew), the ultra-double white faced down with the pale yellow Lemon Ball, both of which you can raise from seed (see *February*) . . . or use this peony foliage, perhaps in a half circle, to shade the roots of white clematis grown against a sunny wall.

These peonies can also be used as a low summer edging along a walk or driveway; in bloom they would knock the viewer speechless and, later, present a line of dark and gracious foliage . . . or they could be used as an edging for a terrace . . . . as foreplanting for evergreens (they go particularly well with junipers) in a country-formal setting . . . . or in front of lilies, so that the tall white or pale pink or pale yellow trumpets rise up above dark peony foliage in July and August . . . . or, massed, in the corner of an old country-style stone wall with a feathery white silver lace vine tumbling along its top.

Peonies will grow almost anywhere, given proper bedding, except in very acid soils, in deep shade, too near roots of trees or shrubs, or so far south that they cannot freeze in winter (this is necessary to bloom). They are tough, easy, hardy, and long-lived, need dividing only when the clumps get too huge. They love sun, and you get more flowers in sun but the blossoms themselves do not last as long as when given some slight afternoon shade. I have had some of these hybrids bloom quite well with only three or four hours of late morning sun.

About planting herbaceous peonies: I am still feuding with

the usual peony-planting directions you read everywhere because most of them contain a hidden pitfall which any number of innocent gardeners tumble into. You are told to prepare a deep, wide planting site, to dig down at least 2′ and preferably 3′, to put a layer of drainage material such as stones or gravel in the bottom (drainage is of greatest importance to all peonies), and then fill this huge excavation with soil well mixed with compost and/or dried manure (not fresh), a cup or more of bone meal, a little coarse sand, and to top all this with several inches of plain earth in which the peony root should be set with the "eyes" (buds on crown) exactly 2″ below the surface. You are also warned that deeper planting may result in failure to bloom.

So you do all this, carefully and prayerfully, and do you know what happens in most cases? After a good hosing and a few weeks of hard autumn rains your peony roots will have sunk down into the soft bedding so that the "eyes" are no longer 2″ below the surface but nearer 4″ or 5″ and, consequently, you get no flowers. I don't know how many times I have been asked about non-blooming peonies and found the crowns so submerged they couldn't possibly have bloomed. "But I followed the directions so carefully!" is the cry of the puzzled gardener.

The pitfall is that these same planting directions usually tell you to prepare the planting site well ahead of time, from three weeks to a year ahead of time, but the importance of this is not stressed, no understandable reason is given and, consequently, most new gardeners pay no attention to it. What's the hurry? The plants haven't even come yet! But the reason for this direction is to allow plenty of time for this settling of the earth, so that when the peony roots are planted they will *not* sink. Why don't garden books explain these things? Probably because most of them are written by professionals who have forgotten how many, many things a new gardener must learn, who assume a reader-knowledge which just isn't there.

If you cannot prepare your peony sites well ahead of time and must plant at the last moment I have found it safest to set the roots so that the buds are just *at* the surface, or a little above, so that you can still see them when the tamping down and watering operations have been completed. In a few weeks, if you have prepared the bedding properly, you will find that the buds have sunk to just about the right 2" depth. If they are still a bit high, which is unlikely, you can cover them with a little earth. But it is better to have them too high than too low.

And do you know why this is important? Because these crown-buds must be frozen, or at least frosted, in order to produce bloom. Consequently, the warmer your climate the shallower should be the setting of these buds, from a final 1" below to, possibly, surface level itself.

Now does all this make sense? Once you understand the reason for a direction it is easy to remember and you follow it gladly. For many years I was puzzled by these matters until I had them explained to me by an authority at a botanical garden who seemed surprised that everyone didn't know such things. Yet in my forty years of reading about peonies in innumerable garden books I have only once come upon this information in print.

Don't expect too much of peonies the first year after planting; they are slow to get into orbit. However, if you have bought good roots of good size from a good nursery you may get a sample bloom or two that first spring. I often have. And from then on they need almost no care, though they do appreciate an early breakfast of bone meal (one cup per plant) plus a sprinkling of wood ashes, both scratched in around the roots; if no wood ashes water in a little ground limestone. During prolonged dry spells they might also need water, as would most plants, but don't just sprinkle; let the end of the hose rest just above the roots and allow a gentle trickle to seep down into the earth; give about half an hour of such watering to each plant.

And do not, ever, use chemical fertilizers on peonies, either in the planting operation or later; they respond much better to organic materials. A light coating of compost mixed with a little dried manure and another cup of bone meal can be scratched into the earth around the roots in the fall but be sure not to cover the crown itself; even this attention they can get along without for a few years so don't worry if you have to skip it. I stick seed-setting forget-me-nots under my herbaceous peonies where, in the cool damp shade, they raise their enormous families for distribution the following spring. This arrangement seems to please all concerned.

The stalks of herbaceous peonies should be cut down in the fall. The reason for this—and, again, if you know the reason you are more likely to respect the direction—is because the old stalks, often flopped over on the ground, offer winter nesting to fungus spores. So clip off these stalks just below ground level, being careful not to injure the crown buds which lie just beneath. Easiest way to do this is to feel around with your finger, locate the buds, then clip only the stalks. You will probably clip your finger as well but this is not important. No winter mulch is either necessary or desirable for established peonies. Newly set plants (all peonies are planted in the fall, preferably in September) can be given a light airy covering of pine branches or salt hay after the ground is well frozen but this is simply to prevent possible frost-heave.

Tree peonies are not trees at all but woody, shrub-like plants which grow from 3′ to 6′ tall with, sometimes, an almost equal spread at full maturity. They lose their leaves in winter but the woody stems remain and should NOT be cut down. In early spring new leaves and buds appear on these stems, often with more new stems springing out of the ground.

The fresh new growth of Japanese tree peonies is a delight, a muted strawberry-pink-pistachio-green business; circle the plants with white arabis (the double *flore-pleno*) and with this as an overture your peony season really begins in April. Furthermore, this arabis can be left there, being a light feeder and shallow-rooted, to be clipped back after flowering into mounds of frosted silver, a nice footing for the uplifting summer foliage of the tree peony.

The Japanese tree peonies start opening their incredible flowers about the last week in May, and even my relatively young plants (six to eight years old) bear from twelve to eighteen 7″ flowers apiece; I believe the count gets up to twenty or thirty 10″ blossoms on older plants. Which is just horticultural cheesecake but ecstasy to most gardeners. In form, these peonies are lifting and spreading, sometimes open in habit, the leaves a delicate greyish-green. The plants are often weighted down by the size and profusion of the blossoms but as soon as these are clipped off, after flowering, the stems spring back to position. Or if your tree peony is hopelessly burdened down by this flowering you can help it by clipping off the largest and heaviest blossoms. If you want to render a hostess speechless with gratitude arrive with an armful of 7″ to 10″ tree peony flowers. Your social image can coast on this for quite a while.

Perhaps you have been afraid of tree peonies because you have heard that they were expensive to buy, difficult to grow, and suitable only to elaborate gardens. Good tree peonies—the only kind worth buying; most of the cheap ones are a waste of time, space, and money—are certainly expensive, but they are a lifetime investment growing more beautiful and more valuable each year. And do you know why they are expensive? Let me quote part of a letter from my friend Silvia Saunders: "It is the casualties in the first and second year which keep TPs still so expensive; most of us who work with propagating lose half the first year, and another half the second year, and end up with three plants for every twelve grafts we made two years ago . . ."

The reason for this may well be because Miss Saunders' standards of excellence are so high, as are the standards of most other top-ranking hybridizers, all of them unwilling to sponsor inferior plants. You will sometimes find cheap tree peonies listed in "bargain" catalogues but these offerings may be discards, or have been carelessly grafted on poor stock so that the plants are weak, the flowers small, the colors unpredictable. I have, occasionally, seen tree peonies of this type produce a few small, meager blossoms but to anyone who knows what a really good tree peony can look like they were a lot of nothing.

Besides Miss Saunders there are, of course, several other tree peony growers you can trust, for the challenge of this peony seems to attract chiefly the devout and dedicated hybridist who stakes his name and his honor on the plants he offers. One of these is William Gratwick of Pavilion, N. Y. who, with his partner Nassos Daphnis who does the hybridizing, offers only beautifully grown, highly selected specimen type plants of a size and quality unavailable at most nurseries. These are frankly expensive, but they are probably the finest tree peonies you could buy anywhere. Even if you are not yet ready for plants of this caliber I suggest that you send for the Gratwick catalogue if only to glimpse what lies ahead of you once you get started on tree peonies. This catalogue is a small one but well put together, well printed, with black and white photographs.

Mr. Gratwick, who specializes in the extraordinary "Daphnis hybrids" originated there in Pavilion, also offers a selected list of Japanese tree peonies and a choice assortment of the famous Saunders *lutea* hybrids. These may be formed like "magnolia blossoms" or "lotus flowers" or "great anemones" and the colors range "from silvery-cream through all the yellows to the color of ripe grain, and from dusty pink through deep strawberry tones to a maroon that is close to black, with a scattering of subtle mauves and shadowed rose colors. . . ."

Well, that should hold you for a while. And if you are ever anywhere near the Gratwick nursery towards the end of May be very sure to take in their Tree Peony Festival—some 4,000 plants all in bloom!—which starts the weekend after Lilac Sunday in Rochester, N.Y. You might telephone ahead to find out the exact dates. The Gratwick nursery is about forty miles south of Rochester on the York-Pavilion road.

There are also other reliable nurseries where, if you are a beginner, you can get good tree peonies, in younger plants, at rela-

A Saunders semi-double white Japanese tree peony, unnamed. The blossoms are almost 9″ across.

EUGENE D. TRUDEAU

NASSOS DAPHNIS

A tree peony named Tria, a yellow Daphnis hybrid introduced by the Gratwick Nursery.

tively modest prices and still be sure of excellent quality. These plants will take longer to develop into the spectaculars you dream of but they will make it in time and the growing of them will be a lasting excitement. Some of these nurseries are listed on page 243.

I have found tree peonies as easy to grow as the herbaceous kind if you give them the bedding they prefer and don't move them around too much. No peony likes moving and tree peonies resent it even more than the herbaceous kinds, unless they are moved to a happier spot. Another hazard is dogs, some of them anyhow. One of our dogs, a you-name-it puppy from Bide-A-Wee, loves to chomp on the winter stems of tree peonies while the other, a very pedigreed Cairn terrier, doesn't touch the peonies, prefers common lilacs. (There must be something of significance in there somewhere but I can't figure out what it is.) And I have heard of

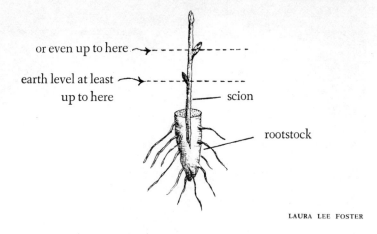

or even up to here

earth level at least
up to here

scion

rootstock

LAURA LEE FOSTER

other dogs chewing tree peony stems in winter. However, this will not seriously harm the plant itself, you will lose whatever bloom that stem would have produced but new stems will rise up to take its place. Once established, tree peonies are strong growers.

The bedding for tree peonies should be the same as for the herbaceous kinds except that they like even more bone meal: about a pound for a small plant, two pounds for a larger one, dug deeply into the planting site. But the most important difference is that tree peonies should be planted quite deeply. Unlike herbaceous peonies, the tree peony root is a stalk-like affair grafted on to a piece of herbaceous root about 4″ long. This root acts like a nurse until the scion can put out its own roots, therefore the more of the scion buried the better chance it has to do this; you bury all the lower, non-budded part and even some of the budded part. The accompanying sketch, which was originally drawn by Miss Saunders herself, shows how deeply to plant a tree peony.

The importance of a large, well-prepared planting site was demonstrated by the experience of a friend. Having read about tree peonies, but not knowing exactly what they were, she ordered one from a reliable nursery and, figuring it was a tree, had her men dig a planting site big enough to take a young maple. This great excavation, prepared well ahead of time just as the directions said, was then filled with all the recommended goodies and my friend impatiently awaited the arrival of her tree peony, wondering if it would come by truck. When it finally arrived by mail and turned out to be a scrawny little stalk only about 8″ long she couldn't believe it. Recovering from her mirth she set the tiny thing in the vast planting site where it looked completely lost, and a little bewildered by its good fortune. This story was the delight of her friends for some time to come.

But the punch line is what happened later. Finding that tree peonies were so small and so easy to plant she ordered several more, but this time did not bother with all that fancy bedding, planted them in just ordinary holes. So—and you are probably way ahead of me—the first tree peony, set in the maple-tree-size site, grew joyfully and extravagantly while the later arrivals, in their cramped quarters, did almost nothing and eventually had to be dug up and replanted properly.

Where you position a tree peony, its exposure to sun or wind, its background, and its relation to other plants, other garden features, is something to consider long and carefully. A spot sheltered from winter winds is recommended by most growers, though I have found my own tree peonies to be far hardier than expected. Ample sun is also important, plus, if possible, light overhead shade during the hottest part of the day to enable the flowers to last longer, the colors to glow more effectively. But of all these considerations I think the setting, the background, is of greatest importance, for a tree peony is not a plant you just stick in with a lot of other plants. In most country gardens it is an item you treat with reverence.

My first experience with a Japanese tree peony was unfortunate. Many years ago a friend who was moving away gave me one I had drooled over in her garden. It was snowy white, a single, with softly fluted petals and a great gold heart; it was the legendary blonde who, arriving at the opera swathed in white mink, steps out of the Rolls to enchant the photographers with her innocent wide-eyed smile.

I was so overcome by the magnificence of this gift that, like a dog suddenly given a whole leg of roast lamb, I went around in a daze trying to figure out where best to inter it. Obviously it had to be in some spot where visitors could appreciate it, and this meant near the front entrance. The only sheltered yet sunny spot in that area was up against a screened porch, so this is where I put it. What I had failed to consider, most unfortunately, was the background, for this was when the boys were growing up and that screened porch was their private territory, so my tree peony lifted its white mink elegance against a backdrop of unmade army cots, model aeroplanes, comic books, and empty coke bottles.

In the twenty some years which have elapsed since then I have learned a little more about tree peonies, how to grow them and where best to place them. I still cannot give them the perfect setting, not having a place of suitable distinction, but have found that they will often fit quite happily into even a simple country garden if given genteel companions, some suggestion of background. They go well with roses, with lilies, against certain shrubs, against almost all evergreens, and can even be used in the perennial bed if neighbored by such aristocrats. I have a ruffled white which looks quite well (to me, anyhow) in a wall corner against a white shrub-althea with groups of Madonna lilies nearby and a footing of evergreen candytuft. This gives four separate periods of bloom in that tiny corner and all the inhabitants are congenial, all like the same soil and setting.

But wherever you put your tree peonies be sure they have plenty of root room, the kind of food and lodging they prefer—a deep, rich, well-drained bedding with plenty of bone meal, a touch of lime. This is particularly important if their neighbors like a little acidity as do roses, most lilies (not Madonnas) and many evergreens. But don't worry too much about this acid-alkaline matter

This tree peony planting in the Gratwick Nursery suggests using these superb plants as a driveway edging.

for most plants, with a few exceptions, are reasonably tolerant if other conditions are to their liking.

Evergreens or stonework provide the best background of all for Japanese tree peonies, so look around for possible settings. Or they could be used on either side of a fine doorway if enough room can be allowed, for these beauties can eventually develop a spread of 4′ or more. They are one of the very few flowering plants distinguished enough to flank a formal entrance.

The *lutea* hybrids are equally distinguished but different in character. They are heavier, more compact in habit with, usually, thicker, darker foliage; I believe there are also some ferny-leafed ones but these I do not have. My own *lutea* hybrids have foliage somewhat like that of herbaceous peonies but there is a lot more of it, more strength and depth. Yet they are somehow simpler. They are simple enough to combine well with common country-garden perennials and annuals in a bed or border. They are also magnificent flanking wide stone steps or walks; they take a slightly larger, heavier planting scale than the Japanese, have almost as much authority as evergreens.

And the flowers! These start opening in early June and continue for almost two weeks. You can have your choice of cupped, flared, ruffled, or furled . . . in the cream ivories through all the yellows, the tea-rose shades through the pinks into the subtle reds to deep maroon . . . .

Or maybe I shouldn't have started you on all this. Especially as you were probably planning to cut down on your plantings, not increase them. Sorry.

Iris Problems

The new bearded (or German) iris, glamorous descendants of the old-fashioned "flags", are one of the joys of the June scene, and one of the most difficult to place well. Especially in perennial plantings. For, aside from perfect drainage, they must have ample ventilation around their sword-like leaves and ample sun on their rhizomes if they are to remain healthy. And trying to find this much space for them in the usual flower bed is like trying to find a seat on a bus during rush hour.

I wish I knew the answer to this problem. I have often seen iris combined with perennials and annuals so that, from a distance, it delights the eye, but closer inspection has usually shown that the rhizomes would shortly be smothered by adjacent foliage, and this is an invitation to trouble. Sure enough, later in the summer or early the next spring I get telephone calls from alarmed gardeners asking what to do about that awful goo on the iris roots.

That awful goo is probably soft rot, usually introduced by borers which frequent damp, close garden areas and are particularly fond of iris. Sometimes you can have borers without soft rot, or soft rot without borers, but the two usually go together like bacon and eggs.

As this soft rot is a major threat to iris let us get it out of the way first of all. It is a fungus infection which, once it gets into the rhizome, produces an open sore which exudes a slimey, evil-smelling pus. If you see such a sore on an iris rhizome, or even a small open spot with pus leaking out, or a thin, paper-like crust which looks as though it had pus beneath, you probably have soft rot and had better do something about it fast. The first thing you are likely to do is rush for your garden books.

This is what I did, the first time I met soft rot, and was appalled by what I read: according to the experts the whole iris plant should be taken up and burned, all neighboring iris removed, scraped if necessary, then soaked in formaldehyde or bichloride of mercury (corrosive sublimate) for several hours, all the soil in that area either disinfected with the above, or dug out and removed to a far place and new soil brought in. It sounded like a bad dream. Also, in my case, the iris affected was a very choice variety I wanted to save. I decided to chance a short cut and just douse the entire area, and all its inhabitants, with the disinfectant.

A quick trip to town got me some bichloride of mercury. But I should warn you that this can be an upsetting experience if you are a timid soul. First you have to sign the Poison Book and furnish identification, and the inference is that you should have brought along your birth certificate, your dental chart, and a letter from your minister. The pharmacist peers at you over his spectacles and asks what you want to use this for and do you know it is a deadly poison? By this time everyone else is looking at you too and, feeling like a criminal, you explain that you want it to treat soft rot on iris. This causes somebody to snicker, and the pharmacist to register such obvious suspicion that you are tempted to add, wildly, that what you really want it for is Aunt Mildred's soup. But this is no time to get funny. Finally, you are given the small but deadly package and you get out of there fast, shaken but triumphant.

This bichloride of mercury comes in tablets shaped, appropriately, like little coffins—or did when I bought it many years ago—and I am not kidding when I tell you that these tablets should be handled with utmost caution. The container in which you dissolve them (I used an old glass jar, quart size) should be smashed when you are through with it, the stick with which you stir the solution should be burned, lest the dog get hold of it, and if any has gotten on your hands you should wash with soap immediately. Also, the remaining tablets should be locked—repeat, locked—away and the key hidden in some place known only to you. This is vitally important if you have small children who climb and like to sample strange "candies". And maybe you should now read this whole paragraph again. I frolic around with a lot of things but not with bichloride of mercury.

I used two tablets to a quart of water. It saves time to mix up a whole gallon at once if you have a container which can be smashed afterwards and which will allow vigorous stirring with a stick, but the usual gallon jug will not and these tablets take a lot of stirring. They should dissolve completely. When I finally got them dissolved I poured this solution over the infected rhizomes, and repeated this thrice more, saturating all neighboring iris and the surrounding soil. It was a lot of trouble but easier than digging up the whole planting, and there was a chance it might work.

It did. The soft-rot sores dried up (I had exposed the whole area to full sun) and most of the iris bloomed that June, just six weeks later. The plant which had suffered greatest damage took longer to recover but flowered the following year. By that time I had learned my lesson and the planting received ample ventilation and sun. The only time I have found soft rot since then is when I have gotten careless and allowed iris to be overrun by neighboring plants. Too deep planting will also invite soft rot.

So this is the problem of working iris into the perennial garden which, in midsummer, usually becomes a jungle. Especially if you follow the close-planting system recommended by so many garden writers as it gives more bloom per foot and discourages weeds. Weeds are indeed kept out by this lack of air and light, and all kinds of fungus diseases are invited in to replace them. Take your choice.

There is one perennial which combines well with bearded iris, yet does not shut out too much sun and air, and that is gypsophila. I have a dream iris planting in mind which I hope some day to work out for myself but, in the meantime, I give it to you in case you already have the setting for it.

This setting would be a long, raised bed, 3′ to 4′ wide, built against a high stone wall, in full sun and with good air drainage. The wall would carry a spreading, fan-like tracery of dark green euonymus *radicans,* clipped flat, against which would rise feathery masses of tall white gypsophila Perfecta which, in turn, would provide background for drifts of bearded iris in blending shades of pale to deep pink, to wine red, pale blue to darkest blue, the lavenders, the cream whites and yellows. Footing this iris drift would be the low spreading gypsophila Pink Fairy, and under this, hanging down over the lower (retaining) wall a curtain of *Cerastium tomentosum* (snow-in-summer) to provide a foam of white in May and a silver-grey edging the rest of the summer. At each end of this planting, to finish it off, would be a lowish Pfitzer juniper, compact form (*J. Pfitzeriana compacta*), nipped back to be irregular and interesting, kept away from the iris rhizomes.

To me it sounds good. Because all the plants would be congenial, all enjoy the same type of soil and setting—a light, limey soil, super-drainage and full sun—and because of the interplay of strength and gentleness, of line, form, and texture. It would not provide the all-summer riot of color most gardeners seem to crave but it would provide an all-summer serenity which, to me, is far more important. I invite comment and criticism from any professional who, for want of something better to do, may be reading this book.

Another setting for bearded iris might be a narrow bed or beds along a path, preferably a winding path. Candytuft edging for this one (*Iberis sempervirens* Little Gem) but be sure the bed is wide enough to allow room for the candytuft to spread without covering the iris roots. This candytuft would provide a white edging in May a gentle, almost solid ribbon border of whitest white, and, after the iris had finished, give a dark, low footing to the uprising grey-green iris shafts. These two are also good companions with the same tastes.

How to Plant Bearded Iris: These can be planted—or lifted, divided, and replanted—any time from July to September, but the best time is right after they finish blooming, which is usually early July in our area. This gives them a better chance to anchor themselves firmly before winter. Late planting renders them liable to frost-heave.

When lifting and dividing iris cut out the old woody parts and discard, saving only the strong young roots. Then—and this will surprise you—let them lie out in the sun for several hours for the cuts to callus over. This bearded iris is one of the very few plants which, after digging, should have its roots exposed to sun and wind, a treatment which would kill most plants. If you are a perfectionist you might dust the cuts with sulphur but I have never bothered to do this.

Bearded iris like a light sandy loam, perfect drainage, and their favorite food is bone meal. Do *not* use manure or any strong fertilizers for they are light feeders. And it is easy to remember how deeply to plant if you keep in mind the old as-a-duck-swims rule. This means that the top of the rhizome should ride just above ground level. Some authorities recommend deeper planting, just below ground level, but after my encounter with soft rot I prefer to play it safe and plant high. To start with anyhow, for the rhizomes are apt to sink a little as they settle in. Poke the roots well down, settle firmly, and then cut the tops back to the classic fan shape. This is not just to make them look flossy but to cut down evaporation and conserve plant strength for root establishment.

Bearded iris usually bloom only tentatively the first spring following division but after that, and for the next three or four years, they produce more and more flowers each season until the clumps get so big and crowded that they have to be divided again. Finally you run out of space. You also run out of friends to whom you can give this surplus iris because they are already giving away theirs. So do you know what to do then? Stop at any bare, new house you see along the road and offer the inhabitant a bag of iris roots, trimmed and ready for planting. The recipient of this gift will be so astonished and grateful that you will drive on feeling very pleased with yourself.

Where to Get Bearded Iris: I maintain that it is a good idea, when buying any plants, to first view them on the hoof, in bloom, so that you see exactly what you are getting. If you live near any large nursery visit their iris fields in June and make your own selections to be dug for you later. However, perhaps even before you do this I suggest that you look over the extraordinary iris menu offered by Gilbert H. Wild & Son, specialists in iris, peonies, and day lilies. This catalogue is a big, full-color spectacular with twenty pages of bearded iris! There are color combinations, shadings, tones you never knew existed, and each one so beautiful you simply must have it. Shaken, you realize that to find room for all these you will probably have to plow up the south forty. Where, as a matter of fact, they would probably do very well indeed.

Two other members of the iris family which I grow with great pleasure are the tiny, creeping *I. cristata,* mentioned elsewhere, and the Siberian iris, *I. sibirica.* These Siberians grow into great clumps, form a mass of bloom in June, and will grow almost anywhere given reasonably good soil. Unlike their bearded cousins they like a rich, moist, slightly acid soil.

But I am not sure how valuable they are in the small garden. Their grass-like foliage is somewhat similar to that of the day lilies (which see, later, in *July*) but their flowering period is shorter and they take up almost as much room when not in bloom. So whether you want to allot them precious space in the perennial garden is up to you. Their summer foliage is pleasant but, in my opinion, doesn't earn its keep. I think they are better used, individually, as accent plants, preferably near a pool or some suggestion of water. While a watery setting is not essential to their well-being, as it is to the Japanese variety, they enjoy moisture and somehow seem to look best near water. They are gentle, simple plants, fit well into a simple setting. Very easy to grow.

But the giant Japanese iris, *I. Kaempferi,* is not simple at all. It is a regal affair, enormous iris-type flowers atop tall stems, too flamboyant to use in a simple perennial garden in my opinion, though you sometimes see them included. But they grow so much, much better in a moist setting, such as the edge of a pond, that it seems a pity to attempt them elsewhere. They should have sun and a humusy, well-drained acid soil (keep all lime away from them) such as usually occurs near natural ponds and streams. The colors are pinks and lavenders and blue-purples and wine reds and there is also a mammoth white job with gold trim. They bloom in July.

The All White Garden for After Dusk

"What is that wonderful smell?" asked one of the guests, hopefully rattling the ice in an empty glass.

We were all sitting out on the terrace in the dusk of a June evening and that wonderful smell was sweet rocket. There was a planting of it nearby, in the corner of the stone wall, rising whitely against evergreens.

It was an all-white garden designed especially for summer evenings. The gaze, roaming around, found white blossoms everywhere, gleaming against the dark of the stone walls, the dark of evergreens. In one area the first white spires of delphinium were rising up against stone . . . in another a cascade of white clematis tumbled over the wall . . . in still another there was the gentle splashing of water, and, tracked by ear, the eye found huge, white lotus-type peony blossoms bending over a tiny pool. By the gate which gave entrance to this enchantment was the white blur of a fragrant, old-fashioned mock orange against the dark grey of the house. It was a blur because most of us were well past middle age and had our glasses off. Which made everything look better.

I couldn't wait to see it by daylight with my glasses on, see if it really was that good.

It was. Even in daylight. The whole thing had been planned for summer only, from Memorial Day to Labor Day, so no space was wasted on early or late bloom. Except for white flowering quinces (*C. nivalis*) at either end of the delphinium planting, mostly for summer foliage, plus groups of white tulips here and there, and white lilacs planted outside the wall but bending over it. These items just for May weekends, hostess said.

The little pool itself was even better by daylight. It was one of those recirculating affairs (more about these in *August*) and seemed to work very well, a delicate curve of water issuing from the lifted head of a bronze frog to splash down, gently, into a small pool which was flat-stone edged with white violas tucked between the stones.

And all of this half shaded by the great white peony which turned out to be White Gull, a single of exquisite form. A stone rabbit crouched under the peony, sniffing the violas. Hostess said that in that damp, half-shady setting the violas would keep going all summer.

Nearby, also in partial shade, tall lilies rising from low evergreens were getting ready to open their great white trumpets in July and August. Further along, sprawled on top of the wall in full sun, a silver lace vine would obviously provide a foam of whiteness later in the summer. And below this, in shade, were groups of white tuberous begonias, just budding. This was a nice contrast in forms and textures, the delicate airiness of the lace vine and the firm, strong substance of the begonias.

Next came some Korean box and hostess called attention to the nicotiana seedlings (the old-fashioned white, dusk-blooming *affinis*) which would shortly rise up in back of the boxwood to perfume the evening air. Seems she had stuck some nicotiana plants in that spot several years ago and they had been self-seeding ever since. Which is a break for any gardener, for this plant when self-sown is far stronger, more vigorous and more flowerful, than any sown by human hand. And this is true of many self-seeders, as every experienced gardener has discovered. Why? I do not know. It is one of the many things I do not know.

And, everywhere, edgings of low white petunias, just beginning their long season of bloom. Hostess said white edgings were important in any area used after dark. Kept traffic where it belonged, like the white lines edging a state road.

The sweet rocket (*Hesperis matronalis,* white variety, see *February* description in plant list) was a surprise in that setting as it is apt to be an untidy grower, and using it on a terrace with evergreens seemed like wearing sneakers with a formal. But in this case it looked very well, the tall, phlox-like heads spraying out against the dark yews, the coarse yet handsome clump of basal foliage, which would be left when the tops were cut down, giving texture contrast to the needled evergreens and forming a good, simple background for the low, white petunias. But perhaps of greatest importance, its rural informality served—as did the old-fashioned mock orange against the house—to tie the whole country-formal planting picture to its background of barns and rolling fields and far hills. This was nice planning.

I asked how long it had taken to get this show on the road, to get all these plantings so skillfully blended. Hostess said, thoughtfully, about ten years of making mistakes. "And", she added, "I am still making them."

I nodded respectfully. The gardener who can recognize mistakes is the gardener who has learned a lot.

The Kitchen-Door Garden For a Fast
Facsimile of Gracious Living

This is a small, bright, practical idea which might be of interest if you do a lot of cooking or entertaining. And if your kitchen door, which carries all family traffic in most country set-ups, is not too cluttered with bicycles, tricycles, push trucks, doll carriages, baseball equipment, the dog's old bones, the cat's half-eaten field mice, and other evidence of the rich, full life. Thankfully, I have completed my period of service in the armed forces of family living and can only hope that you have your life better organized than I had mine. Which wouldn't take much doing.

This is the kind of garden you can dash out to when you need a handful of parsley, a wad of chives, some fresh basil for the salad, a few sprigs of mint for the gin-and-tonic, a flower to clench your teeth on. In such an emergency you have neither the time nor the wits to travel far, and to maintain the illusion that you are a great cook as well as a serene, unhurried hostess, you will have to move fast, so this garden should be very, very close to the kitchen door.

Such a garden can be any size or shape which seems to fit best into the setting of bicycles, tricycles, old bones, dead mice, et al. You can construct this garden yourself while waiting for water to boil or the iron to heat and what better use of your time? You are building up a social image which, hopefully, will rub off on your young when they leave the nest. For whatever good it may do them.

So you dig up a small plot of earth close to the kitchen door. You can rim this job with the stones you unearth while digging, gives a tidy edging. And you don't have to incorporate any fancy additives for the plants you are going to put in are as plebeian as the setting they grace and will be happy with just average soil.

If you do a lot of summer entertaining stick a few roots of mint (either the real or the spearmint, hardly anyone can tell the difference) in each corner of your bed. This mint, unless controlled, will shortly spread into all surrounding areas. The trouble with mint is not how to grow it but how to keep it from growing; but guests who do not know this will say oh, my, mint! and think you are a wonderful gardener as well as a gracious hostess. You let them think this. So to cope with the mint roots take a long strip of heavy-duty aluminum foil and fold it into eight thicknesses, the completed job to be about 7″ or 8″ wide and as long as necessary to insert, deeply, between the mint roots and the rest of the garden. Otherwise you will have nothing but mint.

Parsley can edge the remainder of your bed. It is manageable, does not root-spread, and looks pretty both on the hoof and on the dish. You can buy well-started parsley plants almost anywhere. Or you can raise your own from seed, but it is slow. Inside this parsley rim put a lot of chives; they will spread but not as relentlessly as the mint. Chive plants, also, can be bought almost anywhere.

Inside of all this, and interspersed among the chives, put dwarf marigolds, the Nugget type from Burpee which you raise from seed (see *February* listing of annuals). These, which bloom more constantly and profusely than any other marigold I know of, are just for fun, to liven up this mundane planting and provide a flower for behind the ear if, regrettably, you should feel so tempted. (If over forty, please, no flower behind the ear.)

In the center of this bed put a few plants of sweet basil. These will grow taller than the rest of the plantings and so look best when centered. And if you have always used dried basil you have no idea how much better fresh-picked basil leaves can taste in salads, potatoes, cream soups, almost anything. Fresh basil would make an old plastic sponge taste good.

The mint is completely hardy. Ditto the chives. But the other plants are frost-tender so, in northern areas, June is about the earliest you can plant out this assortment. And if you should have any room left over, here are some other dainties which would come in handy: tiny carrots to be fresh-plucked and fresh-washed for the cocktail tray . . . baby radishes . . . baby scallions . . . and when serving such a tray, stud the whole thing with fresh-cut marigold heads and leaves. These will last almost two hours before wilting and by that time it won't matter what they look like.

Old Gracious Living herself.

JULY

Midsummer—The Flowering

ROSES AND DELPHINIUMS

I do not belong to the rose-growing brotherhood, an august breed apart from common gardeners, so am now proceeding with greatest caution. But I have discovered two roses which are so easy to grow, so relatively bug-free, that even I can grow them. And without spraying, for I refuse to use poison sprays. So possibly these roses might be of interest to other gardeners who feel as I do about spraying. If there are such gardeners.

The floribunda bush rose Betty Prior is one. She is a little elderly as roses go, and new varieties come and go so fast it is difficult to keep track of them, but her gentleness and simplicity make her particularly suitable for the country garden. She is a tall grower, reaching 5' or more in maturity, but slender, with quantities of single, wild-rose type blossoms well carried on strong, lifting stems. The flowers open a clear mid-pink, then fade to pale pink, so that you get a blended two-toned effect. And she blooms—actually—all summer, from late June or early July until after Thanksgiving. I am writing this on November 30th and have just cut a sizable bunch of flowers and buds from half-frozen plants bedded in snow. Maybe there are other roses which act the same way but I don't know about them. I write only about the plants I have grown.

Another feature which makes Betty Prior so valuable in the country garden is her ability to make all neighboring flowers seem more beautiful and important, a quality not found in roses of the prima donna type. I like her with Madonna lilies and the blended blues of delphiniums *Belladonna* and *Bellamosum,* the Connecticut Yankees and, later, with the hazy blues of *Salvia farinacea,* the blues and lavenders of fall-blooming asters. She is not an expensive rose and you can get her, potted or canned, at any good nursery.

The other rose is the now-famous polyantha the Fairy. And you can believe whatever the catalogues say about this one. It flowers almost incessantly, great lifting sprays of pale pink which rise 4' high and spread to 3'. It is hardly ever out of bloom and, like Betty Prior, keeps going into late, late fall; I have cut blossoms from The Fairy when the entire plant was deep in snow. It makes a delight-ful low hedge. Also good for facing down a shrub border, or in a special planting with junipers. In the perennial bed or border try underplanting the lifting sprays with low petunias, white and deep purple. Or, if you have the spot, try this rose by itself with masses of lavender (*Lavandula*), all different heights and shades of laven-der: Hidcote Purple, Folgate Blue, Munstead Dwarf, and the tiny Twickle Purple which grows only about 8" high. Lavender, as you probably know, is not only part of the country garden scene but the traditional companion of roses as it is supposed to keep bugs away.

I have found both of these roses to be remarkably bug-and-blight free. There has been some light leaf damage from chewing insects but never enough to affect flowering, and just one applica-tion of the systemic Rose And Flower Care mentioned earlier took care of this; the new fall growth came out clean and whole and continued that way with, it seemed to me, extra quantities of bloom. Now that I have discovered this new method of insect control I may, again, try some of the other varieties.

And that is all I am saying about roses. If you are a rose grower you probably know more about them than I do and should be writ-ing this part yourself.

Delphiniums I do know a little something about. I have grown them for twenty years, all kinds, both from seed and division, and consider most of them easy. My problem now is finding room for them since I have cut down so drastically on the growing beds for delphiniums resent crowding and if you cannot give them ample space you might as well give up growing them. Regretfully, I must now restrict my delphinium plantings to the smaller ones, the *belladonnas* and *bellamosas,* the Chinese, and the Connecticut Yan-kees. These take up half the room demanded by the giant kinds and need comparatively little staking; twiggy supports are usually enough, and less conspicuous than regular garden stakes. And the flowers, produced twice a season by these smaller varieties, are just as heavenly.

About the towering delphiniums, the Pacific hybrids et al: I think it is a waste of time to grow these unless you have the perfect spot for them, and the time to take care of them. Such a spot would be at the southern or southeastern side of a high wall, or fence, or other wind protection. It is heartbreaking to labor long and lovingly over these majestic beauties, watch the great spires rise up so proudly in the calm sun of late June or early July and then, after a walloping storm, see the whole planting broken and wrecked beyond repair. Even when staked, and almost every spire needs individual staking, the flower heads are often broken down to the ties, flopped over. A high wall will not always prevent such damage but it will at least lessen it.

The presence of nearby water is another factor in the successful growing of all delphiniums, especially the tall ones which do so magnificently in England and along coastal areas; a river, a lake, even a small pond will gentle the air, give it moisture, and all delphiniums will respond to this with stronger growth, better flowers, better colors. They are difficult in dry, windy areas—my own never reached perfection—and yet I once saw a superb planting of the towering Pacific hybrids (the Round Table assembly) backed by a shrub screen and ringing a small farm pond in the bone-dry hills of Vermont. Well, maybe "farm" should be in quotes for it was quite a place, but this showed what the presence of water could do.

Also, remember that the word "perennial" is rather loosely used when applied to those Pacific hybrids. When happiest, as when sheltered and near water, I have known them to last three or four years before deteriorating, but usually they last only two. This is reasonable, for the plants spend themselves so extravagantly on the enormous flower spikes that, in time, their strength is simply exhausted. The English versions, the Bishops, the Blackmore & Langdons, are more truly perennial in habit and, in my opinion, every bit as beautiful. Perhaps more so because they are gentler, less flashy. The colorings are approximately the same but the individual flowerets are more open, less tightly packed on the stalk.

All delphiniums are hefty eaters and the big ones have incredible appetites, which is not surprising when you consider the volume of bloom they produce. They like a rich, humusy, deeply dug bed, a little on the limey side, with excellent drainage. And deeply dug means at least 2′ and preferably 3′ for the big ones, a layer of pebbles or crushed stone in the bottom, and the rest of the excavation then filled with half-and-half compost (or well-rotted manure or dried manure) and good garden earth, all this well mixed with a little coarse sand, two cupfuls of bone meal and about a cup of sulphate of potash. Let this conglomeration come to within 3″ or 4″ of the top, cover to ground level with plain earth, and give the whole thing a good hosing. Do all this as far ahead of time as possible, at least two or three weeks, so that all that bedding has a chance to settle, and help along this settling with more hosings. When it has sunk down a few inches cover with still more plain earth and set your delphiniums in this.

Perhaps here would be a good place to explain why you should top such a planting site with plain earth. A plant which has just been dug up—or, even worse, comes bare-root through the mail—has been through a major operation and should have a bland diet until it has had time to recover, just as you would be given a bland diet for a few days after major surgery. When they are ready the roots will travel down to find heartier food. You don't have to worry about this when setting in trees and shrubs as most of these have a tougher digestive system and, usually, take leaner bedding; also, unless the roots are dormant they are—or should be—balled and burlaped so the plant suffers less shock.

The smaller delphiniums take the same planting procedure except that the holes need not be as deep, 18″ is enough unless you are feeling generous, for all plants are grateful for as much root room as they can get and will usually repay your generosity many times over. And one cup of bone meal instead of two, half a cup of the potash. And always, when planting any delphiniums, allow space between them, and between them and their neighbors: the major delphiniums should be at least 2′ to 3′ apart—3′ is safer—and the minor ones from 15″ to 2′. And that means distance from other plants too. You can sometimes get away with crowding for a year or so but as the delphiniums get bigger, and their neighbors do too, ventilation will be decreased and a prolonged humid spell can bring trouble. When planting delphiniums against a stone wall always set them out at least 18″ to allow air circulation between them and the wall, and remove the lowest leaves if they tend to lie flat on the ground.

Delphiniums are best planted in spring, but if you are impatient and want to take a chance on fall planting (some nurseries will not even sell them in the fall) mulch with salt hay or pine branches, after the ground has frozen, to prevent frost heave. I have often set out seedlings or new divisions in the fall and had no trouble with them but I believe this practice is frowned upon by the experts. Or maybe mine came through so well because I mulched them with vermiculite instead of the classic hay or branches. In fact, all the countless delphiniums I have raised from seed—and they are absurdly easy from seed—have been set out in the fall and, thickly covered with vermiculite, have been brisk and eager in spring. But this is merely my own experience so maybe you should pay it no mind.

In early spring remove whatever mulch you have used and give a good sprinkling of wood ashes to further strengthen stems, contribute lime. Then, on top of the wood ashes, put a wide, deep collar of coal ashes. This, as explained earlier (in *April*) is to repel slugs which crave young delphinium shoots but dislike crawling over scratchy material. If you don't mind the looks of these coal ashes leave them on all summer as they benefit the plant by increasing surface drainage, decreasing under-leaf humidity. It is also wise to dust the young plants with sulphur, or some preparation containing sulphur, to discourage the development of black spot. It is far easier to prevent this than to cure it.

Immediately after the first bloom—of all delphiniums—cut back the flowering stalks to the first major leaves. Of course, if you are cutting for the house you will need longer stalks but, as a general rule, leave as much leafage on the plant as possible. Then give each plant a good belt of manure tea and, in six to eight weeks, you will be rewarded by a second surge of bloom. This, occurring usually in September and sometimes continuing into November, will be gentler than the first, but it has a wistful autumn tenderness which makes it even more appealing. I have had Connecticut Yankees bloom through the snow, well after hard frost.

Where to get delphiniums: Any good nursery—and I repeat *good*. Don't ever try to economize on delphiniums for you may get weak, inferior plants, possibly diseased plants. If you don't have a really good nursery in your immediate area, and must order by mail, White Flower Farm has very good delphiniums, all kinds, and their packing and shipping techniques are said to be excellent. They will ship delphiniums only in spring but better get your order in early.

Or, for fun and games, try raising your own from seed. I usually start seeds in June (Note: all delphinium seed should be kept in the ice box until used.) in those One-Step seed starters described in *February*. Then, when the muffins show roots, I pot them up in half-and-half soil and compost plus a little bone meal and sink the pots in earth. This gives them a good root-ball for planting out in late August or early September and by the time the ground freezes they have established themselves.

THE DAY LILIES (*Hemerocallis*)

These are, traditionally, part of the country scene, the country garden. But if you still think of day lilies as those rather commonplace orange or yellow affairs growing along rural roads you have

Pale citron yellow day lilies (*Hemerocallis*) against a redwood fence.

THEODORA M. PRENTICE

a surprise coming to you, for the new day lilies are a far cry from their simple ancestors. Did you know that you can now get day lilies in ivory and cream white, in snow pink, shell pink, peach, melon, apricot, rose, the raspberry-pinks and wine shades, as well as chartreuse and all tints of yellow and soft orange? That you can have your choice of ruffled, rounded, bowl-shaped, crêped, twisted, or fluted flower forms, many of them up to 7" across? That you can have any plant size you fancy from the regal 40" tall aristocrats down to the little 10" mini-jobs? That many of these bear thirty to forty flowers per plant? And that you can select them to bloom, in variety, for almost four months?

It is something to think about. The world of day lilies has certainly changed since most of us started gardening.

I had no idea there were so many different colors and forms in day lilies until I happened upon the Wild catalogue mentioned earlier in connection with iris. This nursery specializes in day lilies as well as iris and peonies, and the day lily section is astonishing: thirty-two pages listing over four hundred varieties and eighty-nine of them pictured in full color! And this is only one catalogue; there are several others, each, presumably, with its own presentations. Well, the Wild catalogue will hold me for quite a while.

It leaves you feeling a little dazed. Where and how to use such a wealth of color becomes the problem. Though the actual growing of day lilies is certainly no problem; they are one of the easiest and toughest of all plants and will, indeed, "grow anywhere" in any reasonable soil, in full sun or partial shade. So it is only the appropriate setting which is important.

In outlying areas, especially in farming country, it seems to me that the old-fashioned colors and simple forms are still the most desirable—the soft yellow and orange tones which have always been traditional. The difference is that you can now get these colorings in plants which bear much larger flowers, and many more of them, so that the plantings are twice as effective. So consider these day lilies for those areas you never knew what to do with: alongside your country road, against your old stone walls, against pasture fences or old barns, as foreground planting for that far field which, happily, features your neighbor's cows.

Closer to the house you could use the more sophisticated colorings, the cream ivories merging into the pink tones, then into the peach and melon shades, then back through the citrus yellows to cream white. Such a drift planting could be used against shrubbery at the edge of the lawn, or against a wall or building, to border a wide path, or driveway, or parking area. Or, for that matter, to form an entire garden by themselves in some difficult, half-shady spot where nothing else seems to do well. Just remember that the larger day lilies are also large in scale, their handsome grass-like foliage a little on the coarse side, so should be used only in large-scale settings.

However, there are many small charmers like the little Pink Vanilla (ruffled peach pink with green throat, grows only 10″–12″ tall, bears 4″ to 5″ flowers) which could be tucked into small, intimate plantings on the terrace or grouped at the edge of the perennial border. And any number of 20″ beauties to combine with them, or to face down taller plantings. Another feature of these new day lilies is that many of them stay open at night, something their ancestors never did, which makes them valuable for social areas which are used in the evening.

The actual planting of day lilies couldn't be simpler. As they develop heavy root systems they prefer a spacious, well-drained, compost-rich bedding but will philosophically make do with anything they are given. I have found that like most plants which flower generously over a long period, they are especially fond of manure tea, and a good swig of this when the buds are just beginning to form will prolong the blooming period. They increase rapidly and so need division every three or four years (I divide mine in late August) but aside from this they need no care at all, are bug-and-blight free so far as I know, and you don't even have to weed them as the arching leaves shade the soil, discourage unwanted growths.

THE TRUE LILIES (*Lilium*)

The gentle little Madonna lilies (*L. candidum*) are the first to bloom for me. They enter the garden picture in late June or early July and instantly make friends with everything nearby. I cannot think of any plant, blooming at this time, which is not made more beautiful by the presence of Madonna lilies; they have that rare quality, shared by the simpler roses and salvia *farinacea,* which seems to bring out the hidden values in their surroundings. Some humans have this too.

Madonnas love the sun, full sun, and a rich but light limey soil. Actually, they are so easy that they will grow almost anywhere but they make especially good companions for other lime-loving plants which bloom at that time; clematis, the gypsophilas, peonies, and, of course, delphiniums. Try a group of Madonna lilies against the blue clematis Ramona; or, if you want ecstasy, devise an all-white grouping of Madonna lilies and the great white clematis Henryi in the corner of a stone wall, flanked by yews and footed by low white petunias.

Like all true lilies, their stalks, after flowering, present a small problem as they should never be cut down but allowed to ripen and feed the maturing bulbs. If this bothers you, and a screening of some sort seems desirable, I know of nothing better than the light, airy gypsophila, baby sitter to all withering bulb foliage. There is the faithful old Bristol Fairy or the newer and larger-flowered Perfecta, both growing to about 4' which is plenty tall enough to screen the Madonna stalks, and which will keep flowering off and on all summer if trimmed back. Incidentally, look in the White Flower Farm catalogue for a great idea on growing this gypsophila.

Madonna lilies, unlike other true lilies, should have very shallow planting; you put the bulbs just barely under the surface. They should be planted—or moved—shortly after flowering so that they have plenty of time to anchor themselves before the ground freezes; they will soon send up a tuffet of green leaves so you know where they are, that they have taken hold. As stated before, they will grow almost anywhere but if the soil is too acid and no green tuffet appears within a few weeks you had better give a quick application of lime or wood ashes. This will usually do the trick. Once the green tuffet appears you can stop worrying. These Madonnas also enjoy a sprinkling of wood ashes in spring, washed down with a little manure tea.

And that's all I can think of to say about Madonna lilies because they are so easy. And so inexpensive.

The great trumpet lilies, most of which now carry the proud name of Jan de Graaff, are neither easy nor inexpensive but, once established, become major features in any garden.

I have come only lately to these lilies. For years I admired them in other people's gardens, but impersonally and without ardor, as one admires postal inspectors and the unsung artists who illustrate dictionaries. I had not the slightest desire to invite them into my life. Then, about five years ago, someone sent me some lily bulbs as a hostess present. I thanked her politely and intended to throw them out when it occurred to me that this would be a stupid thing to do; they were big, beautiful bulbs and obviously costly. So I looked up lily culture and stuck them into the ground. To my astonishment they grew and flowered, great pink trumpets with silver edgings.

After that I couldn't wait to grow more lilies. It had taken me well over half a century to appreciate them and I had a lot of catching up to do. I have been doing it ever since. I also had a lot of learning to do, for although lily culture is apparently perfectly simple, and every book explains it, every grower sends explicit directions, there are often lilies which simply don't come up.

The commonest reason for this is mice, and the invention of the lily basket is one of the break-throughs of gardening history. This is a wire mesh affair which allows the roots to grow through but prevents mice from getting at the bulb. I get mine from McCormick Lilies (formerly Romaine B. Ware) and although these are somewhat expensive I consider them less expensive than losing costly lilies to mice.* And the McCormick catalogue is well worth sending for; they list the cream of the lily crop, all kinds, and send excellent top-size bulbs. Another McCormick product I have found well worth buying is their special lily fertilizer, called Ware's Lily Food, which is especially blended for lilies, supposed to contain everything needful in a balanced ratio. This comes in a granular form and you simply dissolve it in a watering can and water your lilies twice or thrice a season. Takes the guesswork out of lily feeding.

Another reason why lilies may not come up is, I suspect, too deep planting, not giving the bed time enough to settle before putting in the bulbs. Again, as with peonies and many other major plants, it is best to prepare the planting site well ahead of time to allow for this settling which can alter planting depths by several inches. Lilies, like tulips and several other bulbs, can pull them-

* See page 245 for an interesting account of how these baskets are made.

To show to best advantage lilies should have a background.

selves down, if they wish to, but cannot push themselves up so if they sink down too far, they have had it. Inadequate drainage is another reason for lily failúre, but this is discussed at length in any treatise on lily culture.

Where to use these regal trumpet lilies takes considerable thought. My feeling is that they should be grown only in rather special areas with some sort of background, either underplanted with some interesting material or companioned by plants of distinction such as evergreens, roses or peonies. This brings up the problem of root-room, for lilies must never be crowded below ground, or above ground either as the stems need air circulation. Still, even keeping this in mind, it is often possible to plant them among low evergreens or choice shrubs or peonies where the roots will be shaded.

Or in bays on the terrace, perhaps against the house or a wall. Sometimes you can even clear a space for them at the back of the perennial border, though this should depend on the character, the setting, and the background of the border itself, its distinction or lack of it. Seems to me that to use these haughty lilies in the untended mish-mash of some country borders would be like doing the milking in a mink coat. But a lot of gardeners will not agree with this. Which, perhaps, is just as well. Gardening is to give pleasure to the gardener.

Most of these major lilies bloom in July or August. They like gentle morning sun but the flowers show up better and last longer when shaded from the scorching sun of midsummer afternoons. They also like something around their feet to shelter roots, keep

The invaluable foliage plant *Bergenia cordifolia*. Its thick, shell-like leaves are a dark, semi-glossy green. For me it grows best in semi-shade among rocks.

THEODORA M. PRENTICE

them cool, so if you are using lilies in the open they will need some form of ground cover. The funkias (or hostas or whatever they are now called) have long been the traditional cover-planting for lily beds but I think it is high time somebody came up with some new ideas.

How about some of those shallow-rooted, shade-tolerant annuals to provide a base of summer-long bloom, good foliage? Dwarf bush-balsam, quick and easy from seed (see *February*) might be one, with its wealth of small, dark, shining leaves, its faintly formal flowers; you could use white balsam under colored lilies, rose or salmon balsam under white ones. Or masses of low impatiens, another easy annual but not so quick. Or groups of the low, fibrous-rooted begonias, small-flowered and waxy-leaved, which bloom so profusely all summer. Any of these would give carpeting and continuous flowering whether the lilies were in bloom or not.

I am also playing with the idea of trying the beautiful Bergenia (formerly *megasea*), its great, dark, shining, shell-like leaves to rise up around the lily stalks; this, being one of the *Saxifragaceae,* would need rocks to provide cool root-runs but the lilies should also appreciate this. It might work out very well as Bergenia blooms in spring, the extraordinary foliage remaining a joy all summer. At least it would be a switch from the eternal funkias.

But perhaps the brightest idea of all came from a little old lady who happened to be an African violet addict. She vacations her countless plants in shady lily beds, to the delight of all concerned including the viewers. Any African violet growers reading this?

Midsummer—The Planning

To my way of thinking, most of your July and August gardening should be done in a cool shade with your feet up, a cold glass at your elbow, and a stack of garden books, magazines, and catalogues within easy reach. Don't deny yourself these long, lazy afternoons when, free from any compulsion to scurry around and do things, you can relish the fruits of earlier labors. The whole idea of a garden is that you can enjoy it. And part of this enjoyment lies in the planning for further enjoyment, the consideration of new ideas for improvement. In case you have a New England conscience

about doing nothing in the middle of the afternoon you can comfort yourself with the knowledge that you are indeed doing something; you are planning, and planning is the most important part
of any gardening operation.

Incredibly, with the end of July the season is almost over. There
is little physical work to do now, until fall planting time, except the
eternal lawns, the endless removal of spent flowers, and perhaps one
more feeding of lilies, one more application of systemic bug controls. In our area it is risky to fertilize anything after the first of
August.

And with September comes the actual doing of whatever major changes you have decided upon; changes in grade, perhaps, or
in walks or drives, the construction of new areas, the deep-digging
of planting sites for trees or shrubs to be set in later or the following
spring, the redoing of perennial beds if this seems necessary. Fall
is by far the best time to embark upon any of these projects for
the earth is warm and mellow, easy to work, and you usually have
more time than in spring. So from here on into October these
matters will be considered, suggestions offered.

Maybe you should start your thinking with the front areas as
these are usually considered the most important. And the way your
thinking progresses will depend upon the size and type of house
you have, how far it is from the road, and how you want to live.

To most country dwellers privacy is important. It was one
of the reasons they moved to the country. So a screen of some kind,
somewhere between the house and the road, becomes the first consideration. Though, of course, not every country dweller feels this
way; some people enjoy the public gaze, want to see and be seen. If
this is the way you want to live by all means follow your own in-
clinations, and it is no business of mine, but you might as well
skip the next several paragraphs because they will be concerned
with screening, with the establishment of privacy.

In rural sections and in many small country towns the older
and finer houses used a roadside screen of tall flowering shrubs to
separate the private grounds from the public ones. Such a screen
is not only a pleasant idea with a nice country feel to it but a very
practical one as well, and particularly practical today, for shrubs
and trees absorb dust, noise and air pollution, protecting the house
and its inhabitants. It goes well with almost any traditional type

of architecture, offers beauty to the passerby, affords privacy without seeming forbidding, and needs practically no upkeep. A good shrub combination for such a screen might be French lilacs, beauty bush (*Kolkwitzia amabilis*), and shrub-althea (or Rose of Sharon, *Hibiscus syriacus*) which would offer three separate periods of bloom and grow almost anywhere.

On the inner or house side of this screen could be a planting of low flowering shrubs and evergreens—individual plants to depend on whether this area was in sun or shade—to be enjoyed from the house, from the front windows, across an expanse of lawn. This would provide beauty in the front area yet keep within the landscaping law that there should be no flowers in the public domain. Flowering shrubs are considered an exception on informal properties.

Or maybe your house is so small, so low, so close to the road that such a shrub planting would make it look like Moses in the

This illustrates what can be done with property right smack on a state road; note telephone wires and road sign a few feet away. The woven redwood fence gives privacy, forms the background for these single herbaceous peonies which will be followed shortly by clematis and climbing roses.

EUGENE D. TRUDEAU

THEODORA M. PRENTICE

Clematis Henryi starting up the redwood fence. The blossoms also work their way through and bloom on the other side as well.

bulrushes. Or maybe you just don't like the idea of such a screen along the road, prefer the more welcoming look of an open lawn. In either case you could bring the screen closer to the house, its heft, height and type to depend upon the heft, height and type of your house; a small, low house would take a small, low screen, a taller, two-story house could afford the privacy of a taller screen or hedge.

THE SCREENED PATH

An unbroken stretch of lawn, no matter how small, always looks larger than the same lawn cut in two by a path or interrupted by spotty shrub planting. So, if possible, have your path come from the side, where there is usually a driveway, and keep your shrubs around the edges. This will give you more lawn area, and a hedge or shrub-screen set alongside the path running parallel to the house will give you privacy. Or at least the suggestion of privacy, for even a low hedge or shrub-edging supplies a line of demarcation between the public and private areas. It also gives a sense of enclosure, and any enclosed area immediately takes on fresh interest and importance. So, besides privacy, you also have a tiny intimate area—maybe only a strip of earth between house and walk—in which to plant something special, something which might look lost and absurd if planted in the open. This in itself gives welcome to the caller, gives the sense of being accepted into the personal life of the house.

The type of hedging or screening material you choose should depend as much on the type and architecture of your house as on its size and height. For instance, a little white Cape Codder might take a line of everblooming roses, such as The Fairy, along a stepping-stone path set with small creeping plants, while a split-level house of approximately the same size but strengthened by the sterner lines of contemporary architecture would take a more tailored type of screening, such as a clipped hedge of Alpine currant (*Ribes alpinus*)* which is particularly good in shade

Larger houses, depending upon their architectural heritage, could afford the privacy of taller hedges or screens, either evergreen or deciduous. If you happen to live in a mild climate, or along a coast, and can grow the hollies and boxwoods the way they grow in England, you don't need any advice from me, but in frigid areas we have to take second choice.

Yew (*Taxus* in variety) is probably the most distinguished hedging material for cold sections of the country. It is hardy, tough, slow and expensive, but in time it makes a magnificent evergreen hedge which needs almost no maintenance; clipping once a year is usually enough, and it will grow almost anywhere, given a humusy

* This is one of the few currants not susceptible to the white pine blister rust when planted in the open.

bedding and good drainage. It is formal in character and should be your first choice for really fine architecture.

Canadian hemlock (*Tsuga canadensis*) is next in toughness and in formality. It is thoroughly hardy, of course, but is said to dislike wind and dry soils. At least according to the books, though I know of several hemlock plantings around here which have happily accepted both conditions. The handsome hemlock hedge pictured opposite has been thriving for years on a dry bank in full wind. It was started a little over twenty years ago from 2′ to 3′ seedlings, kept very low and very tight at first to thicken up, and is still kept low and tight because that is the way the owner wants it; without such control it would be far taller by this time. Owner says it needs shearing only once a year (he shears in July) plus an occasional touch-up with hand clippers if a sprig gets out of line. Aside from that he never waters it or gives it the slightest care, and each year it gets thicker and more beautiful. Hemlock is not as expensive as yew and can be formal or semi-formal according to its setting.

Some of the tall deciduous hedges can be almost as handsome as evergreen ones if you don't mind their winter appearance. They are, usually, less formal in character, less costly to install, far faster growing, but need far more maintenance. For you can't get away from the fact that the faster a hedge grows the oftener it will have to be clipped if you want to keep it tidy, so when you see "Fast Growing" in a catalogue maybe you had better think twice. Amur River privet, for instance, needs trimming five or six times a season. I know because we have it; it was one of our early mistakes. Some day, if I can ever scrape up the courage, I hope to have the whole thing dug up and replaced by something else but right now I don't have that much fortitude.

Chinese elm (*Ulmus parvifolia*) makes an interesting semi-formal hedge which carries its small shiny-green leaves well into the fall. It is hardy, easy, and fast growing, can be kept down to around 6′ if you wish, and if you keep after it, for it is really a small tree. Will grow almost anywhere and is not expensive.

Alder buckthorn (*Rhamnus Frangula*), which is thornless, has lustrous, oval, deep green leaves which also last well into fall. The *columnaris* form has recently become popular under the patented name of Tallhedge. This is very fast growing and will shoot up to 15′ if uncontrolled but you can keep it down to a more manageable

THEODORA M. PRENTICE

The hemlock hedge mentioned on opposite page. In this case the owner prefers the sternly vertical trim rather than the slanting one recommended by many authorities, and certainly this hedge could hardly be more beautiful no matter how it was cut.

height if you want a clipped hedge. Actually, as its natural habit of growth is upright and tidy, it needs less maintenance, except to control height, than sprawlier growers. It can be almost formal when tightly sheared, or informal when allowed to grow more naturally. It is fairly expensive, for a hedge.

Euonymus alatus compactus, the popular shrub called burning bush, makes a superb and unusual screen where there is room. It is tough, hardy, easy, grows about 7′ tall and 4′ wide. In summer its upspringing stems are clothed with good, dark green leaves which turn a spectacular strawberry-rose with the coming of cool weather. A whole line of these shrubs in fall is something to remember. It can also be clipped into hedge form but it seems to me a pity to do this when it is so beautiful in its natural state. Particularly good with large, comfortable houses of no special architectural type. It is moderately expensive.

EUGENE D. TRUDEAU

Entrance from driveway, showing walk running parallel to the house, screened from the road by a tall hedge.

Paths, also, should accord with the personality of the house. Contemporary architects and free-wheeling garden designers have devised many new ways of handling paths and paving which carry out the young and courageous character of these new houses. If you have such a house by all means investigate these bright, new functional ideas for most of them are dedicated to ease of maintenance.

For traditional houses of average size, semi-formal to formal, the path of well-fitted flagstones, or patterned brick laid in sand, is still a pleasure to the eye. At least to the elderly eye. Though, personally, I consider brick somewhat overrated. It is what we have, in the front area, and although it has the serenity of a more gracious era, it takes considerable upkeep; weed-killer two or three times a season in open areas, and the hand-plucking of weeds along the edges where weed-killer cannot be used because of adjacent plantings. I have tried to get around this by using small, creeping things, *Antennaria* and the thymes, hoping this will make the weeds less apparent—and also to tone down the formality of patterned brick as our house is not that formal—but unwanted growths still spring up through the sand. Bricks-laid-in-cement is supposed to be a *faux pas,* like blowing on your soup, but it would certainly be a lot more practical.

By this time you may be a little tired of this constant harping on maintenance, but it seems to me that, nowadays, any garden book which does not take a realistic look at upkeep is just drifting through a Never Never Land of dreams. I figure that most readers are more interested in easier gardening than they are in dreamy prose.

THE FORECOURT

Your screened path, then, leads from the driveway along the front of the house to the entrance door where it opens up into a forecourt. A forecourt is a paved area which can be any size or shape you fancy, either small or large depending upon the size and character of the house, and usually backed by a continuation of the hedge or screen.

If you have never considered a forecourt do think about it now for it can be one of the happiest of all gardening ideas. It does for a house what a becoming hair-do does for a woman. It is particularly effective with the small house where it is so unexpected, contributing that priceless quality of surprise which is so difficult to incorporate into small properties. One of the smallest and most de-

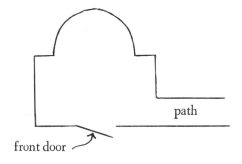

path

front door

LAURA LEE FOSTER

lightful forecourts I can remember was a tiny semicircle of brick, edged by evergreen candytuft in full snow-white bloom against a backing of clipped boxwood. This was in Georgetown, outside of Washington, D.C. and the tiny house was an architectural gem, the scale and simplicity of this forecourt exactly right.

Maybe your house is not an architectural gem but you can still give it personality and distinction by presenting it with a forecourt. One of the few exceptions to this sweeping statement is the house with the front porch. If you have such a house, and want to keep your porch, forget about the forecourt. But the classic front porch is now, in most cases, merely vestigial, a hold-over from the days when it was the only pleasant place to sit; it has been replaced by the back terrace or patio, the TV set, and the world of wheels. This is not to scorn the beloved old front porch, which looks so right and welcoming with big, comfortable, relaxed houses of dubious architectural ancestry, but simply to warn you against further complicating an already confused façade.

If your house is small and simple, a small and simple semicircle or rectangle would best become it. The planting would depend upon whatever planting you had used along the path and should be a continuation of it so that each area blends into the other. For very low houses Korean box makes a good hedging to accompany the path and embrace the tiny forecourt; it is not tall enough to provide screening but it makes a definite evergreen line of demarcation. Pansies in spring, and low annuals in summer, could rim the forecourt to nestle against the informal boxwood. This Korean box is completely hardy and does not need clipping unless you wish to keep it trim and tidy. Or figure out your own plant combinations as the catalogues are now bristling with low hedging ideas for small low houses. There are so many materials of this type now available that I have not even attempted to list them.

For the house of some size and substance there is a forecourt form which is particularly interesting for, besides being pleasing to the eye, it invites so many different planting ideas. This is a rectangle topped with a slightly smaller semicircle (see sketch). It is best used with a house large enough to take a tall hedge, or screen, as this form needs the continuation of a strong backing, is slightly formal in feeling. You can have the hedge swing into the niches at the end with white iron urns, flower filled, at the corners against

EUGENE D. TRUDEAU

Forecourt showing one way of using the design sketched on page 153.

the dark background . . . . or you could use simple garden ornaments such as stone fruit baskets, set in stone pedestals, in the
corners . . . . or fuchsias or lantanas bedded in Italian pottery.

Or you could leave the niches open and plant tall, slim evergreens such as Irish junipers in the corners, wreathing their feet
with potted pale-pink geraniums and low white petunias. Or if the
whole scale of this set-up was large enough, and important enough,
you could allow needful planting space in the niches and set in
Japanese tree peonies, which could be staggering against a tall,
clipped hedge. Or small flowering trees such as *Viburnum Burkwoodi* with its fragrant blossoms in May and good glossy leafage all
summer. Or you could lie awake nights dreaming up still more ideas.

If possible, there should be a tree bending over your forecourt.
This gives a welcome, a sense of loving protection, and seems to
tie everything together. What size and kind of tree would depend
upon the size and type of forecourt; the height and heft of the
hedging or screening material, but such a tree should be open,
spreading, and airy rather than heavy or upright; it should, ideally,
provide blossoms in spring, dappled shade in summer and interesting
branch lines in winter. Leaf through your catalogues, garden books
and magazines and see what trees appeal to you most.

THE FRONT DOOR

On the house side of your paved walk, screened from public gaze and graced by a sense of enclosure, you have whatever small, choice plantings the space will accommodate and these, or some related variant of these, should continue along the front of the house to become underplanting for whatever shrubs or evergreens attend your front door. This will give continuity to the whole small area, tie the different parts together. Spotty planting can be disastrous in a restricted stretch of earth; you end up with a mish-mash.

Such a planting will depend not only on the size and type of your house, but also on the amount of sun or shade this area receives, the amount of space available. For instance, in full sun and to companion a small, simple house you could use a ribbon planting of pansies, for early spring, to be replaced by low, spreading verbenas—perhaps pale pink and purple, or blue and white—to spill out over the walk and carpet uplifting French lilacs on either side of the doorway . . . or you could use a band of the feathery, silvery-grey artemisia Silver Mound (needs a light shearing in mid-July to prevent seed-formation and the middle-aged spread) to do the same thing. In partial shade you could use violas (all white, or blue and white, depending on the color of your house) to edge the path and continue on to underplant untrimmed Korean box on either side of the door. For a more formal house, and a planting area in deep shade, you might choose the low, glossy and very choice European ginger (*Asarum europaeum*) to become a ground cover under a doorway planting of hollies and broadleafed flowering evergreens.

Or—and if you live far enough south this is something to consider,—use the exquisite *Nierembergia rivularis,* mentioned earlier, for the entire area. This has the remarkable quality of being at once formal and informal, and it will grow in either sun or light shade: dark, spoon-shaped green leaves 3″ high with huge white cap-flowers sitting right on top. And it does, actually, bloom from May to October. I only wish it were hardy here.

For the actual doorway planting itself I do urge you to contemplate something more original than the inevitable evergreen muffins or cones, which, in my opinion, are among the most tiresome of all planting clichés. There is so much other material available if only home-owners would investigate this wealth, refuse the

Tiny semi-formal garden fitted into the ell of the house. This is on the other side of the walk shown on page 152. The edging is clipped English ivy, the ground cover Wiltoni juniper, the accents English boxwood and artemisia Silver Mound. Small pavement-creepers, such as the *Antennaris neodioica* in the foreground, contribute informality.

package deals pushed by so many nurseries. Evergreens are certainly desirable for winter welcome but the most beautiful evergreens seldom get planted except by landscape architects. Yet they are available to home-owners everywhere, in any number of nurseries and catalogues.

There are, for instance, the hollies. These come in many shapes, forms and degrees of hardiness and formality, ranging from the tall inkberry (*Ilex glabra*), which is probably the hardiest and least formal, down through the *crenatas* many of which are hardy, even here, in shady sheltered spots, or when grown near water (all hollies like water). And all hollies have beautiful foliage, sometimes glossy, sometimes semi-glossy; they like shade—in cold areas—and a rich, humusy, somewhat acid soil. Go to any fine nursery and look over the many types and forms available.

Pieris floribunda and *Leucothoe catesbaei,* with their larger and more pointed leaves, their attractive flowers, are good companions for the small-leafed hollies and enjoy the same soil and site. Mountain laurel (*Kalmia latifolia*) and azaleas, in variety, are also effective with hollies, give spring and early-summer flowering and strong, serene leafage the rest of the year. But such a planting, such a bank of strong individualists, should only be used in front of a large and powerful house, perhaps with a high foundation to hide; it would smother a small, low house. As a general rule, the greater the architectural beauty of a house the less foundation planting it needs.

Smaller houses, where the entrance is in shade or partial shade, can take a selected few of these broadleafed evergreens but only a very few; perhaps a white Carolina rhododendron on either side of the doorway (R. *carolinianum* var. *album*—the white is better than the lavender) flanked by the glossy, tiny-leafed holly *Ilex crenata convexa bullata*: or, for a very small house, the white-flowering azalea *vuykiana palestrina* with the tiny dwarf holly *I. crenata Helleri*. And these are only two ideas picked out of a hatful. Do investigate the countless combinations offered by these more unusual broadleafed evergreens before surrendering to the hackneyed "foundation planting."

For entrances in either sun or shade, any soil, any exposure, the great euonymus tribe offers a wide choice of shrubby evergreens, most of them thoroughly hardy. The Sarcoxi strain is the toughest, is more or less upright in habit, grows to about 4′ and has leafage somewhat like *vegetus.* The Corliss strain is perhaps a shade less hardy but still plenty tough. The foliage is more like *E. radicans,* dark and semi-glossy, and these Corliss versions, called Emerald, come in several forms: Emerald Charm is tall, narrow and upright to about 5′, Emerald Pride is the compact bush-type about 4′ high and almost as wide, Emerald Cushion is a little dwarf spreader about 18″ high and a reach of 3′.

Any of these, in combination with each other or with low junipers or flowering shrubs, would be excellent for the small house; they go particularly well with junipers, besides taking the same soil, as the feathery grey-green of the junipers gives nice contrast to the firm, glossy leafage of the euonymus. Low, untrimmed Korean box could also join this party. And tall French lilacs to frame the whole thing. When planting a doorway which opens onto a forecourt, terminates a path from the side, always use a tall shrub, or shrub planting, or small flowering tree at the far corner to balance all the busyness on the other side.

If your house happens to be of any masonry material—brick, stone, stucco, or whatever—here is another way to incorporate the evergreen note around the entrance: plant a climbing euonymus vine beside the door and let it swarm up to curve over the doorway, keeping the whole thing clipped flat against the house. When grown like this, clipped flat and tight, the euonymus stems develop beautiful lines and patterns of their own, and these become even more interesting with the years. Sometimes an old euonymus vine so grown will be loosened by strong winds, perhaps torn loose, so it is a good idea to anchor the stems to the masonry with those clamps which are sold for this very purpose; these clamps also enable you to shape the stem patterns, achieve just the right curve over the doorway. A single euonymus vine, grown this way, should be balanced on the other side of the entrance by a tallish evergreen or a flowering shrub of some substance.

Or, if your house is wide enough and tall enough, you could use a vine on either side of the doorway to form a complete frame, being careful to keep the euonymus shoots away from any woodwork as no vine should ever attach itself to wood. Or—and this is *or*, not *and*—you could frame an important front window the same way. This is a particularly pleasant method of handling a large window for, if the window frame is metal, not wood, you can let the vine come close to the glass so that, from within, one looks out through a leaf-edged frame.

Which climbing euonymus to use would depend on the size and height of your house: a large, substantial house would take the large, leathery-leaved *vegetus* with its clusters of orange berries in fall, while a smaller house would take the less heavy, semi-glossy leafage of *radicans*: a tiny, low house might take the tiny-leafed

E. Kewensis (this needs shade, is hard to establish in sun) which can be trained into sprawling, spreading patterns contributing personality to the most ordinary façade. All these euonymus plantings should have only the simplest footing, such as a ground cover, so that interest is centered on the patterns made by the vine.

THE ENTRANCE WHICH HAS GRADING PROBLEMS

All the foregoing has been based on the assumption that your front area is relatively level and uninteresting, that there are no great differences in grade to consider. Actually, differences in grade can be a blessing, as they offer so many opportunities for retaining walls, perhaps dripping ivy, and steps banked with low evergreens and shrubs. In such an area a forecourt would be absurd, would only complicate matters further.

There are many ways of handling such an area where grading is necessary but one of the simplest is to—again—have the path come in from the driveway side, mount a few steps, and then continue along the front of the house as a narrow, paved terrace edged with an iron railing and screened from the road by flowering trees, planted on the lower level, so that their flowery tops rise just above the railing. There would be no planting on the terrace itself; in spring the trees would provide a wealth of bloom, and, during the summer, Italian pottery jars holding fuchsias, or upright lantanas, or tuberous begonias, or whatever, could be set around the doorway to give welcome.

The doorway itself could be made interesting by being slightly recessed with, on either side and half-way up, small niches in which to set potted ivy to drip down and, above these niches, narrow one-way windows. This would enable the owner to peek out to see if it really was the wolf at the door at last. And after all that grading, the construction of such a terrace, the paving, the iron railings, the Italian pottery jars and their contents, it might well be the wolf.

AUGUST

View From A Terrace

I. THE MAGIC OF LIGHT

This part will deal with the area wherein you spend whatever leisure time you are able to snatch out of your day or evening. This area may be at the back of the house, or at the side, may be large or small, may include a view of far fields or woods, or merely of your neighbor's garage. But to you it is probably the most important part of your property for it is where you sink down to put your feet up when Old Kaspar's work is done—temporarily, anyhow —and if you do a lot of entertaining this is where you do it whenever possible.

Garden lighting for evening pleasure is becoming more and more popular. Some people like it and some people don't, but according to those who have mastered the art it can make a briar patch look like a flower show and Br'er Rabbit look like Zsa Zsa Gabor. You work it out so that a soft radiance comes from the side or from below, never from above unless it is merely a luminous glow and all mechanism well hidden; any strong light blasting down from above flattens and distorts, a fact known to every woman who has looked into a mirror under a harsh light.

There are many ways to use garden lighting, and many appliances of various kinds for various effects. If you are interested in this idea I suggest that you get in touch with your local electric company and ask for literature on the subject. Not only will you get, and speedily, a raft of booklets all crammed with pictures and suggestions, but also the active interest of their Garden Lighting Adviser. Some electric companies will even send such an expert to help you arrange lighting effects in your own garden.

The up-lighting of trees can add drama to the evening scene.

Here are some suggestions for invoking this magic: if you have a pool or fountain of any kind—and before you finish this chapter you will probably be planning one—sink the light in nearby shrubbery so that it illuminates the play of water and whatever ornament accompanies it; this is particularly dramatic with a jet fountain. Or if you have a garden seat, or bird bath, or other object of interest tucked into the shrubbery, let the light come from whichever side seems best. And light shining straight up from underneath a tree is always fascinating. I remember once looking up into the great branches of a huge maple, the light filtering up and up through the leaves into a fathomless world of mystery.

All white plants are particularly effective when lighted: white birches, the white spires of delphinium, white vines of all types, white lilies. And should you have a pool with white or pale yellow water lilies, the kind that stay open at night, by all means try out different lighting effects. Shrubs and broadleafed evergreens with glossy foliage also show up well, but don't waste time on dull-leafed plants unless they have white blossoms.

All equipment designed for outdoor use is thoroughly insulated, thoroughly safe to use if directions are followed, but always read these directions carefully, including the fine print, before you start experimenting. Most of these lights use low current. Also, many of them are portable, can be moved from place to place as desired. One of the most versatile is the portable outdoor bullet-type which spikes into the ground, operates on a swivel so that it can be adjusted to various angles.

When you get the mass of literature your electric company will send you at the drop of a phone call you will encounter many new ideas. Ask, especially, for information on bug lights; these attract flying insects to the lights themselves instead of to you. Which makes the outdoor evening far pleasanter.

II. COOL, CLEAR WATER

There is nothing more refreshing on a hot August afternoon or evening than the sight—and, if possible, the sound—of cool, clear water.

Once upon a time even a small pool meant considerable financial outlay. It meant the installation of pipes from house to pool, plus some arrangement for overflow, plus the grim thought that a prolonged drought and consequent water shortage might make the whole thing inoperable. No gardener who has watched his plants and lawns die of thirst is going to waste water on a pool.

But the pump which recirculates the same small amount of water over and over has changed the entire pool picture for any number of country dwellers with an uncertain water supply. This method needs no pipes from the house, no pipes for overflow; the whole contraption comes in a kit which includes everything needed. You simply dig a hole of whatever size and shape pleases you, line it with the plastic liner (included in the kit), set the pump in the bottom and hide it with stones and sand, arrange the hose which returns the water, rim the edges with flat stones and small plants, fill the cavity with water, plug in the electric cord—and you are in business.

These pool kits come in three different sizes and strengths: there is the fountain kit which provides a single jet of water, the fountain-ring kit which gives a circular display, and the waterfall kit which you rig up to cascade—or trickle—down from an elevation. This last is the most complicated to construct, also the most expensive to buy, as a larger and more powerful pump is needed to lift the water so it can circulate; the higher the lift the larger the pump must be.

You can get these kits at almost any good general nursery, complete with literature including photographs and diagrams, plus personal advice. At present writing prices for the simpler kits and smaller pumps start at around $30 and this is the total cost of the pool, not counting your own labor and the small amount of current which will be used. The only problem is that the pool, or fountain, or waterfall must be close enough to the house to plug into an electric outlet, via a possible extension cord, which means some kind of screening to hide this cordage. Or the cord can be buried. All this you will have to work out for yourself.

If the above seems to present too many complications there is the simple homespun hose-method to consider. This, described in *January* for the watering of the Hidden Garden pool, can be worked out for any pool or fountain near the house. Or even further away, for all you need is more hose and the ingenuity to conceal it, snake it through plantings. In most informal country setups the slow drip into the shallow pool is more in keeping than the flashier fountain; it is also preferred by the birds as they are alarmed by water which is too active. And if this small flow is turned off at night, or when not being appreciated, very little water will be used, the slight overflow absorbed by the surrounding area and water-loving plants.

About the pool itself: there are any number of prefabricated pools on the market. Most of these come in odd shapes, supposed to look more "natural", but with flat stones and thoughtful planting around the edges they can be quite attractive. Or you can dig your own pool and make it a proper one, line it with stones and cement and incorporate the necessary drains. Directions for making such a pool can be found in almost any complete garden book.

No matter what type of pool or fountain you decide upon there are two catalogues you should leaf through first, if only to enlarge your own thinking, to glimpse the infinite variety of beautifully designed pool fixtures and ornaments now available. One of these catalogues is put out by The Florentine Craftsmen, the other by the Erkins Studios, both of New York. These will furnish you with a dazzlement of new ideas. All ornaments intended for pool use are piped, ready to be connected, and both catalogues contain designs which can be used with recirculating pumps.

Most of the material in these catalogues is estate type, too elaborate for use in a casual country setting, but you will also find many simple designs—small frogs, turtles, flowers, shells to fasten to a wall—which are so joyous in conception and naïve in character that they would be quite at home in the country garden. Some of the prices may shake you up a little but others are quite reasonable. If you are going to buy any garden ornaments at all they should be really good, and most of these are really good.

Where to put your pool or fountain will depend so entirely on the size, shape, and contours of your property that the only way I can help you is to describe some of the pool treatments I have seen and enjoyed, hoping that one of these may give you ideas.

1. WALL FOUNTAIN WITH SHELL. The setting was a small, semi-formal terrace shaded by a huge beech tree. The center of this area was flagstone-paved and bordered on two sides by flowering evergreens against a 5′ wall of stone. A house wall formed the third side, planted with shrubs and peonies, and on the fourth side was a yew hedge clipped to half-moon shape, low in the center and rising at each end to terminate in tall yews. This framed the view across the valley to the evergreen-studded mountainside beyond.

But it was the little wall fountain which contributed greatest enjoyment to this scene. From a lead flower set in the stone wall issued a gentle stream of water which fell into a lead shell and, from that, dripped down into a small shallow stone pool beneath. English ivy swarmed up the wall to embrace the whole thing, and the azaleas (*Schlippenbachi*) on either side must have been a joy in spring. The little pool itself was attended by shell-leafed Bergenias (*Saxifraga cordifolia*) massed against the wall and white violas massed around the front. The flow of water was so gentle that birds used both the shell and the shallow pool beneath. On that hot August afternoon there was a continuous fluttering of arrivals, splashings, and departures. It was a fascinating floor show.

Owner said that water was piped from the house, which was nearby, to enter the wall at the back, all this mechanism screened by shrubbery. The water was turned off at night, turned on only when the terrace was in use so the overflow was no problem. He said the piping had been surprisingly inexpensive to install, around $50 for the whole job as he remembered. The stone-lined pool he had made himself.

2. IVY-WREATHED POOL, JET FOUNTAIN. This is one of the best pool treatments I have ever seen. It is in back of a small, very old house which has been so lovingly remodeled that it carries a

Ivy-wreathed pool described above.

EUGENE D. TRUDEAU

quality of grace while still retaining its deep-country flavor. The owner is a distinguished artist, also an architect.

A small grass terrace opens out from the back of this house, and three shallow steps of native stone lead down between clipped yews to a lawn in which is set the little pool, ivy-ringed, a single jet of water rising from the graceful figure in the center. When the low western sun shines through this jet spray it creates sheer magic. In back of this pool is an ancient maple which gives shade during the hottest part of the day but does not shut out the view across the valley. On one side of this lawn area is an old barn, its siding silver with age, and on the other side the lawn merges down into meadows and an apple orchard with a sweep of hills beyond.

The pool, which is shallow and lined with native stone, is gravity-fed from an overflowing artesian well (the site picked by a dowser from a photograph!) and the excess water is drained out through a pipe, within the pool, to filter down through the earth and be absorbed by a great willow tree set below the slope. There is a stone control-box so that the amount of flow can be regulated, or shut off.

The jet itself comes from a half-inch pipe topped with a copper petcock. But here is an ingenious feature: if such a pipe gets even a fraction of an inch out of line the jet of water will be canted and unsightly, so the owner took a common pencil, removed the ends and the lead, bound it with plastic tape, and set it into the top of the pipe to rise just a little above the petcock. So if the jet varies even a hair from the perfect perpendicular it can be adjusted by regulating the more flexible pencil top, which is too small to be noticeable.

The low coping around the pool is of native stone, the ring of ivy planted close against it, and here is a special low-maintenance feature: outside of this ivy ring is a second coping (octagonal) of brick-like patio tile, deeply set. This not only keeps the ivy from creeping out into the lawn but also furnishes a second rim, or guide line, so that the job of clipping is made easier and faster.

All this has been gone into at some length because such a pool, no matter how fed, contributes so much to such an area and these details might help other gardeners. It would probably be possible to work out a fairly reasonable facsimile of this pool with a recirculating pump and the jet fountain kit mentioned earlier.

3. HOMEMADE POOL—A SPECIAL FOR CHILDREN. The owners were young and clear-eyed and full of dreams. Someday they hoped to make a real terrace out of the grassy area in back of the dilapidated old farmhouse they were trying to do over themselves, but in the meantime they had to make do with what was there. And with their homemade pool.

All that was there was a tumbled-down stone wall on two sides, a few common lilacs and peonies left by the former owner, an old silver lace vine, and an ancient apple tree, magnificently twisted, which gave courage and character to the whole thing. Under this apple tree, in a corner of the stone wall, was the pool.

It was wide, fan-shaped, and shallow. The owners had simply dug out a sizable area and lined it with small flattish stones, put a thin sheet of clear plastic over the stones and added a sandy bottom on top of the plastic. The edges of the plastic were anchored by larger stones with tuffets of ajuga tucked between them. The whole thing fitted, spreading outwards, into that corner of the wall through which a garden hose had been threaded; water trickled down over a stone lip to splash into the pool beneath. On that hot August day the silver lace vine was a white foam along the sunny part of the wall and was footed by masses of dwarf marigolds, home grown.

The owners said the reason they had made the pool so wide and shallow was so the children could use it as a paddle place, a play place. But the unique feature of this arrangement was the placing of the hose end: by simply shifting a small stone, which the children could do for themselves, the nozzle could be slanted up so that when the water was turned on full and adjusted to spray they could create their own shower bath to cavort in—and all without adult aid.

The young wife said this was one of their brighter ideas. It had also provided good discipline, for the children were held responsible for turning the hose off when playtime was over and if this was forgotten, if the hose was left running, the oldest child had to go back and turn it off even if this meant getting out of bed at night. And no six-year old likes to travel out into the black dark, all alone, with a flashlight. After two such experiences there was no more trouble with the hose.

Luckily, this property included an ever-gushing spring which provided plenty of water. It was one of the reasons they had bought the long-forsaken old house, for with three children and another on the way water was a major consideration. So was money. Owner said the whole pool project had cost less than $5, as he remembered: $2.98 for the hose and around $1.50 for the plastic liner.

But the greatest benefit to all had been the fun of constructing it. The children had been so eager to make their own pool that they had trundled away earth in their small carts, had combed the property for stones to line the bottom; they had even dug out the sand from a sandy spot, screened it through a kitchen sieve, and carted it back to the pool. It was their pool, they had made it themselves, and great was their pride therein.

It also gave pleasure to adults, on summer evenings after the children were in bed, the soft sound of water splashing down to combine with the soft sound of the whippoorwill on a distant stone wall.

4. THE HIDDEN POOL. This one took up almost no room at all. It was tucked into a bit of property so small you wouldn't have thought a pool was possible.

It was hidden amid shrubbery below a retaining wall which held up a small, narrow terrace with an iron railing along the edge. From this terrace a few stone steps led down, between azaleas and hollies, to curve back towards the wall and there, surprisingly, was a little pool catching a gush of water which issued from between some rocks. Ferns and primroses were growing out of crevices, and the whole thing was sheltered and shaded by small trees and tall shrubs which edged the property.

The gusher was one of those recirculating affairs. This was hard to believe for the effect was that of a natural stream bubbling out of natural rocks, but the owner assured me that it was all done by a small pump. The electric cord had been guided up over the terrace and through shrubbery so skillfully that its passage to the house was completely hidden; they had had to use an extension cord but that was a small matter. From the terrace above they could enjoy the sound of gushing water, and the curving steps leading down to the hidden pool gave interest and mystery. The big project had been building the rocky setting.

They had, at first, faced a major problem: their property was too small to include the stones and rocks necessary so a system had been worked out. They were most hospitable, welcomed house guests, but each guest was asked to bring a stone or flat rock—and the bigger the better—as a hostess gift. Great was the glee when guests arrived with a real monster. And they must have had some merry times because some of the stones were majestic in size, and how they ever got hefted out of the cars which brought them is still a mystery to the complaisant owners. It is astonishing what miracles can be wrought by hospitality.

5. SMALL COUNTRY POND VIEWED FROM A TERRACE. The simplicity of this pond is a joy. You sit on the shaded terrace above and look out upon a scene of serenity, a circle of clear water with lawn coming right down to the rim. In the foreground, at the edge of the paved terrace held by the retaining wall, a very old soapstone sink offers bathing facilities to the birds and contributes a special country flavor; a large and unusual metal bird (made by the owner) supplies the water for his small friends. The water is piped from the house a few feet away.

This spacious pool was nothing but a swampy meadow before the owner, a distinguished architect and also an artist, decided that a farm-type pond would accord well with the very old farmhouse he was remodeling. A bulldozer was hired to clean out the muck, shape the simple circle (it is 72′ in diameter), and deepen it to 8′ in the center so it could be used for swimming. A great flat boulder was left at one side for diving. Also for the putting on of skates in winter. The water is piped from a nearby spring which runs gently but constantly—another lucky landowner with plenty of water—and the surplus drains off into the field. The pond is full of fish which keep it clean.

The small terrace at right is an example of what can be done with imagination, unerring taste, and a sensitivity to setting. It lies between the end of the old house, which was probably the summer kitchen at one time, and a shed which shows the silvery siding of age; this is now used for garden tools. These two buildings are connected by a flagstone-paved terrace with informal wooden roofing supported by posts. It is open on both sides so a breeze sweeps through even on the hottest days.

Below this terrace, below the retaining walls as the ground drops away towards the pond, are shrub plantings, naturalized

THEODORA M. PRENTICE

Small country pond viewed from a terrace. To the left, in the foreground, is the old soapstone sink used as a bird bath and presided over by the metal bird which looks enormous in the picture but is actually 24" high

THEODORA M. PRENTICE

EUGENE D. TRUDEAU

View from the other side of the pond, showing the gardens which descend to the lawn, swing out to meet the pond's edge.

masses of sweet rocket, lupins, day lilies, beds of old-fashioned perennials and annuals, all reached by steps of rough wood and native stone which lead down to the lawn-and-water level. Here you turn and look back towards the house, rejoice in the gentle contours and simple planting of this country garden.

6. A CONNECTICUT POND FOR CANADA GEESE. Would you believe that not too long ago the pond pictured on page 174 was non-existent? That this whole area was just a barren, treeless bog, just no-good swamp land according to the farmer who owned it? But this no-good swamp land, plus a fine but dilapidated farmhouse, was bought by a couple who knew what they were doing, who were

not afraid of work, who loved water, and wildlife, and especially birds. They had long held the dream of having their own private wildfowl sanctuary and this meant water, islands surrounded by water where the birds could be relatively safe from foxes, dogs, all four-footed predators.

And would you believe that this spacious pond—only half of which is shown in this picture—was made by this man and wife with their own hands? Or, more accurately, by their own hands operating their own tractor and scoop, for they had no outside help except for a young lad who came in by the day to trundle earth and rocks.

Before starting this major enterprise they made a careful study of the whole situation. They called in the State Conservation experts, the soil specialist, the water specialist, the wildlife specialist, and received invaluable advice on how to proceed. Without this advice, they soon realized, months of work would have been wasted. It is a pity more land owners do not take advantage of this wealth of information which is provided, free, by almost every state.

It took them approximately ten years to complete the series of ponds and islands, stream-fed and spring-fed, to build the necessary dams and fish-ladders, to plant all the trees shown in these pictures. Incredibly, almost all of these trees were either brought in from the woods as little seedlings or propagated from a parent tree; all the willows were so propagated. And all this within the last twenty years. Few people realize how fast most trees will grow when carefully planted in the soil and setting they like best.

The establishment of trees was a separate and equally major enterprise, for the land had become so impoverished by countless years of neglect and over-grazing that almost every foot of it had to be replaced, and deeply, with good growing earth, with endless loads of humus and leaf mold brought in from the woods, with compost and peat moss and manure and all the needed minerals and trace elements. How well this herculean labor has paid off is shown by the vibrant health and vigor of the various plantings in these pictures.

Each spring the geese come back to their islands to raise their young. They are now so tame, so used to people as purveyors of tidbits, that they come honking up to see what you have for them. The owners keep a box of bread and whole corn on the terrace which overlooks the ponds and to have wild Canada geese eating out of your hand is a unique experience.

From the ponds the wide lawns of Merion bluegrass sweep up towards the house which is large, Colonial in character, has been beautifully restored. And from the house you look out over these lawns to the ponds, the willows, the geese. There are perfectly proportioned allées giving a sense of space and serenity, there are wide gravel walks (wide enough to take the tractor), and special group plantings which the owner, who was a professional garden consultant, called garden rooms. Trees, evergreens, clipped hedges, flowering shrubs and vines, ground covers, are everywhere; there are very few perennials or annuals. Each area is so skillfully planned that it merges into the next, effortlessly.

This is one of the most beautifully designed country places I know of. And it shows what can be done with a dream.

A Connecticut pond made especially for Canada geese. This picture was taken in very early spring before the geese arrived.

The geese in residence.

III. TREES AND SHRUBS FOR
SCREENING OR FRAMING

These you use to screen out whatever parts of a view you don't like, or to frame whatever parts you do like. It is the choosing and placing of this material which is important, knowing how tall or wide it will grow, how it will look from where you are sitting right now. Which is, presumably, the terrace.

Suppose, for instance, that your view across the fields includes a delicate white church spire which is presently neighbored by a new shopping center. Or your glimpse of far blue hills includes a housing development in the foreground. By choosing the right trees or shrubs, and placing them accurately, you can blot out the shopping center or the housing development while framing the church spire or the hills and guests will exclaim oh, what a lovely view! I don't say this is easy, because it is not. But I do say it can be done because I have seen it done.

Or, closer by, trees or shrubs can be used to frame a focal point. And a focal point, Virginia, is any unexpected and pleasurable sight, usually framed, which surprises and delights the eye. Like a small alcove of gentle shrubs filled with a carved stone figure of St. Francis. Or an old-fashioned bathtub with claw feet filled with Sophia Loren; your husband would probably prefer this one. The point is that you can create a focal point out of almost anything if you frame it.

With this in mind consider your view, or lack of it, and what you can do about the situation. Here are some of the trees and large shrubs which can be used for screening or framing, their personalities and characteristics. All of them are deciduous, which means that they do not work in winter. But, for that matter, you are not likely to be sitting out on your terrace in winter.

Two of the fastest growing trees for screening out distant and objectionable objects are willows (*Salix* in variety) and tulip trees

Skillful planning and planting make this lawn area, viewed from the terrace, seem much larger than it actually is.

The far steps (just visible in the preceding) lead up between birches, mountain laurel, ferns and wildflowers to the top of an abandoned railroad bank from which one looks down, on the other side, into a rushing brook.

(*Liriodendron Tulipifera*). Both are easy, if established when small, and relatively inexpensive. Both are fast growing if happily placed, the willows rising 3' to 4' a year, the tulip trees 4' to 6' a year.

The common weeping willow, *Salix babylonica*, grows to around 40', though sometimes more, and has a tremendous spread; it is a soft, feathery job, light in value despite its size, and is excellent for horizontal screening. The variety *Salamoni* (or *sepulcralis*) is considered hardier and stronger, has about the same form as *babylonica*, sometimes grows larger. Both are hardy here. Or, if you are

This little fern, shown in a corner of the terrace, arrived under its own steam, settled in amid the cotoneasters and euonymus to the pleasure of all concerned, especially the viewer. One of Gertrude Jekyll's treasured "things that come of themselves".

among the many gardeners who dislike all weeping plants, there is a non-weeping form, *S. fragilis,* which has a lovely lifting head, a strange and beautiful habit of growth, often irregular; this one does not bush out as much, nor can it be depended on to bush out in the right places if used for screening. According to the books it is said to be not too hardy north, except in sheltered spots and along coastal areas, and also somewhat fragile, but I know of a stream-side planting near here which has taken bitter winters for over forty years.

As willows are always associated with water they are particularly suitable for framing any watery view such as a pond, a bit of lake or river. I once saw two great weeping willows used most skillfully to frame a curve in a river while blocking out the unfortunate houses on either side. But be careful where you plant willows for they must have water, and plenty of it, and if they cannot find enough where you have put them those great roots will travel incredible distances in search of moisture, and woe betide anything which gets in their way. So best keep them away from all buildings, all underground pipes, drains, septic tanks, especially if these lie between the willow and a source of water. Willows are also useful for absorbing moisture from a too-wet spot, for binding and holding stream banks, preventing erosion.

Tulip trees grow much taller, well over 100'. The common tulip tree, *L. Tulipifera,* is apt to be upright in form in its native woods but spreads out when grown in the open, attains a more rounded shape; it should always be pruned, when young, to a single stem to develop a good head; the foliage is very heavy. The leaves of the tulip tree are distinctive, look as though the tips had been cut off. This tree is good to use at a distance, or on a slope, for screening out unwanted sights, is hardy well up into New England, being a native of northern woods. It can be moved only when very young.

There is also an upright-growing form of this tulip tree, *L. Tulipifera* var. *fastigiatum,* which is more unusual and far more beautiful. This one has the slender shape of a Lombardy poplar but much larger and heavier; it is perfect for framing anything at a distance. You seldom see it used except by landscape architects on large, sweeping estates as it is too big for small properties, but it is available at better nurseries and can often be well placed on hillsides. Like its plumper sister it can only be moved when small. Both like a deep humusy loam full of peat moss and leaf mold.

Among the smaller trees for screening or framing is one which is unusually desirable yet, apparently, known to comparatively few gardeners. This is *Sophora japonica,* the Japanese pagoda tree or Chinese scholar tree. It grows to about 40' around here with strange, beautifully twisted branch lines (see photographs) which are best revealed by cutting back the end growths very early each spring. So treated it can be used most effectively for framing steps, a special planting, a vista, almost anything worthy of a distinguished frame. Uncut, it forms a heavy, round-headed, widely spreading tree for either lawn or screening, has feather-like leaves and, in maturity, bears panicles of creamy-white flowers in late summer. It likes a deep, sandy loam.

The little Russian olive (*Elaeagnus angustifolia*), spoken of so often throughout this book, is equally valuable for framing or screening but only in deep-country settings for it is a most informal tree. For any framing job it should have a single stem and be so pruned that it shows the dark and lovely stem-lines of which it is capable; for screening get low-branching ones which promise bushy, rounded heads and let them bush out. These versatile little trees can be grown in almost any shape or form which fits the need and, always, they are beautiful with their feathery masses of silver leafage, their black stems. Eventual height is, usually, around 25′ and they will grow almost anywhere in average well-drained soil, love sun and wind, and are astonishingly inexpensive.

They can also be grown, massed, as a high hedge or continuous screen. If you need them for this purpose best order the hedging size from one of the big mid-western nurseries listed on page 243. Out there in the Blizzard Belt where winters are winters and what big teeth you have Grandma this gentle little tree is used for snow-breaks, wind-breaks, dust-breaks. It is that hardy.

There are also many, many other trees, flowering trees of about this same size, which can be used for framing or screening. The catalogues are full of them so take your choice. But if you should be searching for a very special tree in a very special shape for a very special spot here is a small story which might give you a new idea.

There was this couple, fresh from New York, who had bought this old place and were carried away by its New England flavor. They planted all the old-timey shrubs and flowers and planned an old-fashioned herb garden which was to have a twisted old apple tree bending over it at just the right angle; but this tree had to have just the right twist to it for the owners were both artists and line was terribly important. They combed the local nurseries but all the apple trees offered were firmly upright in character, had no bend, no twist.

They had almost given up when, driving along a country road, they spied the apple tree of their dreams. It was small and young, in a cow pasture, and the cows had apparently nibbled it, or rubbed against it, or in some manner distorted its habit of growth so that it was all curved over on one side. Enchanted by this discovery the couple stopped at the farmhouse and asked the farmer whether he

A sophora tree trimmed back to reveal the lovely stem lines. These trees happily accept underplanting.

would be willing to sell them that little tree if they arranged for the moving of it. When the farmer had collected his wits and rubbed them together he said yes, maybe, but he kind of liked that tree himself and forthwith named a price he was afraid would stop them. It didn't. Papers were signed and, shortly, a local tree-moving service dug up the tree and replanted it by the herb garden where it presented exactly the lines desired.

Which of the parties involved in this transaction had the best story to tell was a matter of mirth for some time. The New York couple, enthralled by their find, told all their city friends how they had persuaded the farmer to let them have this exquisite little tree for almost nothing. The farmer, meanwhile, was telling all his local friends how crazily city people will throw away money, how they paid him a fat price for a stunted, bent-over, no-good tree which didn't even bear eatable apples, and when they could have gotten a nice straight one from Monkey Ward for half the price.

If, instead of a delicate tree, you need a big heavy shrub to screen out your neighbor's garage, your own incinerator, or the sun-bathing blonde on the next property you might consider plain, common Amur River privet (*Ligustrum amurense*). This, surprisingly, makes a very handsome shrub when untrimmed, given plenty of room to develop. It grows 12' to 15' tall and almost as wide, presents a great billowing mass of dark green, semi-glossy leafage. It is not only a fast grower, which is what makes it too demanding as a hedge, but it is easy, hardy, and inexpensive, will grow almost anywhere in any kind of soil. However, it has two drawbacks: you cannot grow anything else close by as it is one of the robber barons, taking all nourishment out of the surrounding soil; also, its so-called flowering has an unpleasant smell so that it is unsuited to social areas when grown untrimmed. But if you are interested only in a big, heavy screen this privet will give it to you fast and cheaply. Plant about 5' or 6' apart for such a screen.

The taller (6' to 10') and heavier viburnums, in variety, are also useful for screening and offer a flowering period as well. The typical viburnum foliage is dull and coarse, the whole personality coarse and heavy (now watch the hackles rise on viburnum lovers!) but the large flower-heads and bright berries are effective from a distance. Hardy, easy, will grow anywhere in sun, and the commoner varieties are not expensive.

The above does not apply to their little cousins, *V. Carlesi* and *V. Burkwoodi* which have made the Social Register. Both bear very fragrant, pale pink flower-heads, are smaller and more delicate in structure, not much good for screening but delightful on a terrace, near a doorway or window where the fragrance can waft into the house. *V. Carlesi* has soft grey-green leafage; *V. Burkwoodi* has, surprisingly for a viburnum, an open, airy habit of growth and small, dark, semi-glossy leaves. This one would be a good choice for framing some nearby object such as a garden seat, a bird bath, a small pool. If possible, get it on a single stem so that it can be grown as a very choice little tree, somewhat rounded in form, to about 8'.

Another open, airy shrub for framing scenes perhaps a little further away would be the Daphne lilac (*Syringa microphylla superba*) spoken of earlier. This blooms twice a year, in May and again in August; it is light and graceful for a lilac with slender willowy stems burdened with fragrant pink trusses. The catalogues say it seldom grows over 5'. Maybe so, but mine are topping 8'.

And then, straight out of a fairy tale, is the little honeysuckle "tree", *Lonicera Korolkowi,* described at some length in *January* for use in the Hidden Garden. This one, which grows to about 10', has a wildwood quality which recommends it for some spot of natural beauty, though I have seen it suggested by distinguished garden designers for foundation planting. In my opinion, this strange and enchanting little tree is best used to frame a path leading down to a brook, or into woodlands. Get it on a single twisted stem, if possible, to provide the lifting, tree-like quality.

A major shrub, which can also be grown as a low-branching tree, is the corky, winged *Euonymus alatus* with its stern and striking branch lines. This one, not often seen, is a larger and more open version of the *E. alatus compactus,* or burning bush, which is seen everywhere and makes a fine thick shrub for screening. But the big one has far more character and is more beautiful the whole year round, from early spring when the flat winged stems—flatter and more winged than those of the *compactus*—turn pistachio-green and ashes-of-roses pink, through a summer of clean, dark leafage which becomes, in fall, a brilliant strawberry-rose, into a winter when every flat, outreaching stem carries an icing of snow. *Hortus II* lists this one as growing to 8', but mine is over 9'—and almost as wide—and I have seen even larger specimens. It is much too big and powerful to use in small areas or near small houses; the exception to this might be the small house of contemporary architecture, for in this case the stern, clean strength of the architectural lines could balance the stern, clean strength of the *alatus.* When associated with other types of architecture it is best used in large areas, for framing something of sizable importance; it is too open for screening.

Here are a few more explicit suggestions for using small trees to frame or accent your view from the terrace:

1. Individually, or in pairs, to frame a doorway, steps, a path.

2. At either end of a special planting to frame it, give it importance.

3. To mark an entrance, such as a driveway, perhaps under-

planted with low junipers. Be sure this planting does not interfere with visibility.

4. To line one or both sides of a long driveway.

5. Singly, as the central feature of a swing-around driveway, again underplanted with low junipers or some other ground cover.

6. To give height and vertical interest to an evergreen planting, perhaps at the edge of a lawn.

7. To soften the corner of a house or a bare house wall; to give horizontal (spreading) contrast to a chimney.

8. To use, singly, as the central feature of a paved terrace, ringed with vacationing house plants in summer.

9. As a crescent-shaped background for some special planting which blooms at another time (peonies, day lilies, low roses, etc.), or as a straight background for a perennial bed.

10. For planting, at a lower level, below a retaining wall so that the flowering or fruiting tree tops rise up to furnish beauty along the top of the wall and a background for upper-level planting. This is a good way to handle the edge of a terrace where the ground drops away sharply. Also gives privacy, should that be desirable, and screens out unsightly views should that also be desirable.

But before you pick any of these trees or shrubs out of a catalogue, just because they look so pretty in the pictures, I urge you to view them on the hoof, in nurseries or in gardens, either private or botanical. And now, in late summer, is the best time to do this; now most of them present nothing but structure and leafage and you can get a clearer idea of the character and personality. For the way a plant looks when out of bloom is, to my way of thinking, even more important than the way it looks in its hour of flowering (which is when it is photographed for the catalogue) as you have to live with it a lot longer in this less glamorous state. Choosing a tree or shrub is like choosing a husband or wife; you can be bewitched by the blossoms but when these are gone it is the character of the plant, its serene foliage, its intrinsic grace—or lack of it—which will be important to you for the rest of the course.

That Velvet Lawn

The best time to install a new lawn or conduct major repairs on an old one is early spring, and the second best time is early fall. September is preferred by most gardeners, for there is apt to be more time then than in spring when the dust is on the curtain and the moth is on the tweed and you are so overwhelmed by things to be done that you end up sitting in the sun and doing nothing.

Questioning the unquestionable desirability of the velvet lawn is like questioning the sanctity of Motherhood; the reaction you get is pain, shock, and the suspicion that you are not quite right in the head. Which is indeed possible. But the fact remains that the velvet lawn, like sanctified Motherhood, can sometimes demand more upkeep than you are able to give it.

If you have a sweep of property distinguished by fine architecture, superb trees, banks of flowering evergreens meticulously tended, and all the other mink and pearls of gardening you have no choice; you will have to have that velvet lawn no matter what it costs you in time, money, and maintenance. And it will cost you plenty. You should dig down 18" to 2', investigate drainage and install same if necessary, then replace the soil well laced with compost, peat moss and bone meal, allow the whole thing time to settle, fill up with more of the above if necessary, roll it, and then buy the very best grass seed. Which may or may not be Merion bluegrass. Anyhow, good grass seed will be expensive, but after all the work you have put into this enterprise it would be silly to pinch pennies at this point.

Then for the next year or so you will have to roll it, water it, and pray over it; adjust the cutter blades just so, twitch out any weeds which have the audacity to appear, pray over it some more. By that time, if you have survived either physically or financially, you will have a lawn of lush and unbelievable beauty which will, with care, last you the rest of your life, which will survive heaven, hell, drought, and high water and be the pride of your heart. And which you will have to mow constantly in order to maintain this beauty you have wrought.

Such a lawn deserves the awe and reverence of every gardener and don't think for one moment that I am speaking of it lightly. I view such a lawn with even more awe and reverence than most people because I know what it cost to install.

But not everyone has property of this type. If yours is small and broken up, your house merely a house, your time and money constantly gobbled up by other demands, you might want to consider a substitute for grass, some way out of the eternal lawn-mowing problem. Such a way out is ground-covers.

Mysteriously, this seems to be a dirty word to a lot of home owners, and usually the ones who would profit most by its consideration. Perhaps this is because a lawn, any kind of a lawn, has apparently become a status symbol along with the lovely home and the gorgeous drapes, the color TV, and the latest model car glistening in the driveway. It all depends on what is important to you.

I was once asked by a sweet child, the overtired and overworked mother of four tiny children, how she could plant their new place so that it would look pretty but not be any work to take care of as she would have to do the taking-care herself. Noting that both house and property were very small and new, the terrain broken up and difficult to mow, I suggested various flowering shrubs for around the edges, low everblooming roses (The Fairy) on either side of the door, a small flowering tree by the driveway, and all the rest of the area planted with an ajuga ground cover.

She looked at me in horror. "No *lawn*? No flower bed?"

No lawn. No flower bed. I left shortly thereafter in a cooling atmosphere. A few years later I happened to drive by and, just as I expected, there were no shrubs, no roses, no flowering tree, no ajuga. Just the inevitable evergreen muffins by the door, the inevitable "flower bed" of dismal, neglected annuals, and the sweet child herself, obviously pregnant again, wrestling with the lawn mower in the 90° heat. It seemed such a pity.

Ajuga makes an attractive, interesting, labor-free "lawn" if you can detach yourself from tradition. It seems to me a natural for the young, for new houses, new types of architecture, especially contemporary architecture which, already, has so courageously detached itself from tradition. Ajuga needs less than half the soil preparation necessary for a fine lawn. Even 6″ to 8″ of stirred topsoil mixed with a little humus or compost, a sprinkling of bone meal, will make ajuga blissfully happy as it usually has to make do with far less.

And it needs almost no upkeep. In May it will cover the area with a sheet of lovely blue and, after the flowering has finished, you can mow down these spikes if you want to, or leave them alone to fall over by themselves. After that, with no further attention from you, your lawn will be clothed all summer in flat rosettes of a semi-glossy metallic green which will take a surprising amount of traffic. Or, if you fancy a more formal effect, a tight, brocade-like carpet, you can mow it—once—when it has completed new growth, usually around July. Furthermore, ajuga will grow almost anywhere, in sun or shade, wet soil or dry, and the only upkeep it needs is a sprinkling of dried manure in early spring. It will even do without that.

Sticking the neck out even further, I personally like ajuga creeping into a conventional grass lawn to form strange swirls and patterns. Or maybe this is because our so-called lawns, which were never properly prepared but just grew, could be benefited by almost anything interesting. Visitors often say "Oh, I see you have that stuff" to which I reply, with a bright smile, "Yes, I like it." They look at me with some alarm.

They are even more shocked by the tiny, creeping *Veronica repens* which also invades our lawns, to my great pleasure. This mite, hardly more than 1″ high, spreads like the classic wildfire, becomes a flat, swirling sheet of palest blue in spring, a flat, swirling sheet of pale green during the summer after mowing. I am well aware that conventional gardeners are offended by these variations from the norm but this is simple deep-country property, not an estate, and I enjoy these diversions.

Another ground cover to consider, if you have the terrain for it, is the enormous family of thymes. I once saw these used as carpeting around a very simple old house in a dry, rock-strewn, sunny area and the effect was most interesting, great spreading swirls of flat, variously colored foliage, many of the swirls a mass of bloom. There are far too many thymes to go into here—look up the number and variety of thymes available in any rock garden catalogue—but if you happen to have a rocky site in full sun, and impossible to mow, do investigate this possibility. The owner of this display said it took no upkeep whatsoever.

About zoysia: you see this type of grass advertised constantly and have probably wondered whether it was really that good. From my own experience I should say yes and no and maybe. It depends on your problem and where you live. In this cold region it is endlessly slow to green up in spring—all regular grass will be a fresh bright green while the zoysia is still a straw-colored mat—and, in late fall, the zoysia is the first to lose color. Yet during the summer it is a deep green carpet, feels like foam rubber to walk on and so thick that hardly a weed can poke through. I believe that in milder climates it greens up faster and stays green longer.

Its ability to thrive in poor dry soil is unbelievable. We tried it on our terrace a few years ago during that five-year drought which wiped out so many carelessly planted lawns. With no rain for weeks on end, and no water for watering, and no bedding of humus to comfort the grass roots, our casual lawn almost disappeared. Something had to be done, and we had heard that zoysia was remarkably drought-resistant. It was and is. Stuck in hurriedly, and with almost no soil preparation, it took over fast. We did not do the whole area, only the worst spots, so now, each spring and fall, we have spreading patches of dead-looking zoysia amid relatively good grass. This is a little too far out even for me. Some day I hope to have the whole thing dug up deeply and properly and sown to Merion bluegrass, for this is one part of our property which should have a velvet lawn. Tradition will probably welcome me back with some surprise.

This zoysia spreads fairly quickly, pushing aside weeds and grass alike in its progress, but it spreads fastest towards the sun. I have never seen this fact mentioned in the ads but it is important to know, so if you decide to try zoysia start it at the northern or eastern side of the area, and if you have the patience to plant it carefully, with a little compost or humus around its roots, it will take hold faster than if you follow the quick-and-easy plugger directions which come with it.

About Evergreens

For most evergreens early spring planting is desirable, in some cases essential, but for many others, and depending on where you live, September offers another planting period. Consult your local nurseryman on this matter.

Directions for planting evergreens are included in almost every garden book and encyclopedia, but here is one trick I learned from an expert and which I have seldom seen in print:

After you have settled the root-ball into its bedding, filled in the earth and tramped it down firmly, take the handle of a shovel—or a broomstick, any straight handle—and poke deep holes all around the perimeter of the root-ball, the more the better. Then, and not until then, do the watering. This poking is to close up some of the countless air pockets which always exist in any deep-planting operation, also to allow deeper penetration of the water. You will usually see air bubbling up through these holes. Continue watering until no more air bubbles up, until the whole area is really saturated and the holes begin to cave in by themselves. Then apply the final covering of earth, plus a light mulch of compost, *and do not tramp down after this*. The soil will settle naturally, allowing the proper amount of ventilation; if you tramp wet earth you compact it so that no air at all can penetrate. This same procedure, the poking of deep holes before watering, should be employed in any deep-planting operation whether trees, shrubs, or major perennials but is especially important with evergreens as their roots are more sensitive to air pockets.

Another matter not always included in planting directions is the after-care of evergreens. The tops should be hose-sprayed daily for at least a week if there is sun or wind, after that every few days. Or, if the evergreen is small, spray and cover immediately with a large peach basket, allowing plenty of room for ventilation; or if too large for a peach basket shade with burlap draped over sticks. The idea is to prevent all possible strain on the roots, caused by evaporation and the withdrawal of moisture from leaves or needles, until the roots themselves are able to tap their own moisture.

There is still another important matter often omitted in garden books. Many evergreens, especially the flowering broadleafed ones such as azaleas, rhododendrons, mountain laurel and the like, are allergic to lime in any form and so should not be planted close to a newly-made foundation because of lime seepage from same. Most experienced gardeners know this but few beginners do. I know of one costly disaster which happened to a friend who had just built a fine new house; to save money he had not consulted a landscape architect, had decided to do all the planning and planting himself as he knew exactly what he wanted, which was mostly broadleafed evergreens. He went to a nursery and bought a lavish assortment of rhododendrons and azaleas, hollies and andromedas, and planted them all around his new foundation. Every single one of them died and he was out almost two hundred dollars, far more than it would have cost him to get a few hours of advice from a professional who could have saved him this loss. It is not always cheaper to do it yourself unless you know exactly what you are doing.

Also, be cautious about buying evergreens. This caution was stressed in *May*, in the article on buying plants, but is so important that I am giving it again.

It is often a waste of time, space, and money to pick up those "bargains" offered by chain stores, supermarkets, and many roadside stands. Usually these cheap evergreens have tiny root-balls which, more often than not, have been allowed to dry out thus signing the death warrant of the plant, for evergreens cannot go long without root moisture though the tops are slow to show this creeping death. The root-ball of a well-grown, well-dug, and well-packed evergreen should be almost as large as its top growth, should be firm and moist to the touch, the whole thing heavy and solid when you try to lift it. If it is surprisingly light, or the soil shifts, don't buy it. You will save money by going to a good nursery and buying a well-grown plant which has been properly dug and packed. Of course, many roadside stands are operated by accomplished and trustworthy gardeners who offer equally well-grown and well-dug plants, can afford lower prices because there is less overhead, but you should know what to look for when considering their wares.

All the above will greatly amuse my friends who know that I am constantly bringing home forlorn, half-dead plants, the kind I am telling you to avoid. But this is because I am a bird-brain about plants; I feel so sorry for the poor things, want to give them comfort and a second chance. They are my little loves and I put them in the

Intensive Care Unit, clucking over them like a daft mother hen. Some of my most cherished plants have come into my life this way, have developed strange and—to me—beautiful forms. But I do not recommend this practice if you want the show-place type of garden most admired by normal people.

To many gardeners, and I am one, evergreens offer more beauty per inch than almost any other form of plant life. Like trees, they have an enduring quality, give form and structure to a setting as no mere flowers can. Also, evergreens are apt to have more individuality than other plants. Perhaps, someday, somewhere, you may encounter an evergreen with so much personality, such strength and

This small country-formal garden, outlined by well-laid stone-work and well-clipped yew hedges, features evergreens, has been so well designed and well placed that it seems far larger than it really is. At the far end the rectangle is softened by a semicircle (same design as shown in sketch on page 153 holding a half-moon of herbaceous peonies footed by native stones laid in a circular pattern around an old mill wheel.

EUGENE D. TRUDEAU

Detail of this small garden showing how evergreens can be combined with perennials. Note the dark yew in the far corner, the clipped blanket of euonymus along the top of the wall. The silvery edging is veronica *incana*.

gentleness, that your heart will stand still. Take it then, if you can get it, or you may spend the rest of your life regretting your indecision.

It seems to me a pity to confine evergreens to the conventional plantings around the house when they are so valuable in other areas as well. They can be used to give authority to a weak spot, to balance a major tree or clothe an ugly bank; tall evergreens, along with flowering shrubs, can firm up a property edging, small ones can be used to define, accent, or terminate a flower border. And, of course, evergreens form the perfect background for flowers, making even a few blossoms seem more important than a whole riot of color. So with all these opportunities in mind look around your property and see what can be done.

Garden rooms, mentioned earlier, offer one possibility. This idea—small, semi-enclosed areas of individual interest—is one frequently employed by landscape architects when dealing with large estates, but it can also be simplified and scaled down to fit smaller and less formal properties. It is a refreshing way to add interest to an otherwise uninteresting spot.

Evergreens are almost essential in such plantings, especially if viewed from the house in winter, for these garden rooms should present, primarily, a sense of quiet strength and repose, and nothing gives these qualities in greater measure than evergreens. Except, perhaps, trees, which also belong in this picture: a single tree to preside over the whole, or trees as a background to furnish shade or shelter. You can have flowers or not as you choose; they relax the formality but perhaps this is what you want. The flowering broad-

Another small garden featuring evergreens. This one, viewed from the house, gives pleasure in winter as well as summer.

THEODORA M. PRENTICE

leafed evergreens, in variety, contribute this softer type of beauty as well as their own distinction. Or, in casual rural settings you could use deciduous material for the enclosure, a flowering tree to give shade, and simple evergreens to mark the entrance.

Where to tuck in such a garden may be a problem. Sometimes a simple one can be fitted into a shrub border, perhaps in a corner of the property. Or if you have a path leading to some other area a garden room might, surprisingly, be encountered on the way. Or a path curving down—or up—stone steps, shrub-edged, might terminate in a garden room. Or, if you have the space, an allée of flowering trees could lead straight to a semi-formal garden room. There are any number of possibilities.

If evergreens are part of this room's basic structure the carpeting should be the velvet lawn, meticulously maintained; or, to save maintenance, the small area could be flagstone-paved. If the enclosure is of deciduous material you could use pebbles-on-plastic: to do this you first clean the area of major vegetation, then spread out a sheet of plastic with holes punched in it and cover this with a thick layer of pebbles; the plastic keeps weeds and grasses from arising and the holes allow drainage so that the footing stays dry. Or you could simply carpet the area with an ajuga ground cover. Or use flat stones, sunk in sand, with small flowering creepers in planting pockets.

To convey a sense of invitation and repose some sort of seat should be included in your garden room. This should be of whatever type, or material, best accords with the room and its setting. Strictly formal settings we can skip, they are out of the range of this book, but many country properties include fine old houses which invite the gentle grace of faintly formal treatment.

Such as a clipped hemlock hedge with a white iron bench set against it, a spreading dogwood in back and a little to one side to provide shade, low azaleas at the entrance . . . or the same hedge in semi-circular form with a white iron table and two matching chairs arranged against the dark background, potted pale pink tree-fuchsias at the entrance.

Perhaps your property has a woodsy background. If so, consider a backing of native pines to shelter a curved planting of white Carolina rhododendrons (*R. Carolinianum* var. *album*), a simple cast-stone bench with potted tree-fuchsias on either side, the entrance

A serene and beautiful garden room, hemlock-hedged. It occurs as a surprise off the main path which leads to another area.

marked by low, glossy, semi-clipped Japanese hollies (*Ilex crenata convexa bullata*) . . . or use the hollies on either side of the bench and the fuchsias to mark the entrance.

In sunnier, more casual areas, a semi-circular backing of tall Pfitzer junipers could enclose two half-circles of white iris, stone-edged, with a white wooden bench in the center flanked by tall, coral-pink geraniums (potted), Korean boxwoods marking the entrance . . . or the same juniper background, the half-circle plantings of silver-grey stachys edged with evergreen candytuft, the bench flanked by coral flowering quinces, the entrance marked by circular swirls of low, compact lavender (*Lavendula officinalis* Twickle Purple; sorry, but that is its name).

And so on and so on ad infinitum. In any informal country setting where a casual evergreen background or screen is needed remember these tall Pfitzer junipers. They also make an excellent backing and wind-screen for a perennial bed or border as all flowers seem doubly effective against this soft grey-green. These junipers are very hardy and, in fact, stay healthier (less apt to invite red spider) in exposed, sunny, windy positions.

You may be puzzled by this reference to "tall" Pfitzer junipers as one reads everywhere, and endlessly, that Pfitzer junipers are "low and spreading". Well, I can tell you from thirty years' experience with them that some are and some are not. The males, which can be identified even when young by their vigorous up-shooting branches, can grow to 8'. I know because I have them that high. The females stay low, spreading, and demure as is more seemly, stop at around 4' usually; these too can be identified in youth by their softer, spreading habit. So it is always best to go to a nursery and pick out the individual junipers you want, to grow tall or stay low as may be your need. If you order by mail you never know which form you will get.

And if the nurseryman assures you—and many of them will—that there is no such thing as male and female in junipers, no difference in form, you can refer him to L. H. Bailey's *Standard Cyclopedia of Horticulture*, Vol. II, page 1728, upper right-hand paragraph, which clearly lists these male and female forms of *J. chinensis* and their differing habits of growth. And if he doesn't recognize the name of L. H. Bailey you had better take your business elsewhere as he probably knows even less about plants than you do.

The same applies to the little Sargent juniper, *J. Sargenti,* another form of *chinensis,* mentioned so frequently throughout this book as it is one of my favorite plants. Again you have two different personalities, habits of growth, although they are both sweepingly classified in most catalogues as growing about 2' tall with a spread up to 6'. Yet the strong, often craggy male form with its lifting, twisting branches and crisper needles is quite different from the softer, spreading female. This male Sargent has far more character, and its spread can be controlled by nipping back so that you get a comparatively upright plant with strange, curving stem lines. This juniper, too, you should choose personally to make sure which form you are getting. In my opinion, the male form is the only one worth buying.

The compact forms of the Pfitzer juniper (*J. Pfitzeriana compacta*) do not seem to vary as much in character, at least the ones I have seen have all been about the same in shape and habit. This is a most useful juniper in the middle-size range; grows to around 5' and is tighter than its parents. It is informal enough to be used as end plantings for a simple flower border, good to step-down a background of tall Pfitzers. Or it would make a nice medium-height enclosure for a garden room in sun with a Russian olive rising above to give dappled shade—or a whole ring of Russian olives in back—with groups of potted geraniums on either side of a white bench, the entrance to all this marked by white single herbaceous peonies.

There are any number of low spreading junipers of the *horizontalis* type, most of them well known, all of them excellent for ground-covering banks or largish areas in full sun, but there is one little creeper which is not so well known. This is *J. Wiltoni*. It is the flattest of them all, seldom more than 2" high, and forms a spreading carpet of plume-shaped branches which hug the ground; it has short, crisp needles shaded grey-green with, in late summer, fat grey berries which sit right on top. It is pictured on page 157. Its lineage is unknown to me but I have been told that it was discovered on an island off the coast of Maine by the owner of the Wilton nurseries, Wilton, Connecticut, who was so delighted with this rare form that he took a few reverent cuttings back to his nursery to propagate. All the *Wiltoni* now on the market are supposed to have come from these original cuttings. It is absurdly easy from cuttings; I have rooted any number of them by simply nipping off the shoots and sticking them back into the earth, weighed down by stones. It will also stem-root.

This little gem is too choice for large areas—there are plenty of other junipers for these—but perfect for carpeting small rather special spots. It will spread to about 3' and cover the ground so completely that, after a few years, only a very few weeds come through, and its curving lines are a delight, especially when they swirl out over stone. You may have to hunt around for this *Wiltoni* as it is not well known but in our area it is carried by the Rosedale Nurseries in both their Hawthorne, N.Y. and Millbrook, N.Y. branches. I have heard that some mid-western nurseries trim it back so that it forms a tiny bush, which might be interesting.

Good Companion Evergreens: Junipers combine particularly well with all the broadleafed forms of euonymus (the *Fortunei* group), like the same soil and setting, and the dark, firm, semi-glossy leafage of the euonymus contrasts effectively against the feathery grey-green foliage of the junipers. Boxwood is also good in such a group, offering a different leaf form. The so-called English boxwood (*Buxus sempervirens suffruticosa*), which may or may not be hardy in your area, is considered the most beautiful and the most formal; *B. sempervirens Welleri* is almost as beautiful and a lot hardier but very slow growing. The Korean box (*B. microphylla koreana*) is the hardiest of all but slightly coarser and far less formal; this one also comes in a dwarf, tiny-leafed form, *B. microphylla koreana* Arnold Arboretum strain, which is a charmer, grows only about 12″ high when untrimmed and has a lifting, spreading habit of growth, a delightful small evergreen for informal use. The low, silvery-leafed *Stachys lanata* makes a good edging for such a plant grouping and all of them combine well with flowering trees and shrubs. All like sun, average good soil, though the euonymus is equally happy in shade.

Properties which are sheltered by nearby woodlands and have shade problems can usually afford the luxury of the flowering broadleafed evergreens which need an acid soil and protection from wind. These beauties seem particularly right against a background of pines or hemlocks. Such a planting could be highlighted in spring by sweeps of daffodils, sweeps of the pale blue wild phlox *divaricata,* small nests of primroses. Later, after the broadleafed evergreens had finished blooming, you could have the shining gleam of lilies in some half-sunny spot, the white and pink foam of astilbes, the towering cream-white spires of *Cimicifuga racemosa* and the lower *C. simplex* with, in late fall, a carpet of colchicums. Consult any good garden book on shade bloomers. *Gardening In The Shade* by Harriet K. Morse is one of the best.

Such a natural setting would not lend itself to the more planned type of garden room spoken of earlier, but you could devise wide, shallow alcoves to hold special combinations of these plants, the selection to depend upon the formality or informality which prevails throughout the rest of the area, also upon scale. A small, simple house set in deep woods would take only a small, simple alcove. Perhaps groups of mountain laurel, and the tall, loose inkberry holly (*Ilex glabra*) backing a pale pink azalea *Schlippenbachi* for May bloom, all this set against an irregular backdrop of Swiss mountain pine (*Pinus Mugo*) with a ground cover of sweet woodruff (*Asperula odorata*), the seat a cedar slab laid across native rocks.

Larger properties, carefully maintained, could take a spectacular sweep of the more distinguished flowering evergreens. This type of planting would be particularly desirable if the area were viewed from the house. In the background, against the woodland, you could use groups of the big, white, rosebay rhododendron (*R. maximum* var. *album*) which will grow to 10′ or more, has enormous leaves and also enormous flower heads, is spectacular even from a distance;

A Norway spruce, close to a building but with a woodland background, is underplanted with shade-tolerant mountain laurel, ferns, pale pink astilbes.

THEODORA M. PRENTICE

A massed planting of *kaempferi* azaleas in a half-shady woodland setting of birch, dogwood, hemlock.

this is a massive job, large scale, needs plenty of room. In front of this could be sweeps of lower rhododendrons and azaleas, the different kinds and colorings (your choice) defined by groups of the inkberry holly and blended by the creamy-white *Pieris floribunda*. In such a wide, large scale planting you could go psychedelic on colors. Towards the front, and at the sides, taper down and merge all this into the cultivated area with groups of low white azaleas and the choicer forms of holly, the *I. crenata* in variety and including the glossy-leafed *convexa bullata* for highlighting. For early spring bloom you could edge the entire area with sweeps of daffodils, yellow and white.

All the above evergreens are available at most fine nurseries, so you would have no problem there. The problem might be paying for them as, I am sorry to say, most of them are expensive. So here is an idea:

Want To Save Money On Evergreens?

Did you know that you can buy infant plants—trees, shrubs, evergreens of all kinds—from nurseries which specialize in these sizes, and raise them yourself? Don't be alarmed, this is not difficult, and in a few years you will have any number of sizable beauties ready to set in place. At a fraction of what they would have cost in regular sizes at a regular nursery.

These babies take up very little room for the first few years as they can be placed, closely together, in rows; all you need is a small space protected from wind and strongest sun. Or a cold frame. If you don't have a cold frame you can rim the open area with boards or cement blocks and put lath over the top, or chicken wire to hold pine branches. The soil should be well drained, deeply dug, and soft with humus and sand. Planting directions usually accompany each order.

Some of these infant plants can be started in the fall and some can't; the nursery will advise you on this and withhold shipment until spring if they feel this is safer for your locality. But you can at least prepare your nursery bed this fall, let it settle and mellow over the winter so that it will be ready for spring planting. You will have a lot of fun and save a lot of money, which is one of the happiest combinations I know of.

Two of the nurseries which specialize in such baby plants and sell retail are Girard Nurseries, Geneva, Ohio, and Green Ridge Nursery, Madison, Ohio. I have had many plants from both and can recommend their wares, so send for their catalogues. There may be other nurseries of this type but I do not know them. Most growers of such small plants sell wholesale only.

OCTOBER

Perennial Beds—New and Old

I envy anyone who is starting a new garden, new plantings, new perennial beds. So many of my own I would like to rip out and do over, knowing so much more now than I did when I first planted them. But, like so many other gardeners, I have to live with my mistakes until they can be repaired.

Fall—September or October—is the best time to prepare a new place for perennials as the soil is then soft and easy to work, the weather pleasant, and you have more time—well, comparatively—than in spring. Also, a bed deeply prepared and left rough over the winter has time to mellow and settle itself and is then ready, in early spring, to receive its new inhabitants. And for most perennials, in this area anyhow, spring planting is far safer than fall planting. So prepare the beds now and, during the winter, mentally arrange and rearrange all these plantings you are dreaming of It is a lot easier to do this in your mind and on paper than in the earth.

First of all, what kind of a perennial bed do you want? One of those legendary affairs close-packed with continuous bloom? If so, it will have to be sizable to accommodate all the plants needed to give successive sweeps of color without looking spotty. If it is to be a border you should allow a minimum width of 6′ and a length of 60′, preferably more each way, and even such a comparatively small area will take skillful planning to look well at all seasons. Also a lot of upkeep.

More and more experienced gardeners, faced with labor problems, are questioning the desirability of even attempting continuous bloom in one massive perennial bed. It is just too much work and worry except on large estates where knowledgeable helpers are available. The trend seems to be to smaller plantings laced with maintenance-free shrubs and evergreens, each planting devoted to a special display area during its special season yet all related, the shrubs and evergreens plus a few annuals to carry it at other times. This can sometimes be a flowery and more open version of the garden rooms spoken of earlier. It means less work and, usually, healthier plants as there is less crowding than in the classic "garden" where insufficient ventilation so often invites disease.

If your property is small you could, perhaps, have two areas for perennials, one to bloom from May to July, the other to take over in July and bloom until frost. The Wayside Garden catalogue offers two such planting plans and although I personally do not care· for some of their color combinations the idea is a fine one. You could use these plans but choose your own colors in the plants recommended, adding a background structure of evergreens or flowering shrubs and finishing off the ends with terminal plants which furnish good all-summer foliage strength, such as herbaceous peonies or low evergreens.

If your property is large and blest by differences in grade, a planted slope is both a delight to the eye and reasonably easy to work, different parts of the area blooming at different times but all tied together by evergreens and both major and minor shrubs. One such hillside garden is pictured on page 204. The areas not in bloom in the photograph will be masses of annuals or midsummer-flowering perennials later in the summer.

Another garden utilizing differences in grade is the circular one pictured on page 205. This was constructed out of what was a small sloping meadow rimmed with old stone walls. A low retaining wall holds up the back, allows a wide and fairly level area which offers the circular garden with lawn center, the background and corners planted with flowering shrubs and small flowering trees. In spring this garden is a sea of early bulbs and small flowery things, followed by masses of azaleas which, in turn, are followed by the circular planting of iris and peonies. And all of this, including the stone-step entrance, screened off from the rest of the property by the aforementioned shrubs and trees. During the summer, while this circular garden is resting, a nearby border of brilliant July-to-frost-blooming perennials and annuals immediately absorbs the eye.

Sometimes the corner of a property offers possibilities, if it is

A rocky and fairly steep hillside garden over which one looks to the blue hills beyond. The planting—spring-flowering shrubs and, later, masses of low perennials and annuals—has been deliberately underplayed so as not to detract from the superb view.

open to the sun. Possibly you already have a tree in such a corner. If so, you are lucky, for a tree, some kind of tree, would be necessary to give structure and height. An apple tree would be ideal if the terrain is open and sunny as apple trees are so easy to underplant (see picture on page 206). Or a Russian olive for a smaller scale planting, or a flowering crab (both of these to be high-headed). Or a Sunburst locust, such as the one pictured in another setting on page 207. Or a dogwood against a woodland background.

   With such a tree as the central corner structure you could plant, under it, a wide sweep of small spring bulbs interplanted with May-flowering blue phlox *divaricata*, arabis, doronicums. Or primroses, forget-me-nots, ferns and mertensia if the tree were a dogwood. Then on either side of this tree, but beyond the spread of its branches, could be groups of white and blue shrub-altheas, kept lowish, to step down the tree and provide maintenance bloom in late summer when the spring-flowering numbers were resting within a deep edging of dwarf white and yellow (mixed) matricaria, a Snow Ball and Lemon Ball. In front of each shrub-althea group a half-circle of herbaceous peonies would offer masses of color in June and foliage strength the rest of the summer.

From these central groupings would stretch out the arms of your perennial beds, one arm to hold June-July bloomers, the other to hold August-September bloomers, both of them backed by tall purple and white lilacs to provide May flowering in these areas, and both terminated by outcurving plantings of massed peonies to give June color and dark, foliage-finish.

The June-July arm of such a perennial planting could hold

A circular garden fitted into existing old stone walls. The great charm of this is that it accords so perfectly with the rural simplicity and country flavor of its setting.

EUGENE D. TRUDEAU

groups of the medium-tall (up to 5′) species delphinium *Belladonna* (light blue), *Bellamosum* (dark blue) and Casa Blanca (white), at the rear, foreplanted with masses of the 2′ ultra-double white matricaria faced down by the dwarf matricaria Lemon Ball. The delphiniums would bloom again through September and the matricarias would keep going all summer. The August-September arm could hold a background planting of tall blue Michaelmas daisy asters (3′ to 4′, your choice of variety; see White Flower Farm catalogue for these) interplanted with tall, white August-flowering lilies (Silver Sunburst is one) and foreplanted with the late-flowering phlox Dresden China, which is a heavenly shell-pink; this planting faced down by dwarf matricaria Snow Ball. All these matricarias you can raise from seed (see *February*).

Or, smaller and simpler versions of the above, using the same plant values and flowering sequences, might be arranged as a swinging serpentine border against a straight shrub or evergreen back-

An apple tree underplanted with daffodils, tulips, doronicum, and anchusa *myosotidiflora.*

THEODORA M. PRENTICE

A Sunburst locust here terminates a tiny, narrow terrace along the side of this euonymus-swathed old house, forms the corner planting of a shrub-and-perennial which edges the lawn. Just below this narrow terrace is a small pool embraced by low cotoneasters and junipers.

ground at the edge of your property; or even broken up into two separate beds if this seems suggested by the size and shape of the area involved. Or, the dwarf matricaria edgings might be better replaced by evergreen candytufts, or by dwarf Korean box (clipped) which would give a more formal finish.

In planning any perennial bed or border against a shrub or evergreen background always be sure to leave ample space—at least 2′ and preferably more—between the major plants and the perennials. Remember that the shrub or evergreen roots usually extend out to the tips of the branches and will grab all the nourishment within reach. Also, to have such an open space at the back, which is not noticeable from the front, will enable you to get behind the perennials and attend to them from the rear. Also to attend to the shrubs or evergreens.

And do you know the easiest way to lay out a curved or curving perennial bed, any kind of curved planting? Use the garden hose, arranging it in whatever lines are most pleasing to you. And don't be chicken about curves. Small, wiggly curves are weak and meaningless. If you are going to have curves let them swing out in strong sweeps—if you have the room. If you don't have the room better give up the idea of curves and settle for a straight, narrow border with, perhaps, circular ends for emphasis.

And do you know how to make circular ends? Measure out from the back of the bed to a mid-point and drive a stake in there. Then fix a piece of cord with a looped end, drop the loop over the stake and with some sharp implement attached to the other end of the cord mark a circle by swinging the cord around the stake. Do the same thing, measuring carefully, at the other end of the bed and you will have two matching circular ends for terminal plantings. Small flowering trees make enchanting terminal plantings for a long border; shorter borders could take peonies or low evergreens. Or these circular ends could be filled with massed plantings of evergreen candytuft, or of the silver-grey *Stachys lanata*.

But no matter what size or shape you make your perennial bed or beds be sure to mark the outlines immediately and securely with many stakes, firmly set, and laced with cord, preferably white. Especially if you have children or dogs. It is maddening to find, after all the work and worry you have been through, that the children have tripped over an unseen cord, yanking it out, or that the puppy has removed the stakes to chew on.

Now to the bed itself.

The deep and thorough preparation of a perennial bed is so important to the health and welfare of the plants it will house that I urge you to consider this a major project. It will prove the best investment that you can make in garden beauty. I know this from bitter experience for I never took the time and trouble to prepare my own beds properly and have regretted this ever since. Yet, several years ago, I supervised the preparation of a perennial bed for a friend, insisted on deep digging, the installation of adequate drainage, and a generous filling of rich, humusy loam, and the perennials in that bed happily survived a long and tragic drought which left most other perennial beds in that area—my own included —a wreckage of dead and dying plants. This was proof beyond doubt that deep digging, or trenching as it is called, is the best insurance you can give any planting of perennials.

So here is my own version of trenching. As you read on, the idea of all that work may fill you with horror but it would probably seem slip-shod to most English gardeners who think nothing of digging down to 3' or more. Ever wonder why English gardens are so famous? Well, one of the reasons, aside from climate, is the way they prepare their perennial beds.

First of all, you will need a strong spade, shovel or spading fork. A big wheelbarrow. A pile of crushed stone or gravel such as is suitable for a driveway. A bale of peat moss. A bag, or possibly two, of dried cow manure. If your soil is unusually heavy you may also need some coarse sand. And, most important of all, you will need a digger with a bright mind as well as a strong back.

Starting at one end, dig out an area approximately 2' to 3' square and at least 2' deep and pile all this earth into the wheelbarrow. Then loosen the bottom (which will be sub-sub-soil) and throw in about 6" to 8" of gravel, depending on how good or bad the drainage looks. Then, on top of this gravel, shovel in the top layer of earth from the next 2' or 3' area, mixing in approximately one third peat moss and a good sprinkling of cow manure. Keep adding earth from this adjoining area, mixing in an increasingly greater proportion of peat moss and manure as the soil gets progressively poorer, until you are again down to the 2' depth and the first excavation is piled high. Then again loosen the bottom, add gravel, and the top layers of soil from the next area. Continue in this manner until you reach the end of the bed, then trundle down the wheelbarrow and use its contents, mixed with peat moss and manure as above, to fill in the last excavation. You and your digger then take time out for a beer.

If this perennial planting is to be a wide border start digging at the back, keeping well away from any shrub or evergreen roots, and go all the way to the end, then come up on the near side. This will bring you back to the wheelbarrow for the last load of fill. If it is to be an open bed which you can·walk around go down one side, turn the corner at the end, and come up the other side, again fetching up at the wheelbarrow. Beds or borders which are full of curves, first wide and then narrow, are best done in sections.

How much peat moss, manure and—possibly—sand should be added will depend entirely upon the type and quality of soil you encounter. Heavy or clayey soils, or very sandy soils, will need more peat moss and manure than average or reasonably good garden earth; very heavy soil may need some sand to break it up. But if you meet solid clods be sure to chop them up as you go along for, if they get together, they can hinder drainage and the penetration of plant roots, and many major perennials, such as peonies, send their roots down almost 2′.

Phosphorus and potash, in one form or another, are both essential in any perennial planting, any planting at all for that matter. These can be incorporated as you go along if you prefer, or you can wait until spring. Seems to me simpler to wait until spring rather than to further complicate an already complicated digging procedure. Most forms of phosphorus and potash don't begin to work until spring anyhow and are easily added when you spade up the bed to prepare it for planting.

Superphosphate is the quickest acting form of phosphorus but I prefer bone meal. Approximately one-half to one cup of either, per square foot, spaded in deeply, is generous measure. Potash can be incorporated either as sulphate of potash or muriate of potash at about the same rate per square yard, but I find wood ashes just as effective and a lot cheaper; give the whole bed a good coating (I never measure) in earliest spring preferably on top of snow so that the ashes have plenty of time to leach down and mellow, then dig it in deeply, along with the bone meal, when the earth is dry enough to work. The lime in the wood ashes helps balance the acidity of the peat moss, giving the more neutral soil preferred by most perennials.

But for the present leave this whole mounded area rough, don't try to smooth it out, make it look pretty. It should be left coarse and open so that frost can get in deeply to work its magical softening and mellowing, especially if the soil is heavy.

After you have finished your beer go back to the bed and give it a good, deep, thorough hosing to moisten the peat moss and manure and start the settling process which will be continued by fall rains and winter snows. You will be surprised by how much that huge heap of earth will settle before spring. Actually, you don't want it to settle too deeply because a raised bed is always more desirable for perennials than a level one, allows better drainage and better ventilation around the plant stems. A perennial border should be higher in the back and slope gently towards the front.

My guess is that by this time you will be very sorry you read this chapter. So now pick up a garden book which tells you that just digging down 10" or 12" and turning over the earth is ample preparation for a perennial bed. I know, I have read that too. It is one of the reasons why my own perennial beds have not done as well as they should.

What you do about old perennial beds in the fall depends on what kind of a person you are: whether, after your party, you bustle around washing glasses, cleaning ashtrays, and fluffing up the couch, or whether you go straight to bed and leave everything for the morning after.

Each system has something to recommend it. In case of a bitter cold winter with little snow the old stalks and dead foliage of the neglected bed will catch and hold leaves and whatever snow there may be, and all this resting on top of weeds will help protect plant roots. This is nature's way of attending to this matter. It is not as sightly or effective as a proper mulch but it is a lot easier for you. It is also a lot easier for the bugs and spores which can look forward to a happy winter nestled deep in all that dead matter.

A perennial bed which is scrupulously cleansed in the fall, every stalk cut down, every dead leaf removed, every weed dug out, is far less likely to harbor bugs and spores. It is also far more likely to suffer from deep freezes in winter and erosion in spring torrents. Also, it will still look so tidy come spring, after a casual raking, that you will probably pay no further attention to it. This would be unfortunate, for every perennial bed should be stirred as soon as frost is out of the ground, the winter-compacted soil loosened around the plants. When you are faced with a mess of weeds to clean out in spring this important stirring and loosening of the soil is automatically taken care of.

After thirty years of trying both systems I have settled for a blend of the two: I cut down any stalks which might give comfort to bugs and spores, especially peony and phlox stalks, yet leave the weeds and such which have moved in during late summer; often in cleaning these out in spring I have found precious seedlings—delphiniums, forget-me-nots, mertensia, self-sown annuals—which would have been destroyed in a fall clean-up. Then, after the ground has frozen, I give the whole area a loose coating of humus mixed with dried manure (avoiding peony roots which should not be covered) and on top of this lay branches, preferably pine branches. At least, this is the theory though I sometimes don't get around to all of it. Salt hay is commonly recommended for such winter mulching but I have found it too tiresome to clean out in spring as it blows when dry, settles into every cranny, and each wisp has to be plucked out by hand.

What to cut and what not to cut: The dead leafage of most perennials can be removed if you feel so inclined, but there is one little perennial which should be left untouched and that is artemisia Silver Mound. Its dead top growth is important for its winter protection, if you remove this the plant may winter-kill, so leave it alone until new growth appears underneath, in spring. This also applies to many of the shrub-type summer bloomers such as caryopteris, the buddleias, etc., which die back in winter and come up from the roots in spring. And, of course, never cut back any live woody plants— roses or shrubs—as this, come a late Indian summer, might stimulate new growth which would not have time to harden off and so would winter-kill. Many perennials such as delphiniums, Madonna lilies, Oriental poppies, countless others, make new green growth in the fall but this is hardy and should be left alone. If mulching with humus or manure encircle these little green tufts, do not cover them.

Planting, moving, or dividing perennials: When to do this to which perennials puzzles any number of gardeners, though such information can usually be found in any complete garden book or encyclopedia. As a general rule, with the inevitable exceptions, most perennials which bloom in spring can be planted, moved or divided in early fall; those which bloom in summer or autumn take spring attention. Two of the exceptions commonly grown are bearded iris and Madonna lilies, both of which should be moved or divided as soon after blooming as possible, which is around July in this area. Another exception is Oriental poppies; in this case you wait until the old foliage has withered and new green shoots appear, which is usually August.

The advisability of planting, moving or dividing other perennials in the fall will depend upon the hardiness of the perennials involved: if border-line hardy in your area best wait until spring. Where you live is another important consideration. In our cold hills where winter often cracks down hard and early, the planting or moving of perennials in the fall is risky, yet less than fifty miles away, down-state or nearer water, it is common practice. I have often taken such risks, and so have countless other gardeners around here, but it is not recommended.

No matter where you live one rule is universal: never apply any mulch until after the ground has frozen. A winter mulch is put on to keep the ground cold, to prevent the alternate freezing and thawing which causes frost-heave, tears and exposes plant roots. Also, a premature mulch encourages mice. These little creatures spend the fall looking for a cozy spot for the winter, and to find warm earth under a warm mulch would be the equivalent of your finding a New York apartment with a garden in back and wood-burning fireplaces in every room, and at a rent you could afford to pay. So wait until the ground is well frozen and the mice have found other quarters before applying a winter mulch.

Fall Planting of Deciduous Trees and Shrubs

Although a new perennial bed is best prepared in the fall and not planted until spring—in any area, to allow for settling—the trees and shrubs which grace it can often be planted in the fall, and the sooner these planting sites are prepared the better. This refers only to the shrubs and small trees you intend to plant yourself, not to major trees which are best handled by a nursery as these usually involve a huge root-ball and professional know-how.

Planting time for deciduous trees and shrubs is late October through November, sometimes even December, depending on where you live. In any case, such items should not be moved or planted until after the leaves have fallen, indicating the onset of dormancy. If it is absolutely necessary to move a shrub or small tree before this happens you can lessen the danger of such a premature move by stripping off the leaves and cutting back one-quarter to one-third of the woody growth. This reduces the strain on the roots while they are trying to get established. A heavy mulch of peat moss mixed with compost is also desirable—mice or no mice—to preserve ground

EUGENE D. TRUDEAU

Planting Suggestion to Consider: A Climbing Tree for children. If you are young and starting a family a relatively safe climbing tree is an excellent investment. This Japanese walnut (*Juglans sieboldiana,* hardy to Zone 3, growing to about 40′) starts branching close to the ground, invites tree houses, attains a magnificent spread. The nuts are very good if you can beat the squirrels to them.

warmth as long as possible, as the roots are still active. And stake-and-tie, or guy-wire, any freshly planted tree or major shrub to keep it from blowing over in strong fall winds. Detailed directions for guying will be found in any garden encyclopedia.

As with perennials, most trees and shrubs which flower in spring can be fall-planted, those which flower in summer or fall are spring-planted. But, again, there are many exceptions, usually depending upon the hardiness, in your area, of the plant involved so consult your nurseryman about this. In any case the planting sites should be prepared now. Trees and shrubs are heavy and will sink deeply into a freshly-dug setting, and more plants are killed by too-deep planting than by too-shallow.

If you have gotten thus far into this book, which is doubtful, you will know all too well what my favorite trees and shrubs are.

These are chosen because I have found them easy to grow, bug an l
blight free, and distinguished by good foliage, or long periods of
bloom, or both. Maybe you will want to try them and maybe not.
But as you have your own preferences, as I have mine, here are
some of the other colors and forms which are available.

SHRUB-ALTHEA (*Hibiscus syriacus*). The reason I prefer the
white, single Wm. R. Smith is because its flowers are larger, more
open, and the whole plant stays in bloom longer than any other
white I have tried; and Blue Bird because its blossoms are so large
and such a heavenly blue, even though its blooming period is shorter
than that of Mr. Smith. But there are many other colors and forms
in these shrub-altheas, pinks and reds, single and doubles and
blends. There is even one extraordinary affair which blooms red,
white and blue on the same plant; this one is for the property which
features pixies, gnomes, and plastic ducks. All shrub-altheas should
be cut back early each spring to keep them reasonably low, bushy
and flowerful. If you don't do this they will soon be a towering
array of stems with flowers only at the top which, unfortunately, is
the way they are so often grown. And don't be alarmed if they seem
dead in early spring, they are very slow to show signs of life. Spring
planting only.

DOGWOOD (*Cornus* in variety). The simple *C. florida* usually
seems most suitable to the country garden with a woodsy background but there are many other dogwoods which are more spectacular, if that is what you want, though they don't always have
the lovely branch lines of the *C. florida,* which also comes in various
shades of pink and red. Spring planting only in this area.

MAGNOLIA, Star Magnolia (*Magnolia stellata*). The simple
form of this magnificent plant is my favorite because it is simple.
But there is also an "improved" form, Dr. Merrill, which is more
spectacular, better suited to the show-case type of garden. However,
all magnolias are valuable for their dark, shapely summer foliage so
take your choice. Early spring planting here.

VIBURNUM in variety. I have said little about any viburnums
except the *Burkwoodi,* one of the smallest and perhaps the least
showy, but there are many others which you might prefer. The well-

known and long-loved *V. Carlesi,* with its grey leafage and fragrant flowerheads, is a joy anywhere and particularly good against a dark red or dark grey house. There is also a hybrid form of this, *V. carl-cephalum,* which grows a little larger and is said to·be even more flowerful. And then there is the great, spreading flower-laden *V. tomentosum Mariesi* which, when happy, will grow 7' or 8' tall and almost as wide. This is another spectacular for large scale plantings. Like most viburnums it bears masses of brilliant berries in the fall. Most viburnums can be fall planted.

Almost all the larger viburnums display quantities of berries in late summer and autumn so if you are particularly interested in this form of fruiting investigate some of these. The *V. setigerum (theiferum),* growing to 10' or more, is a particularly heavy bearer of these glistening scarlet berries. Excellent for the back of the shrub border.

And here are a few—and only a few!—of the many other shrubs and trees which will present you with a rewarding fall display. But, and perhaps more important still, most of these will also furnish spring bloom, and good foliage all summer, a most necessary combination where space is limited and every plant must pay its way all season.

The cotoneasters are perhaps the most versatile of all, from the uprising and outspreading *divaricata,* which will grow to 6' or more with an almost equal spread unless controlled, to the little *apiculata* which stays low, around 2', and spreads out flat. All bear small pink flowers along the branches in spring, small shiny leaves all summer, and lines of scarlet berries in fall. The *C. dielsiana,* especially, is literally burdened down by its berry display. All like sun, very well drained soil, and are easy to grow if moved when young.

Pyracantha coccinea Lalandi, or firethorn, is most famous for its wealth of orange berries but it also bears white flowers in spring and good, semi-evergreen foliage the rest of the year. According to the books it is supposed to grow best in a sunny and protected spot, preferably against a heated wall, but the happiest specimen I ever saw was growing in a northern exposure on a bitter cold hillside! Gardening is full of these individual contradictions but better not count on them. This firethorn is especially effective trained against a wall.

The evergreen *Euonymus vegetus* (which has any number of common names) is another climber, or clamberer, or ground cover, which pays its way all year round with handsome foliage and masses of orange berries in late fall. Sometimes called evergreen bittersweet, its leafage is far preferable to that of the common bittersweet which is *Celastrus*.

Ilex verticillata, a hardy deciduous holly, is a large shrub, (to 10′) in its native form, or a small tree (to about 30′) in the variety *vestita*. Both are slathered, come fall, with brilliant red berries which hang on long after the nondescript leaves have fallen. Best used as background planting for shrubs with better summer foliage, or at the edge of the wild garden. Like all hollies these like water but will also grow in average soil. Or, if you live where the evergreen hollies are hardy look up some of these beauties.

Of the many honeysuckles (*Lonicera*) which bear attractive berries the *L. tartarica* is one of the best. Grows to about 10′ and bushy, presents a cloud of pink flowers in spring, soft greyish leafage all summer, and scarlet berries in fall. It is thoroughly hardy and easy to grow anywhere in sun. Excellent background shrub.

Almost all the flowering crabs (*Malus* in variety) are hung with berries in the fall, sometimes yellow, sometimes red. Birds love these, and if you plant a lot of flowering crabs you will get many migratory flights stopping off for a snack. I do.

And everyone knows the magnificent berries of the mountain ash (*Sorbus* in variety). Growing to around 25′ it is a most valuable tree, easy and hardy, well shaped and with good foliage. And now it comes with different colored berries—white or orange as well as the classic scarlet.

Tulip-Planting Time

October, as every gardener knows, is the time to plant tulips. And countless devotees of the spring scene are going to be putting these bulbs into the ground with fingers and eyes crossed, praying that the planned displays will emerge in due time. And countless gardeners are going to be disappointed and blame it on moles.

The belief that moles eat tulip bulbs is widespread and almost impossible to eradicate. But they don't; they belong to the order

Insectivora and eat earthworms, insects, and grubs. If you don't believe me look it up in the Encyclopedia Britannica. But they do create the turnpikes along which cruise the bulb-eating mice and chipmunks, and these little beasties greet with pleasure any tulip plantings encountered on the way. Sort of an unexpected Howard Johnson. But this distinction is unimportant, it hardly matters which animal eats your tulips. The grim fact remains that your tulips get eaten and do not come up.

How to prevent this is a major concern of gardeners everywhere. One preventive measure, which I have found works fairly well, is to dust the bulbs, before planting, with one of the insecticide-fungicides prepared especially for this purpose; at least I have had more dusted plantings come up than undusted ones, if that means anything. The preparation I used was Henry Field's Bulb Dust.

However, I recently heard of another system which I have not yet tried but certainly intend to: you plant your tulip bulbs in tin cans from which both top and bottom have been removed. This sounds like the best idea of all and gardeners who have tried it say, gleefully, that it works every time; not a bulb lost! Ordinary-sized cans were used but I should think that the larger fruit-juice size (#2 or #2½) would offer more protection, also offer the bulb space in which to grow more bulblets. I hope your family likes canned fruit juice.

Another reason why tulips may not come up is because you have put them in too cold or too wet a spot, or in an area with insufficient drainage. Daffodils would likely do better in such a spot as they enjoy a certain amount of moisture. Tulips need excellent drainage and a warm place in the sun.

About planting depth: most authorities say 6″ to 8″ but don't fret too much about this. Once, several years ago, a large tulip order did not arrive until late November, and I had to get it into the ground immediately as a hard freeze-up was predicted for that night. It was a bitter cold day with freezing rain and by the time I was half way through that planting I was wet and miserable and bone-chilled. Never did tulips go into the ground faster! The last two dozen got stuck in barely 4″ deep; I figured on digging them up the next fall and replanting properly, but in the meantime I just didn't care. All of them came up and bloomed well, to my surprise, and when I dug down to correct their planting depth that October I couldn't find them—they had sunk down to 8″ or more! I have found that tulips, like many lilies, will often pull themselves down to their preferred depth.

But something you should fret about is preparing the planting site properly. I have no use for those circular tulip-planters which merely cut a hole in the earth. The bedding in which you set tulips should be soft and friable for several inches around and beneath the bulb and with about half a cup of bone meal stirred into it. You will get better tulips if you give them this kind of bedding and they will last longer. Especially if protected by tin cans.

Other fall-planted bulbs: most of these are so easy that you will need no help from me. Daffodils are especially simple, will grow almost anywhere and, as they are poisonous to all animals, are never eaten. And the tiny bulbs, which are such a joy in spring, seem equally unpalatable to wild life. Just follow standard planting directions and delight in the results.

Dahlias and Chrysanthemums

My father had two hobbies: dahlias and snakes. The snakes were all harmless, of course, and many of them affectionate, which can be a little disconcerting if you are not used to snakes. Most of the time they were kept in the conservatory, in cages, but often they were allowed the run of the house; snakes are very clean and make wonderful pets. The dining room was their favorite spot and whenever they heard the clatter of dishes they would head for it, to coil under feet or climb up legs hoping for the tidbits they usually got. I enjoyed the snakes.

But not the dahlias. One of my jobs was to help my father with his dahlias, and he had what seemed like thousands of them. Not only did I have to keep the things weeded all summer when I wanted to be flashing around on my bicycle, but, each fall, I had to help dig, sort, label and store them. This was punishment and I vowed that never in my whole life would I get snarled up in gardening. I dreaded dahlia time.

But one year the scales of justice achieved a beautiful balance. My father belonged to a small dahlia society which, each fall, would meet at the home of one of its members for a tour of the garden followed by a luncheon. So our turn came, and when the dahlia addicts were all assembled at table I sneaked down the back way and released the snakes. Needless to say, they all headed for the dining room . . .

I couldn't sit down for a week afterwards but it was worth it.

Which is why there are no dahlias in this book.

Chrysanthemums, in variety, I have tried with varying degrees of success and pleasure.

The big, puffy kinds, the ones usually associated with the name chrysanthemum, I attempted at one time and finally gave up—except as last-minute fillers, bought in pots at a nursery, to give glamor to the border for special occasions. And this, as any shocked chrysanthemum-grower will tell you, is no way to grow these handsome plants. Yet when I tried the proper way, growing them slowly from infancy on, I ran into troubles. In the first place, their foliage, which is only mediocre in my opinion, took up valuable space for five months of the summer without giving anything in return; they needed division every year; they were susceptible to any number of ailments—blight, leaf spot, mildew and rust—and when, at long last, they finally bloomed, after a fashion, I found that they looked out of place in my simple country-garden border and still more out of place in our farmhouse living room. On top of all this, the varieties I tried were not dependably hardy, often winter-killed. Yet I have seen magnificent displays of these chrysanthemums in other gardens, other houses. It depends on how and where you live, how much time and trouble you want to spend on these plants. With so many easy, undemanding, long-term bloomers—delphiniums, roses, monkshood, matricaria, marigolds, Boston daisies, petunias—carrying the gardens well into October it seemed silly to fret over these chrysanthemums.

But some of the other varieties I grow with ease and pleasure. The single Korean daisies (see *February*) have, for me, proved hardy, trouble free, and most rewarding. I grow these in the cutting garden for, like most chrysanthemums, they are vigorous spreaders and here it doesn't matter; they seem to keep right on blooming, from early September to hard frost, without the annual division demanded by most of their kin. And the colors, as mentioned earlier, are heavenly for cutting, for combining with the soft blues of fall asters.

I also grow the *Chrysanthemum rubellum* Clara Curtis, but

this one as a summer ground-cover in odd spots. It has proved easy, hardy, and trouble-free, with a long and prolific blooming period from early August straight through to killing frost. It forms a rapidly spreading mat of low (15"), pink, daisy-like flowers which are slightly touched by magenta. Depends on whether you are allergic to magenta. But one way of handling Clara is to surround her with low white petunias which, like the make-up supplied by TV artists, gives her surprising beauty. I have found her a tough, affable, undemanding girl and most responsive.

But my favorite chrysanthemum, and one I could not live without, is *C. frutescens,* the pale yellow Boston daisy (or Paris daisy, or marguerite). This has such a gentle, poignant quality and is such an incessant bloomer that it belongs in every country garden. It flowers profusely from the time it is set out—late May in this area— until killed by frost in October; I believe it is hardy in milder climates. I take hardwood cuttings late in the fall, dip them in Rootone, and stick them in the One-Steps described earlier. They are easy and quick from such cuttings and when roots have developed I pot them up and set them in the cool room over the winter. I have found that they can also be rooted in plain water, then potted. By May they are eager, bushy, and covered with buds. It is a lot cheaper and more satisfactory to grow them this way than to buy them each spring from a grower.

Cold Business

In this area the light frosts begin in September and continue, with increasing severity, into October. But in between these frosts are warm Indian summer days to be enjoyed, and to preserve the flowering scene as long as possible you cover the tender plants on frosty nights.

I have found that the easiest way to protect plants from these frosts is to cover them with old curtains, organdy or nylon. Such materials are light, do not squash the flowers, yet are adequate against slight frost. As the frosts get heavier I use newspaper under the curtains (newspaper is a surprisingly good insulator) fastening the light material around the pots with safety pins. Stretches of tender annuals in the garden can be protected the same way, the long curtain lengths, either with or without newspaper, anchored down by stones. Always save old curtains of this type for they are endlessly useful in gardening: they can be draped over freshly moved plants to screen out hottest sun; or laid over a seedling bed to prevent washing in heavy rains; or, when weeding, spread out alongside to hold the weeds which can then be bundled up and taken to the compost pile, a lot lighter to carry than baskets.

Of course, these curtains look terrible when draped around and you have to get out early the next morning to remove them, but they will save your plants for many weeks more. Being a tighter weave than cheesecloth they are more effective, and being lighter than burlap do not injure the blossoms.

But by November you have probably taken in the tender plants —fuchsias, geraniums (these are actually *Pelargoniums,* not true *Geraniums*), begonias, et al—for winter storage, and have made cut-

tings from Boston daisies, impatiens, and such. Fuchsias are easy
to carry over; I simply leave mine in their pots, or pot them up if
taken out of urns, and put them in a cool dark place for the winter,
watering only enough to keep from drying out entirely. Then, in
early spring, I bring them into light and warmth, repot every two
years, cut them back here and there, and feed with fish oil which
they like very much. I have read that fuchsias should be raised from
fresh cuttings each year but find the old ones bloom quite well,
and I like the queer branch lines which older plants develop. I
grow only the upright varieties. Or, more accurately, I train what
ever I have to grow upright and branch out. I have never tried
them in tree (standard) form but have been told that this is quite
easy, that you simply select an upright leader, fasten this to a stick
with wire tape, and keep on doing this until the desired height is
attained, then cut back the top to encourage branching and a
rounded head.

Every gardener has his own way of carrying geraniums over
the winter. After many years of trying many systems I have found
one which is very easy and works well. First, before unpotting, you
water the plant just enough to dampen the root system, then you
unpot it and put the whole root ball into a plastic bag, fastening the
bag around the stems with wire twisters and leaving the top exposed; then lay away in a cool, dark place. You can pack a lot of
geraniums into one bushel basket. In early spring you pot them up
again, bring into light and warmth, cut back moderately, and feed
with fish oil. As with fuchsias, you can encourage interesting lines
in the older plants and as these tall up they are useful for backgrounds. I saw one elderly geranium once which was really magnificent; it must have been almost 5′ tall, a brilliant coral, set against
a dead-white cement-block wall which showed up the curiously
curved branch lines. It used to be quite a chore to raise geraniums
to such an age as the heavy pots had to be lugged indoors each fall
and lugged out again each summer but unpotting into plastic bags
simplifies this.

If you want to start new geraniums from cuttings use the
pieces you cut off, first exposing them to air for several hours until
the ends callus over, then dipping into Rootone and sticking them
back into the pot around the parent plant. I have found, surprisingly, that they seem to root faster this way than when potted up

singly. Apparently they like the close comfort of family life. Many plants display this gregarious quality, do better when companioned by their own kind. But as soon as the little cuttings have rooted they should be taken out of the family nest and potted up to start life on their own. As soon as they have settled themselves give a mild solution of fish oil.

Speaking of fish oil, or fish emulsion as it is often called, here are a couple of warnings you should heed. Almost all plants (except lime-lovers) relish this type of fertilizer and it does work wonders, especially on potted plants, but don't use it outdoors in early spring or your plants may be dug up by raccoons who are enticed by this tempting smell. Later, when the raccoons have taken themselves off to the wildwood and streamside—until time to come back for your vegetable garden—it is safe to use.

The other warning concerns your own person: do not handle this fish oil before a social engagement because it has a tenacious fragrance, even the deodorized version, which haunts the nostrils. Once, after using this stuff, I carefully prepared for the evening's gaiety, showered, got all gussied up, and left the house feeling comparatively charming. The hostess's very young daughter, plus daughter's cat, came in to practice the social graces and the cat made one cat-line for me, displaying extraordinary affection. The daughter also seemed fascinated and I thought, smugly, how easy it was to make friends with children and animals, all you needed was a heart of gold and a winning personality. Then the daughter trailed her mother into the kitchen from whence came the dear little childish treble: "Mummy, who is that lady who smells like a dead fish? My kitty likes her very much."

It is not yet time to apply winter mulches as, even here, the ground is seldom sufficiently frozen until early December. But it is time, before the ground does freeze solid, to set up whatever winter screenings you may need. Hardy, well-established evergreens and shrubs will not need such protection but fall-set ones may. It is wise to screen these during their first winter.

One of the best screenings is afforded by upright pine branches, the pointed butt-ends set deeply in the earth, the tops gathered together by that green wire tape you buy by the roll; the many openings around the sides can be partially closed up by weaving in short pine branches, wire fastened. Shrub roses can also be protected this way; they make a faster comeback in the spring. Very small evergreens, or those which may suffer snow-damage, can be sheltered by inverted peach baskets; larger ones by circles of chicken wire filled with salt hay. Major or cherished evergreens, such as old boxwood which is especially susceptible to snow-damage, should be protected by wooden frames, burlap covered. But in any screening operation involving burlap (which can ice up and freeze) always allow ample room for air circulation between screening and plant; the screening should enclose the plant on all sides but clear the tips of the branches. If pine branches are used for screening they can be set more closely as their very structure encourages ventilation.

Where you are going to get all these pine branches is your problem. But I know someone who has found the answer to this one: she invites up, for Thanksgiving, various city friends who crave real fresh air and real exercise, equips them with pruning saws and hatchets, and sends them down to her pine grove to trim out excess growth. This greatly benefits the pine grove, and even the dead lower branches are valuable as leaf-catchers on the perennial beds. If some of the guests are elderly or very young she gives them large plastic bags (garbage can size) for the collecting of pine needles, also valuable. So, in due time, all return with treasure, aglow with fresh air and the happy feeling of having contributed a major service—as indeed they have—to find a blazing fire and tea or cokes or Irish coffee.

Chicken wire is also valuable as a leaf-catcher, especially on ground-cover plantings such as ivy, euonymus, or prostrate junipers, or around sprawly shrubs, such as the lower cotoneasters, which attract every leaf that blows and are so exasperating to clean out in spring. This chicken wire, laid over such planting in fall, will be almost unnoticeable yet will catch and hold the major part of this leafage and, in spring, can simply be lifted off together with its burden. Saves a lot of work.

Warning: do not use salt hay or pine branches around entrances for there is always the half-wit who tosses away the lighted cigarette without looking to see where it will land. I know of one case where a bad fire was started by such a thoughtless action and the cocktail party was busted up by the fire department.

As mentioned many times before, you should not apply flat mulches until after the ground has frozen, but it is a good idea to get all materials ready now. Besides the branchy stuff you should also have a good supply of vermiculite in case of a bitter winter with little snow. This, as noted before, is a remarkable insulator and you may need it to pile around delphiniums, Madonna lilies, iris, and such come real winter in January and little snow cover. (The best time to stock up on vermiculite is spring as it is often difficult to find in the fall; few gardeners seem to appreciate its value as a winter mulch.) Apply thickly and loosely and do not pack down. It has saved many plantings for me.

If, at the last moment, you cannot get vermiculite anywhere you can use pine needles and a snow mulch; pine needles alone do not supply sufficient insulation. Wreathe the plants, thickly, with pine needles and, on top of this, shake on whatever snow you can scrape up anywhere. Collect this snow, which must be dry, with a dust pan and whisk broom and whisk it lightly over the needles, then pile more needles on top, again thickly, to prevent the snow from melting and crusting. Do not touch this snow with your hands or you will compact it, shut out air; it should be feather-light when applied. I have used this type of emergency mulch in mid-winter and, in April, found the snow still snow under the needles, the plants green and eager, while similar but unmulched plantings nearby were deader than frozen cod.

Deer Damage

Despite the number of animal repellents on the market I have yet to find one which keeps deer from eating yews. At least our deer and our yews. I tried one spray, highly recommended by a friend, and our local deer thought it was delicious, gave a real tang to the needles.

I have also tried the cheesecloth gambit. Yes, that's right, cheesecloth. You drape it over the yews, or whatever you want to protect, and it is supposed to frighten the deer away, or at least prevent them from getting at the yews. So one year I tried it, fastening it securely—I thought—around the base of each plant with safety pins. So comes the first real blow of winter and away goes the cheesecloth, wrenched from its moorings, to land on nearby lilacs where it tossed about. The deer, feasting on the suddenly available yews, must have had a gay time munching away and watching the undulating apparitions on the lilacs. Sort of a floor show. And I heard later, from another friend, that she had an old three-legged buck who actually liked cheesecloth. She saw him eating it.

Another idea, far more reasonable, is that you set up protective screening around the yews, stakes with nailed-on burlap coverings. So the next year I went through all this trouble and expense and do you know what happened? Not a yew was eaten. Not even the unprotected yews were eaten. That winter, which was a mild one, we had no deer at all around the house.

The only solution I have found for this problem is a dog. Which can bring on a whole new set of problems. The bouncy puppy we have now eats flowers, prefers peony buds but will make do, for snacks, with tulips, iris, and the fresh young shoots of lilies. I can only pray that she will outgrow this.

Ivy For Your Mantelpiece

For the past ten years I have been rooting clippings of hardy English ivy in the house over the winter—in plain water and sand— and, when well rooted, setting them outdoors to grow more clippings to root in the house, etc., etc.

If you have outdoor ivy you want to propagate you might like to try this method; it makes a pleasant winter interest and a pleasant winter decoration, for outdoor ivy is usually far handsomer than the indoor stuff you see everywhere. It is especially good on a mantelpiece where the strong, outreaching sprays have room to spread and curve in graceful lines and where, usually, it is safe from sun. And has a background. The background is important; a plain wall is best so that the pleasing lines and dark glossy leaves show to best advantage. It can be quite dramatic against a stark wall.

After years of trial and error I have discovered the following:

1. It roots best in tinted glass, possibly because the roots need a certain amount of screened light, and should be kept out of sun. About 2″ of coarse sand or pebbles in the bottom of the container not only holds the stems firmly, makes them easier to arrange, but also seems to encourage rooting.

2. You should NOT change the water. Nor need you add the

bits of charcoal so often recommended to keep the water "pure". Apparently this ivy does not like it pure, it likes to grow its own algae. The first year I attempted all this I followed the books and used charcoal and nothing happened. No roots. The second year I was all out of charcoal so decided to skip it and, lo, roots soon started to sprout. The water gets a little murky but don't let this bother you, just add fresh water as needed.

3. Not all your clippings will root. Some will die within a few weeks, the leaves limp and drooping. Pull these out. Usually clippings with a bit of hard wood at the end will root faster than soft-wood clippings but this is not always the case. Those which have decided to root will stay crisp and alert and, after about a month, pale green new growth will appear at the tips. This means that feeding roots have begun to form, though what they feed on is a mystery.

Planting Suggestion to Consider: Do you have a tree where you want to put a paved terrace and don't know exactly how to handle the situation? Leave an open area around the trunk and plant it with ivy to spread out over the stone. Perfectly beautiful and no upkeep.

THEODORA M. PRENTICE

4. If you are the impatient type you can take these out next spring, cut them back, and root them for further growing in a humusy-sandy soil mix, in individual pots, to be sunk into the ground in a shady spot. By the following fall they should be strong enough to be unpotted and planted wherever you want to plant them. It is a good idea to keep cutting back the top growth until it forms a vigorous bush. After that you can let it rip.

5. Or you can leave the sprays in the house for another winter, which will give them still stronger roots. I have one arrangement which has been in the same place for three years and it is still doing so well I can't bear to disturb it. Perhaps this is because it is in a room which is, usually, kept cool in winter, though I have also rooted this ivy in a normal temperature of 70°. You just have to experiment but it is a lot of fun and will give you a continuous supply of ivy to use outdoors.

A Project For The Winter

I offer this cautiously, somewhat in the manner of the Pilgrim father who hoists his hat on a stick to see how many arrows will fly into it, for I am not at all sure how it will be received.

The project would be to gradually familiarize yourself with the true botanical names of the plants you grow, the plants you love best, for these names will help you place them well in your garden. For instance, any plant with *sax* in its name will appreciate the comfort of rocks around its roots; *heli* means that it needs sun so don't attempt to grow it in shade; *microphylla* means small-leafed, *macrophylla* large-leafed, so when choosing shrubs you know how to combine them for leaf contrast; *sempervirens* means evergreen so this one you can count on in winter. And so on and so on.

But there is an even more important reason for knowing the botanical names of plants. Common names, popular names, vary widely in different sections of the country, sometimes meaning one plant and sometimes another, so you can never be sure of getting exactly what you want unless you know its botanical name. Which is why I have included so many of these names in this book.

All nurserymen who know plant material depend upon botanical names for accuracy. Take, for example, the woman from New

Jersey who ordered her nurseryman to plant six of "those big fragrant white syringas" and found she had six white lilacs. (No slur on New Jersey, I came from there myself and also called it syringa.) What the woman had wanted was *Philadelphus,* probably *P. coronarius,* but to a nurseryman a syringa is a lilac so that is what she got.

The amount of confusion attending common names is incredible. Consider, for instance, the shrub-althea mentioned so often in this book; I finally settled on that for a common name as it seemed the most recognizable to the greatest number of gardeners. Yet this well-known plant (actually *Hibiscus syriacus*) is also known as Rose of Sharon, Rose of Heaven, Rose-mallow Bush, Shrub Hollyhock (the true hollyhock is an *Althea*) and just plain Althea. Then move to another part of the country and Rose of Sharon or Rose of Heaven is a *Lychnis* (a coarse and common perennial) which is also called, variously, Mullein, Campion, Dusty Miller, or Agrostemma while Agrostemma itself is called Corn Cockel, or Maltese Cross, which brings you back to *Lychnis* . . . and you can go on and on like this indefinitely, getting more and more mired in confusion.

Or take Winterberry. I have heard this common name applied to Firethorn (*Pyracantha*), to Bittersweet (which can be either *Celastrus scandens* or *Solanum dulcamara*), to Inkberry (*Ilex glabra*), to *Euonymus europaeus* (which is also called Spindle Tree), to *Euonymus atropurpureus* (which is known elsewhere as Wahoo or Burning Bush which, in turn, is the common name for both forms of *E. alatus*), and to the evergreen euonymus creeper *E. vegetus.* . . . Ask a nurseryman for Winterberry and it's anybody's guess what you will get.

Yet for some obscure reason many people cherish the delusion that botanical names are silly and unimportant, merely affectations. They couldn't be more mistaken. True, some combinations of letters are real teeth-snarlers and fall strangely upon the ear unaccustomed to such sounds, but in every case they mean something, some special plant. And most of these botanical names are no more difficult than *Delphinium, Chrysanthemum, Rhododendron* and *Ageratum.* It is simply a matter of getting used to them.

I am not urging any profound study of botanical names—you couldn't possibly learn them all and it would be a waste of time to even attempt this as most of them will never enter your life—but merely the ones which apply to the plants you grow, the plants which enjoy your climate and which you would like to grow. Perhaps learn just one or two each day. Even at that rate you would have quite a vocabulary come spring and would find the knowledge gained a great help in growing these plants, a deep and personal satisfaction.

The best book for this study would probably be *Hortus II*, which is a stripped down mini-version of Liberty Hyde Bailey's *Standard Cyclopedia of Horticulture*, the bible of all serious American gardeners and their final authority. (Possibly the final-final authority would be the British *Dictionary of Gardening* put out by the Royal Horticultural Society, but this is an esoteric distinction which need not worry you.) *Hortus* gives pronunciations and detailed descriptions, sometimes cultural hints. But maybe for a starter you would find the going easier in the White Flower Farm catalogue which, although its listing is infinitesimal compared to *Hortus,* concentrates on some of the plants you would be most likely to grow, gives phonetic pronunciations and extensive cultural directions.

Still another reason for learning botanical names is that this will enable you to communicate with gardeners all over the world, for these names are the same in any language. I once had a Russian visitor, an elderly but still beautiful and radiant woman, guest of a casual caller, whose only English was How-do-you-do, Goodbye, Please, Thank You and Okay. Which was far more extensive than my Russian and only slightly less extensive than my French. But she was an ardent and informed gardener and, cruising along the plantings, she would touch each plant and, joyfully, give its botanical name as a question.

By the time we were halfway through we were sisters, arm in arm, aglow with this new-found magic of communication. Then she came upon one plant which apparently rang great bells for she cried out with delight "Perovskia! Perovskia!" and flung her arms around my neck. This was followed by a great flood of Russian and, with tears streaming down her cheeks, many gestures. Her friend and interpreter, strolling up, explained that this plant had been in her family's garden in a Russia which was long ago and far away and that she had never seen it since. When she left, with mutual embraces, I felt that I was losing a long-loved friend. I have no idea who she was. But I hope that some day I may meet her again.

DECEMBER

Dept. of Miscellany

At the moment you probably have neither the time nor the temperament for serious garden reading so here are a few casual bits of information to glance at if and when you get the chance. Maybe just as a switch from the current magazine material which tells you, so enthusiastically, how to make dead-twig-and-gumdrop decorations for the home and caterpillar stuffing for the turkey.

So take five. Put your feet up and think beautiful thoughts. Like how to hold a steep bank.

HOW TO HOLD A STEEP BANK

Use willow logs. Laid parallel. In horizontal courses. So that they root back into the earth thus anchoring themselves and the bank at the same time. For willows have only one desire, which is to get to water, so the shoots head back into the damp interior of the bank.

Here is how you do it:

Get willow logs approximately 4″ to 6″ in diameter (anyone who cuts firewood could probably supply these) and bury them about the depth of the logs so that the tops are flush with the grade you want to hold. The logs should be easy handling length, about 4′ to 6′, and *freshly cut;* this is important. The number of logs you will need will, of course, depend upon the size and steepness of the bank: the steeper the grade the more logs will be necessary.

Starting at the bottom, which is where the greatest wash-pressure will build up, lay the logs parallel and butt-to-butt. Then lay

your next course 2′ to 3′ above this (again depending on the steepness of the grade), staggering the butt-joins so that you do not get
a straight gully-run coming down between these joins. As you move
up the bank, or the grade gets flatter, you can increase the distance
between the courses, though they should never be more than 3′ to 4′
apart, and on slight grades you can even stagger the individual logs
(about 2′ to 3′ apart) instead of butt-to-butt. Get the idea?

The best time to start this operation is in earliest spring and,
as noted before, the logs must be freshly cut so that they are still
full of vigor. And tell the woodcutter not to trim off any shoots as
these are especially valuable, you bury them for a fast start. In fact,
the more shoots the better as these will be the first to greet moisture
and start the rooting process. Once these logs are firmly in place
trim off, closely, any shoots which are sticking up as you don't want
trees growing out of the top.

When all this has been done, the logs well bedded and neatly
trimmed, you can plant, between them, whatever ground-cover material you have decided upon. Low, spreading junipers are excellent
for full sun; euonymus *vegetus* or *acuta* for either sun or shade.
Both will contribute their own roots to further strengthen the bank.

I got this valuable information from an engineer who worked
for years with the New York Park Department and this is one of
the ways they hold the banks on the Parkways.

THE HELPFUL AJUGA

And, speaking of ground covers, here is another suggestion.
When you first set out fairly major plants such as the spreading
junipers you will, naturally, place them several feet apart. This
leaves a good deal of the area temporarily uncovered, and these ex-
panses will soon be taken over by weeds unless you do something
about them. What you can do is set in ajuga, quite closely spaced,
which will spread far faster than the evergreens, keep out many of
the lesser weeds, and clothe these bare areas until the larger plants
take over this job. This ajuga will also help prevent surface erosion
in severe rains, yet is so shallow-rooted that it does not interfere with
the major plants. Later, the ajuga can either be taken out and used
elsewhere or left to die out gradually for want of air and light. It is
endlessly useful almost anywhere.

THE VERSATILE CEMENT BLOCK

If your property is small and gay and casual you should investigate the wide and wonderful world of cement blocks. Alone and unadorned they are certainly ugly, but they can be used and planted in ways which transform their grim character into interesting and often delightful garden structures. They can, after their own fashion, take the place of stone when speed and economy are the chief considerations, though they can never contribute the deep serenity and distinction of well-laid stonework on formal or even semi-formal properties. Still, not everyone has property of this type.

These cement blocks come in different sizes. There is the 8″ x 8″ x 12″, the 8″ x 8″ x 16″, and the 4″ x 8″ x 16″. They are greyish-white and have hollows down the middle. It is these hollows which make them adaptable to so many uses. Planting pockets, for instance; you can make a tiny, low, retaining wall with them, planting the open tops with small goodies. Or you could make a higher and stronger retaining wall by setting them on top of each other and anchoring them with steel stakes driven down through the hollows, the cavities then filled with cement. This would make a very strong wall indeed, and you can then plant this wall with creepers to swarm up it—*Ampelopsis lowi* would be good in sun, or euonymus *kewensis* in shade—or leave the top layer open to supply planting pockets for plants which cascade down. (By the way, did you know that you can train clematis to grow down instead of up if you give it guide-wires?) Or, if your terrace or patio is in shade, you could make a low, free-standing wall of these blocks and use cascading fuchsias along the top.

And you can paint your cement-block wall any color which pleasures you, use it as a background for tall plants which need wind-protection; such painting makes it seem less cement-like. I saw one once which was painted a soft pale blue and against this rose delphiniums, dark and mid-blue, spaced by groups of white foxgloves, a few pink tea roses, with the white clematis *Henryi* and the deep purple clematis *Jackmani* climbing the wall on wires; later there would be masses of phlox in white and deep pinks with lavender-blue petunias (Blue Lace) as edging.

Or you could use such a cement wall, painted dead white, as background for espaliered trees, or semi-espaliered shrubs such as

Cotoneaster dielsiana which bears small pink flowers in spring and incredible masses of brilliant scarlet berries in fall. . . . Or create a whole, tiny, enclosed garden; I remember one, at a flower show, with espaliered fruit trees on each of its three walls, a footing of pebbles and, in the center, a simple bird bath on a stone pedestal, its foot wreathed by a circle of myrtle.

But one warning to keep in mind when using these cement blocks: do not plant, close to them, any of the acid-loving evergreens such as azaleas, rhododendrons, and the like, as these may be injured by lime seepage. Keep to the plants which are lime-tolerant.

Another way to use these cement blocks would be as an edging for a walk or flowerbed. Deeply sunk in sand, and placed close together, they would form a barrier against any cultural exchange between the different areas, yet the open tops could be soil-filled and planted with edging items which would hide the cement itself; you might have pansies in spring, later replaced by low petunias or dwarf marigolds or lobelias. Or for year round effect they could be planted with the compact candytuft Little Gem to give a neat evergreen edging.

Cement products for garden use now come in other forms as well. You can get an edging with a scalloped top which looks like brick, is about the same thickness but twice as deep; or if you didn't fancy the scallops you could turn them upside down and use the flat bottoms for a brick edging. There are also flat cement blocks which can be used as paving; these, I am told, come in different colors. But best go to your local garden center, or dealer in building supplies, and look over the many new—and inexpensive—ideas in garden materials.

RHUBARB

Have you ever realized that common rhubarb is a magnificent plant? Well placed, and in the right setting, it can be strikingly effective. But the setting should be stark and simple, against wood or stone, so that the great spreading leaves fan out to show their robust beauty. Being a hearty and plebeian plant it does not belong in areas dedicated to the social graces but in other areas—and most deep-country properties are chiefly other areas—it can surprise and delight the eye. The picture on page 236 shows it against the basement of a house with a footing of pebbles (for practical purposes) which emphasizes the clean, strong lines of the simple plant.

In my opinion, it would be an excellent plant to use with contemporary architecture because of this strength and simplicity. And because its use, especially as a decorative planting around entrances, would indicate the courage and independent thinking of the owners. It should contrast well with the lowish, spreading cotoneaster *C. horizontalis,* and the autumn berries of this would brighten the rather tired appearance of the rhubarb at that time; or the rhubarb could be cut back entirely leaving the cotoneaster in command. If I was young and gay and had a new house with strange, stern lines I would love to experiment with common rhubarb as planting material. And certainly nothing is easier to grow. Or less expensive.

Rhubarb also belongs, definitely, in the rural scene but placed, not just grown in a vegetable garden where it is merely another plant. If you happen to have a great rock try a clump of rhubarb

Just common or garden rhubarb, but a magnificent plant to use in a strong, simple setting, especially in utilitarian areas which are usually so dreary.

THEODORA M. PRENTICE

against it, the massive leaves spreading out, the cream-white blossoming spires rising up against the grey stone. Or maybe you have
an old barn, silvered with age; plant clumps of rhubarb at one
corner. . . . Or try a massed planting in the corner of an old stone
wall, perhaps with a foam of sweet autumn clematis (*C. paniculata*)
tumbling over the wall in back.

There are so many things you can do with rhubarb besides
eat it.

HOW TO MAKE A WOODLAND PATH

Do you have a wildwood, even a small one, through which you
would like to have a permanent, weed-free path, pleasant to walk
upon, along which you could escort guests? The kind of path you
see winding through rhododendron plantings in English garden
books? I don't know how they make them in England but, a few
years ago, I walked along such a path in America and found out how
it was made.

This is what you do:

First dig down about 12", more or less, taking out all native
growths and cutting back any minor tree-roots. Keep away from
major trees, let your path wind through relatively open areas of
underbrush which can later, perhaps, be planted with mountain
laurel or azaleas or ferns, or small things like hepaticas or bloodroot
to be enjoyed at close range.

Then dump in about 6" of wood chips. You can get these chips
through whatever tree-cutting service cuts and grinds up the unwanted wood along your local town or state roads; if you don't know
who does this in your section ask the foreman of any road gang
working nearby. These wood chips are spewed into a huge truck,
and when the truck is full it must be dumped somewhere, the
nearer the better to save time and trucking, unless a load has been
ordered. If you want a load dumped on your property get in touch
with the tree-service and the next time a truck is operating in your
vicinity you will get a mountain of these chips which will cost you
very little.

On top of this woodchip layer put a good sprinkling of rock salt,
which you can buy by the bag almost anywhere. Then fill to the
top with sawdust mixed with sand and more rock salt (sawdust you

can get at any lumber mill) and allow all this to settle for a few weeks. It will sink. Then refill to ground level with more sawdust and sand. In a short time this will pack down to a firm footing; the sand will supply drainage and the combination of woodchips, salt, and sawdust will prevent any growths from springing up. You will have a permanent, weed-free path which will be a pleasure to walk on and which will attain a soft neutral coloring suitable to its setting.

All this may sound like a lot of work—and, let's face it, it is—but you don't necessarily have to do the whole path at once. I know of one gardener who has been working on such a path for several years, in his spare time, and has completed quite a stretch. Each year it goes a little further and each year he gets new ideas for plantings along the side. One section goes through a vale of ferns; there were a few ferns there to start with and noting that these particular ferns liked that spot he started bringing in more. These multiplied, and now he has billows of the lovely things on either side of his path. Further along he found a patch of arbutus, some hepaticas, so turned his path that way, tucked in bloodroot to enjoy the dampness between rocks.

Unusual Gifts For Serious Gardeners

Gardeners are the easiest of all people to please with inexpensive gifts (they are also easy to please with expensive gifts) so all you need is a little forethought and a recollection of your own gardening problems. Of course, if you can afford to give electric compost grinders or three-decker plant lamp outfits you have no need of my advice, or anyone else's. The following is only for people who have No Money.

For instance, no gardener ever has enough baskets—peach baskets, bushel baskets, half-bushel baskets. These, in variety, are endlessly needed for covering things, carting things, as containers for the plants you want to get rid of (i.e. give away with gracious gestures). Also, they wear out with usage and must be replaced, are usually hard to find as they are seldom for sale except in fancy versions at fancy prices. The best place to get these common and invaluable baskets is from your local grocery store or supermarket,

Planting Suggestion to Consider: If you have a great rock, in shade, think about surrounding it with ferns. Here ferns are shown growing most happily around a rock under a magnificent maple tree.

if you can wheedle them out of the clerk, and the best way is to send your teenage daughter on this mission, for in most such stores the clerks are young and male and a chick in a mini-skirt is likely to come home with more baskets than you ever could. She may even come home with the clerk.

Now enters the spirit of Christmas, which means painting the baskets for the Personal Touch. If this is a gift for a male gardener you had better stick to the more conservative shades, Gravy Spot Brown, or Spinach Again Green, or Pot Roast Grey, but with female gardeners you can usually let yourself go; I know one gardener who paints all her baskets School-bus Yellow so that she can spot them, even from a distance, when they have been borrowed by a friend for an unduly long time. Then paint on the recipient's name in big clear letters for a further personal touch which will also insure the return of the baskets.

Such a basket, even empty, would be a welcome gift but a filled basket is still better. What to fill it with is the problem. Of course dried manure would be ideal, but it is possible that this fragrant gift might not be appreciated by other members of the family. So how about filling it with vermiculite? Or, if even the children's piggy bank is empty by this time, you could use pine needles. Or wood ashes. Maybe old nylon curtains such as mentioned earlier?

If, miraculously, you still have a little money left you can easily fill the basket with small, useful items such as another trowel or pruning shears. Again, no gardener ever has enough of these for they are constantly being lost or mislaid (by me, anyhow) and can never be found when needed. And a good way to prevent their recurrent disappearance is, again, to add the personal touch and paint the handles some bright color—red, or yellow, or even dead white— so that the object can be quickly spotted when left on the grass or amid a pile of weeds. Why don't the manufacturers of such garden tools catch on to this idea? Most trowel or clipper handles are either brown or green or a dull metal so that they immediately become invisible when put down. Or maybe they sell more of them because of this.

And there are countless other treasures you can employ in the filling of the basket. How about a big bottle of fish oil? Nothing says loving like a nice bottle of fish oil . . . or a bag of bone meal which costs very little and takes up a lot of room . . . or a package of seed-starting mix complete with old pie tins. Or, if the gardener is a spray-addict, a bottle of insecticide which carries the Yuletide message in its poison warnings followed by a list of emetics?

See how easily and inexpensively you can please a gardener? And where else could you find gift suggestions of this type?

A Brisk Winter Walk

This is probably the last thing you want to contemplate after a holiday stuff but nothing could be better for you. Which is a

dubious recommendation. Such a walk cuts through the post-pran-
dial stupor, brightens the eye, reddens the nose, tightens the figure.
The trouble with most winter walks is that they are usually pointless
and consequently dull. All you get is exercise.

So if you are a serious gardener—and you must be if you are
still reading this book—here is a way to put fresh interest into winter
walks: you make them treasure hunts for the many useful materials
you can gather, for free, from wood or field or country roadside.
You collect these treasures and lug them home to store wherever
you store such things, then return to the fireside so full of health,
virtue and thrift that you are insufferable to others.

You will need much equipment for this safari. Round up several paper shopping bags with loop handles, some old gloves, a good
length of light cord, scissors, clippers, a piece of discarded sheeting
to tear into strips, and several large plastic bags with wire twisters.

And here are some of the treasures you look for:

1. Strong, slim, well-twigged branches tall enough to support
clematis grown in the open bed or border. Such branches are often
found, blown down, along a country road or in a woody area; they
will be dead wood, of course, but still strong enough to carry the
lighter forms of clematis. And they should be quite tall for they will
be driven into the earth fairly deeply. If well twigged the clematis
will climb readily, or they could be used to support a length of
chicken wire. In either case the clematis leafage will soon cover the
supporting mechanism.

When you find a likely candidate for this job trim it (with the
clippers) to a flat, spreading shape and, if you are travelling a road,
tie a length of cord to the stem end so that you can drag the thing
after you; easier than carrying it. Or if you are coursing through the
woods and expect to return that way stand your branch against
something and tie a strip of sheeting to it so you can spot it on your
way back. You may also find a slender maple seedling which offers
just the right height and spread; tie a piece of sheeting to that too
so that you can come back on your next walk with a saw or hatchet.
Assuming, of course, that this baby maple is on your own property
or that you can get the owner's permission to cut it.

2. Watch for old, fallen trees, well decayed, and investigate
the rotted trunks. Inside these trunks you will often find wood so
decomposed that it crumbles in the fingers. This is treasure as it is

a fine soil-conditioner and will be especially useful in your spring seedling-trays; all infant plants seem to love it and often, when transplanting seedlings, I have found the tiny roots clamped tight on a relatively enormous chunk of such wood which they insist on taking with them. Sort of a security-blanket maybe.

So gather up as much of this crumbled wood as you can (here is where the gloves are needed) and cram it into the plastic bags, fastening the tops with the wire twisters. A handy way to carry these bags, which will be light, is to cut a length of cord, fasten each end of the cord to the bag neck with wire, then hang the whole contraption around your neck. This will endow you with voluptuous contours where you may—or may not—need them most.

3. Pine needles. You should realize by this time how valuable these are. They make an almost perfect mulch for most evergreens, are also good on rose or lily plantings, so the more of these needles you can get the better. Stuff them into the shopping bags. Easiest way to carry these, so that your hands still remain free, is to run a length of cord through the handles and tie this cord around your waist. These bags will add still further distinction to your figure.

4. Flat, lichened rocks can be priceless if you are planning a path, a pool edging, almost any kind of flat stonework. You can often find these treasures on or alongside dilapidated old stone walls. They will be too heavy to take with you now but mark the spots—again with torn sheeting tied to the nearest bush or tree—and plan to come back for them soon, hopefully with a strong man and a car. Also hopefully with the owner's permission in case they do not belong to you.

By this time you will probably have had enough. What you do now is pray that you don't meet any of your fancy non-gardening friends as you trudge along, ballooning bags of rotted wood and pine needles, dragging old branches behind you, your nose running (you forgot the handkerchief), your person disheveled, your head full of spring dreams for next year's garden. . . .

But of course you do. The elegant car stops, the amenities are exchanged, and your friends drive on, commenting upon what gardening can do to an otherwise normal and intelligent person.

It is surprising.

INTERESTING NURSERIES
YOU MAY NOT KNOW ABOUT

The nursery descriptions and catalogue prices given below are, to the best of my knowledge, correct for the summer of 1969, but by the time you read this they may have changed. I can only give you the information I have at the moment.

WARREN BALDSIEFEN, Box 88, Bellvale, N.Y. 10912. Catalogue-handbook $1.00. Specialist in choice rhododendrons, azaleas, and a few other plants of this type, all of exceptional quality, unusually well grown and shaped, several rare varieties. The handbook contains many color photographs and a wealth of information on the growing of these beauties. If you live in an acid-soil area this one is for you.

BRIMFIELD GARDENS NURSERY, 245 Brimfield Road, Wethersfield, Conn. 06109. Listing 25¢. Specialists in rare trees and shrubs, also evergreens, hedge plants, and vines. Landscaping service. This is one of the best sources I know of for hard-to-find varieties of the above.

BROOKSIDE NURSERIES, 228 Brookside Road, Darien, Conn. 06820. Handbook-price list $1.00. This nursery sells only organic fertilizers, composts, composting materials and equipment (bins, shredders, etc.), ground covers and mulches, but should be of great interest to organically-minded gardeners as much of the material listed is often difficult to find. The handbook is a gold mine of information on all phases of organic gardening and soil building. Mr. Stanley Bulpitt, owner of this enterprise, was written up in the August 1969 issue of *Reader's Digest,* as an expert on lawns. He is available as a lawn-builder over a several-state area.

W. ATLEE BURPEE CO., Seedsmen, Philadelphia, Pa. 19132. Catalogue free. This one is so well known that it hardly belongs on this list but I am so often asked for the address that I am including it here. Also, like most of the other leading seedsmen, they have specialties of the house not usually listed in other catalogues.

ERKINS STUDIOS, 8 West 40th St., New York, N.Y. 10018. Catalogue free (?). Garden ornaments and statuary of great beauty and distinction. See *August* for details. Catalogue contains photographs of almost everything offered.

FLORENTINE CRAFTSMEN, 650–654 First Ave., New York, N.Y. 10016. Catalogue 25¢. Ditto the above concerning Erkins Studios, but you should have both catalogues as each contains individual offerings.

GERARD NURSERIES, Geneva, Ohio 44041. Catalogue free. This is one of the few nurseries specializing in infant-sized plants (trees, shrubs, evergreens, etc.) which sells these sizes retail. They send excellent plants. See *August* for further details. The other nursery of this type, Green Ridge Nursery, Madison, Ohio 44057, also sent me excellent baby plants, many years ago, but never replied to my inquiry concerning present stock, catalogue price, etc.

WILLIAM GRATWICK, Pavilion, N.Y. 14525. Catalogue free. Mr. Gratwick and his partner, Nassos Daphnis, are tree peony specialists and offer only the finest plants superbly grown to blooming size, including famous Japanese varieties, the best of the Saunders *lutea* hybrids, and a number of their own new introductions. These are probably the most beautiful tree peonies you could buy anywhere. See peony article in *June* for details. The small but very elegant catalogue contains a few black-and-white photographs of some unbelievable flowers.

GURNEY SEED & NURSERY CO., Yankton, S. D. 57078. Catalogue free. This is one of those huge mid-western mail order nurseries usually viewed with skepticism by many eastern gardeners, this one included. In fact, the first catalogue which came my way went straight into the waste basket before I realized that this was the nursery I had heard about, the one which listed unusual (in the east) and super-hardy material at very low prices and sent very good plants. So I retrieved the catalogue and am glad I did. I have been enjoying it ever since.

As a catalogue it takes a little getting used to. It is homey and cosy, its enormous pages larded with brisk color and snapshots of happy Gurney customers, their pets and their kiddies, usually displaying flowers or vegetables of incredible size. And you are cordially invited to send in your own photographs, join in the fun. Once you get used to this approach, unique to most eastern gardeners, it gives a nice, warm, friendly feeling. This catalogue should be of great interest to all gardeners in extremely cold areas for Gurney plants are super-hardy—they would have to be in South Dakota! I call your attention particularly to the section, towards the back of the catalogue, which deals with hardy trees, shrubs, and evergreens for windbreaks and snowbreaks, offers planting plans and diagrams. I have never seen this worked out in such detail in any other catalogue. It should be of value to land owners, everywhere, who have snow or wind problems.

MAYFAIR NURSERIES, Nichols, N.Y. 13812. Catalogue 25¢ or free with order. This small nursery, long distinguished for the quality of its plants, its excellent packing and shipping techniques, now offers only dwarf shrubs and evergreens, heaths, heathers, ground covers, etc. Included are many rare and choice varieties, collectors' items. I have had many fine plants from Mayfair over the years and have always been delighted with them and their condition on arrival.

WALTER MARX GARDENS, Boring, Oregon 97009. Color folder apparently free. Iris specialists. Many unusual forms and varieties not commonly found in most iris listings. Well worth sending for.

MC CORMICK LILIES, P.O. Box 700, Canby, Oregon 97013. Color catalogue free. This was formerly the enterprise of Romaine B. Ware, distinguished lily specialist, who has turned it over to Dorothy and Pat McCormick who will continue the Ware tradition. This means the finest lilies you can buy, and most of them are shown in color in this slim but handsome catalogue. Many of these Jan de Graaff lilies are available at other good nurseries also, but the McCormick catalogue contains two prosaic and valuable items I have not seen listed elsewhere: one is a wire-mesh planting basket to protect the bulbs from mice, and the other is Ware's Lily Food which takes the guess-work out of lily feeding. I use both and am thankful I discovered them. A letter from Dorothy McCormick is so interesting that I am including it here.

"The mesh is of a galvanized type and comes from Germany. We obtain it in rolls and have the baskets made by hand by the United Cerebral Palsy Assn. in Portland. Their workshop is a miracle in action. Some workers can use only one hand, others only their feet, one in particular is brilliant but cannot speak so he uses a typewriter and handles their correspondence (he's studying law part-time) another rides a 3 wheel bicycle to work every day, but cannot walk; and this whole workshop of severely handicapped people is guided by a Mr. Ken Hockensmith who gave up a car salesmanship because he was so taken by the courage of these individuals that he wanted to be a part of them. They have a sort of recreation room where they encourage other handicapped people to come each day to view T.V., visit and keep in touch with the outside world—a type of therapy in itself. This workshop receives 25¢ for each basket we have made and the individuals are paid at a piece rate—some only making a little over their bus fare but they have a sense of independence!

"I'll admit it was quite an emotional strain the first time we visited the shop; but there's never any bickering—just serious attention to the job each one is trying to perform. I'm sure there are companies that could mass produce our basket at a lower cost but we'd loose that warm feeling of having given a helping hand—and I like it."

MERRY GARDENS, Camden, Maine 04843. Handbook plus price list $1.00. This nursery, specializing in unusual house plants, does not properly belong in this book but the handbook they send is so delightful I thought you might like to know about it. After all, a lot of outdoor gardeners are also house-plant addicts. Also listed are choice varieties of plants which could be grown outdoors in summer: geraniums, begonias, herbs, cacti, etc.

MISSION GARDENS, Techny, Ill. 60082. Catalogue free. Specialists in peonies, including tree peonies and the herbaceous singles and Japanese types. Many Saunders peonies are listed. This nursery also carries trees, shrubs, and evergreens for local customers but only peonies and day lilies are shipped.

GEO. W. PARK SEED CO., Greenwood, S. C. 29646. Catalogues will arrive free at the drop of a postcard. This is my favorite seed catalogue, as you may have gathered if you have read this book through from the beginning, which is unlikely. After years of studying other catalogues, sampling their seeds, I have chosen Park's for several reasons: (1) it contains the most extensive seed listing I have yet seen in an American catalogue, including seeds of trees, shrubs, ground covers, etc. and also many of the hard-to-find separate colors in annuals and perennials, (2) the index gives, and quickly, all vital information in condensed form, and, (3) I have found Park seed to be consistently excellent and, in most cases, less expensive than similar offerings listed elsewhere. See *February* for further details on Park seed and various gardening aids. Incidentally, Park also sends very good and very well-packed plants including annuals and perennials, ground covers and vegetables. These plants are offered in a separate catalogue which arrives in early spring.

DAVID L. REATH, Box 251, Vulcan, Mich. 49892. Listing free. Dr. Reath, a veterinarian by profession who loves peonies as much as animals, is "inheriting" the famous Saunders peony stock from Miss Silvia Saunders who is, gradually, retiring from the nursery business. See peony article in *June*. His first listing, which is modest but distinguished, includes only herbaceous hybrids but some lovely ones.

SILVIA SAUNDERS, Clinton, N. Y. 13323. Listing free. Possibly Miss Saunders should not be included in this nursery list as her stocks are running low and it is anybody's guess what she will have left by the time you read this, but she has such superb plants and is such a joy to deal with that I am taking a chance. Her 1969 list shows that she still has several of the herbaceous hybrids mentioned in the peony article (*June*), also Japanese tree peonies and *lutea* hybrids in different sizes and heavenly colors. A post card will bring you her current listing, whatever it is, and also, if you ask for it, her last catalogue (1965) if she has any left. This gives more detailed descriptions of the plants.

WILLIAM TRICKER, INC., Saddle River, N.J. 07458 or Independence, Ohio 44131. Catalogue free. Mr. Tricker is a water-garden specialist, offers only those plants which grow in water, pools of all types and sizes, pool equipment (recirculating pumps, etc.), fishes, fish food. His catalogue contains an eye-popping assortment of water lilies, most of them pictured in color, aquatic plants of all types, and cultural directions, plus diagrams, for planting the pool.

WAYSIDE GARDENS, Mentor, Ohio 44060. Catalogue $2.00 (present price) refunded when you become a customer. See *January* for description and details. This is a valuable reference catalogue, especially if you are a beginner, and well worth the price.

WHITE FLOWER FARM, Litchfield, Conn. 06759. Catalogue $1.00 (no refund); sent free to customers ordering $10.00 or more a year. This catalogue, which is called *The Garden Book,* is unique in horticultural literature, delightfully written, filled with unusual information, and a treasure to own. See *January* for further details. In my opinion, it is a MUST for all serious gardeners, especially those in hilly, frigid areas.

GILBERT H. WILD & SON, INC., Sarcoxie, Missouri 64862. Catalogue 50¢. Specialists in herbaceous peonies, iris, and daylilies. Big, handsome catalogue, full of color, an incredible array of beauties in all three catagories. More about this catalogue will be found in *June* and *July*.

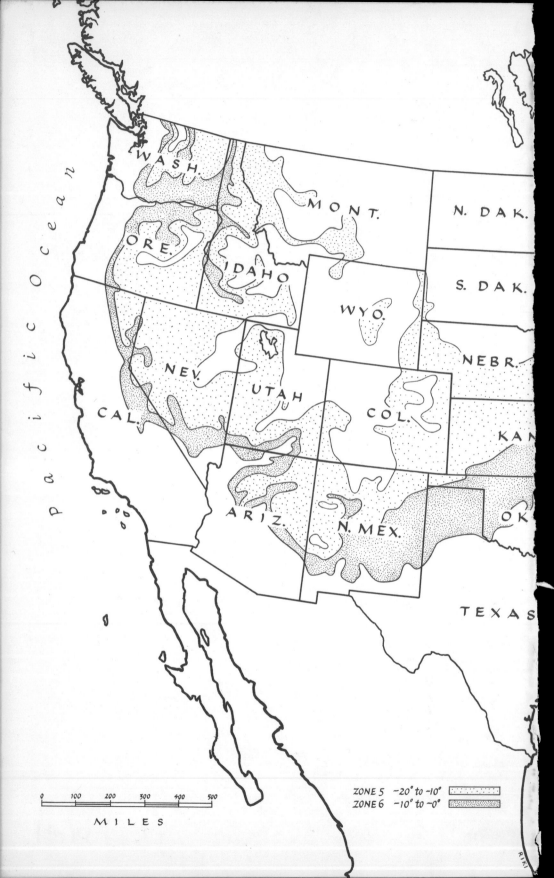

Pacific Ocean

WASH.

ORE.

IDAHO

MONT.

N. DAK.

S. DAK.

WYO.

NEBR.

NEV.

UTAH

COL.

KAN

CAL.

ARIZ.

N. MEX.

OK

TEXAS

0   100   200   300   400   500

MILES

ZONE 5   −20° to −10°
ZONE 6   −10° to −0°

RIKI